THE STORM AT SEA

THE STORM AT SEA

POLITICAL AESTHETICS IN THE
TIME OF SHAKESPEARE

CHRISTOPHER PYE

Fordham University Press New York 2015

Fordham University Press also publishes its books in a variety of electronic formats. Some content that appears in print may not be available in electronic books.

Visit us online at www.fordhampress.com.

Library of Congress Cataloging-in-Publication Data

Pye, Christopher, 1953–
    The storm at sea : political aesthetics in the time of Shakespeare / Christopher Pye. — First edition.
        pages cm
    Includes bibliographical references and index.
    ISBN 978-0-8232-6504-6 (hardback) — ISBN 978-0-8232-6505-3 (paper)
    1. Shakespeare, William, 1564–1616—Political and social views.   2. Politics and literature—Great Britain—History.   3. Aesthetics—Political aspects.   I. Title.
    PR3017.P95 2015
    822.3'3—dc23

                                                                    2014040670

Printed in the United States of America

17 16 15   5 4 3 2 1

First edition

For Renna

Contents

Figures

Acknowledgments

One happy consequence of a project too long in the making is the accumulation of profound intellectual debts and with them, I hope, friendships. I regret having known Helen Tartar only in the attenuated form of e-mail exchanges—I am so grateful to have had her support. Tom Lay has been a generous and reflective editor throughout. I had the good fortune of three superb readers through Fordham: Andrew Daniel, Philip Lorenz, and Graham Hammill, each rigorous, each light-touched. My debt to Graham is deep and long-standing—he has shared guiding insights on this undertaking in just about all its varied and desperate manifestations. Eric Newman and Michael Koch provided thoughtful late-stage editorial advice.

   I owe particular thanks as well to Julia Reinhard Lupton and Hugh Grady for their helpful published responses to a portion of the project published in *Shakespeare Quarterly*—I am grateful to Jonathan Gil Harris for organizing that exchange, and for his thoughts in other contexts. Julia Lupton has been her usual insightful and sympathetic self at many other points as well as this project has evolved. I owe thanks to Richard Wilson, my copanelist along with Drew Daniel at a session on Shakespeare's political aesthetics at the Shakespeare Association meeting, as well as to the audience members at that event. Although she would be hard put to recognize her imprint on a project such as this, I am indebted indeed to Victoria Kahn for her support and her comments at a panel she organized for the RSA, and to Richard Halpern. I am grateful to Walter Johnston and Daniel Hoffman-Schwartz and all the participants in the marvelously intense and collegial panel—"Autonomies"—they organized for the 2014 ACLA convention. Thanks to Frances Restuccia, William Carroll, and audiences at the Harvard

Humanities Center. I am grateful to the Oakley Center at Williams College and to fellow participants in our shared research seminar on Schmitt. I am indebted as well to François-Xavier Gleyzon, Johann Gregory, Richard Burt, Kim Noling, Matthew Biberman, James Siemon, and Grant Farred. I am absurdly lucky to have had such smart and generous colleagues at Williams over the years—I inflicted myself particularly this time around on Theo Davis, Laura Ephraim, Walter Johnston, Gage McWeeny, Peter Murphy, Anjuli Raza Kolb, Mark Reinhardt, Bernie Rhie, and Christian Thorne, all of whom offered support and weighed in in ways that made a difference. Evelyn Pye provided crucial help with translations. I am grateful as well to Ian Balfour for his friendship and insights, and, as always, to William Flesch. My debt to Neil Hertz is indirect and pervasive.

A version of chapter 2 appeared as "Leonardo's Hand: Mimesis, Sexuality, and the Early Modern State" in *Representations* 111 (Fall 2010), and a version of chapter 4 as "To Throw Out Our Eyes for Brave Othello: Shakespeare and Aesthetic Ideology" in *Shakespeare Quarterly* (Winter 2010). A version of chapter 5 appeared as "Against Schmitt: Law, Aesthetics and Absolutism in Shakespeare's *Winter's Tale*" in *South Atlantic Quarterly* (Winter 2009). A modified segment of chapter 3 was published as "Senseless Ilium" in *Shakespeare after 9/11*, ed. Biberman and Lupton (Lewiston, NY: Mellen Press, 2011).

My deepest resources have been closest to home. When they were not driving me to distraction, my students at Williams have been a source of the sheerest kind of intellectual happiness—many of the ideas here emerged out of seminars with them. Anna Swann-Pye has been a favorite literary interlocutor. My thinking has been shaped most profoundly by old friends: John Limon, Anita Sokolsky, Karen Swann, and Steve Tifft. The unreckonable debt is to Renna, without whose patience and support nothing would have been possible.

THE STORM AT SEA

Introduction

At a certain point in its evolution, this book was a project on distraction, perhaps even a history of distraction, beginning from a perception of the persistence and the equivocalness of that psychological category in Shakespeare. Associated with madness—the familiar early modern usage of the term—distraction is also, for Shakespeare, what saves, unbinding the self from solipsistic closure on the one hand and object fixation on the other. The indeterminate character of that state—salvific, but only insofar as it is without object or aim; a betwixt-and-between moment that is also a habitable condition—lead to the intuition that Shakespeare articulates in such moments the condition of aesthetic subjectivity as such: distraction concerns art in a significant key, and is the index of larger transformations in the era.

Transformation is the right word—I will be describing a genealogy of early modern political aesthetics here. But the developmental orientation—whatever had offered the promise of something like a *history* of distraction—also ran up against an obvious dilemma. What does it mean to speak of the aesthetic in advance of the aesthetic, as it were, that is, in advance of its appearance as an articulated philosophical category? The difficulty can be finessed by leaning, for instance, on the distinction between literary and philosophical manifestations, or even by claiming the aesthetic as a universal phenomenon. In fact, the untimely or metaleptic aspect of "the early modern aesthetic"—everything that feels uneasy about such a nomination—is just what makes it compelling especially for political inquiry, for it relates to what makes the aesthetic not just a historical phenomenon but a category that bears intimately on the problem of history and historicization.

Such a preoccupation—"early modern political aesthetics"—places the current project athwart some dominant critical trends in the field. For much politically or socially oriented criticism, the aesthetic has played a significant role in early modern studies largely by virtue of its derogation. The strong fit between cultural materialism and the early modern period has been underwritten in good measure by the claim that the notion of the work of art as an autonomous form did not yet exist historically speaking; New Historicist analysis, for instance, was energized by a conviction about the historical misguidedness of those more or less new critical approaches which considered the work in its own terms and according to its own logic. Even now, when the aesthetic is invoked at all in relation to the Renaissance, it is more often than not with strong provisos about its porousness or negotiability, the fact that it exists in free circulation with the full range of cultural and economic categories. Such an argument tends to be explicitly or implicitly underwritten in turn by a larger assumption about the ideological stakes of aestheticization: the literary critical tradition which treated the Renaissance work as autonomous form, so the argument goes, severed art from its material conditions, and thus systematically obscured its political dimensions.

In part, this book is a rejoinder to these claims and assumptions. The aesthetic was in fact fully engaged during the era, if not as a philosophical category, then as a self-conscious preoccupation of literary and visual work. It is *there*, though we will need to keep in view the complex relation between aestheticization and such designative gestures. And the aesthetic is thought through explicitly in relation to the problem of autonomy. Moreover, it is precisely in relation to the question of the autonomy of the work that art engaged the political most profoundly. To recognize that, we need to be precise about what aesthetic autonomy means in the era. It is not the autonomy of the artist that is at issue— the concern of a latter era of proprietary authorship and individualism— but the autonomy of the work, that is, its capacity to constitute its own grounds as a representational formation. The work is, I will argue, the privileged space in which the problem of foundations as such is engaged.

The aesthetic engages the political in relation to that question of foundations. With the loss of extrinsic or transcendental referent, the early modern socius became the problem of its *mise en forme*, of its ability to constitute itself as an immanent, self-creative domain. The appearance of the aesthetic as a self-conscious formation is indissociable from that problem of autogenesis of the social domain as such; the aesthetic work is where the intractably political because structurally irresolvable question of society's own capacity to "incarnate" itself is most directly enjoined. Within the ambiguous post-theocratic interval of early modernity, the aesthetic assumes a significant relation to an array of political categories, including sovereignty, law, the state, and the subject.

In terms of its historical trajectory, the project moves from what Walter Benjamin describes as the turn from ritual to exhibition value—the always-allegorical moment of the emergence of art "as such"—to the beginnings of the aesthetic as a determined and limitable category in relation to reason and deliberative judgment. The latter is the point at which the artwork will become at once, or by turns, instrumentalized in its association with proprietary authorship and declaredly purposeless as fully developed aesthetic form; thus the progression of the chapters from Leonardo to Thomas Hobbes, from the Machiavellian polis to the "rationalized" state. The bulk of the book focuses on the interim between these moments, the space within which what I term an early modern "creationist" political aesthetics takes shape. Art during that interval is associated with *poesis,* that is, the work's world-creating capacity. But it is also associated with autonomy and totalization. And in the drive toward its own radically conceived autonomy, the work inevitably engages the problem of foundations, including the abyss of its own grounds. Subterranean in the work of a figure like Leonardo da Vinci, an untoward effect of the very scope of that artist's claims for the work's autogenetic power, that problem of art's nonfoundation and its social implications will be engaged as such in Shakespeare's work. For that reason, Shakespeare has a significant place in the narrative I pursue here.

At the same time, even as we speak of the development of something like an aesthetic consciousness, the category of the aesthetic is worth renewing for current early modern studies because it situates the question of the political at a point that cannot be easily reduced to such a historicist narrative. The overdetermined character of modern political society—the fact that it is a society formed around its constitutive divisions and differences—is of a piece with its status as a manifestly historical society, that is, a society founded in relation to its own contingency. As the operation that translates—or persistently does and does not succeed in translating—such division into phenomenal or cognizable form, the aesthetic is inextricable from the operation of historicization itself. That process of translation is also the condition of the appearance of aesthetic subjectivity insofar as the subject is itself a function of such an overdetermined condition; the modern aesthetic subject is, in that regard, a being oriented around the question of its ability to make knowable its own contingency and noncoincidence. As the effect of that fragile process of phenomenalization, aesthetic subjectivity, and by extension political subjectivity, is situated at the irresolvable juncture between empirical history—including the kind of sequential narrative through which one makes claims for something like a history of the subject—and what exceeds because it opens the possibility of such forms of causal accounting.

I will refer to the book's historical concern as proto-aesthetics, though it might be more accurate, though even more ungainly, to call it the interval of the aesthetic/preaesthetic, with a nod to Freud's description—or positing—of a sexual/presexual period in human development. For Freud, that period of infancy occurs before sexuality proper: it only makes sense if understood as a condition of undevelopment. And yet, just insofar it is out of phase, the sexual/presexual figures sexuality most completely precisely as what is inherently disruptive of temporal sequence and categorization, as what is by definition ahead and behind itself.[1] It embodies sexuality "as such," but only to the extent that we do not forget that it is not yet sexuality proper. Similarly, the proto-aesthetic is not yet the aesthetic, and it's crucially important to maintain the genealogical perspective that construes the early modern aesthetic as what is in the process of becoming. And yet the early modern aesthetic is also already and fully there. That contradiction, which leaves irresolvable the distinction between historical development and retroactive projection, is what aesthetic phenomenalization seeks to manage. It is also why the politics of early modern political aesthetics is never purely separable from the dilemma of ones interpretive relation to it.

I intend the Freudian analogy lightly; for one thing, as an analogy, it is itself already within the orbit of aesthetic thought. Although the psychoanalytic perspective is present here only as an undercurrent, I do not see this work as discontinuous with earlier projects of mine where the psychoanalytic orientation is strongly marked, particularly inasmuch as that work sought to analyze the conditions of early modern political subjectivity. Aesthetics as I explore it here, however, does imply some perhaps paradoxical differences. Psychoanalytic consideration of the early modern subject can and should be given a self-conscious historical valence insofar as it dwells on the threshold of the Cartesian structures around which its own method is oriented. Even so, the phenomenological caste of psychoanalytic description tilts it toward claims that can feel transhistorical, whether or not that's a fair perception. By focusing on the aesthetic, I intend to zero in on a specifiable, and even relatively narrow, historical moment—the interval between theocentric institutions and the appearance of the formal state; the claims I want to make for Shakespeare relate to an aesthetic turn I take to be particular to and decisive for that moment. Yet, insofar as it is situated at the constituting limits of phenomenalization, the aesthetic poses the problem of historicization as such in a more radical, or at least in a more outright, way than psychoanalytic inquiry.

Chapter 1 fleshes out the claims broached here, focusing on the relation between aesthetic autonomy, history, and political formation. I will discuss a few literary works—*As You Like It*, *King Lear*, and *Dr. Faustus*—to specify the aesthetic as a problematic generally and for early modernity. I will also engage the relation between aesthetic autonomy and early modern conceptions of sovereignty, suggesting in the process how such an orientation is distinct from the kind of social/psychoanalytic perspective embodied by Claude Lefort's structural analysis on the one hand and Giorgio Agamben's biopolitical analysis on the other. In part, the chapter argues that early modern aesthetics needs to be dislocated from its familiar affiliation with economy and commodification; instead, the aesthetic bears on the prior, intractably political constitution of the very space of the social. That foundational aspect of the aesthetic brings to view the dimension of the works of the period that inevitably resists efforts to reconcile the defining antagonisms of historical society, whether that reconciliation is sought through reference to the totalizing claims of the state, to economy as an organizing metaphor, or by recourse to an artificially imposed distinction between civil and political spheres.

Chapter 2 explores aesthetic autonomy through Leonardo da Vinci's depictions of the incarnation. Registering the divisive turn from *poesis* to *auto-poesis*, those images enact the contradictory logic of mimesis in its distinctly Renaissance form, suggesting the conditions for what can be termed the modern invention of immediacy. At the same time, the status of such absorptive representations as at once mere images and constitutive forms bears on the larger question of the political stakes of the image during the image. The work of the incarnationist image is, I will argue, intimately bound up with the question of the capacity of the polis to constitute itself in immanent form—to incarnate itself, as it were. In enacting such a form of *ex nihilo* creation, Leonardo's work inevitably evokes the exorbitant underpinnings of that political, sexual, and aesthetic formation.

Shifting to the post-Reformation context and to literary concerns, chapter 3 focuses on revenge drama—*The Spanish Tragedy* and *Hamlet* in particular—in part as a way of bringing into focus Shakespeare's distinctive contribution to political aesthetics. The unique and perhaps surprising conjunction between revenge and meta-dramatic reflection can be understood in terms of aestheticization's relation to the difficulty of giving form to the deontologized social space manifest in the illimitability of the revenge cycle. The relation between aesthetics and the social domain is equally evident in these work's engagement with economy and law as structuring categories. With Shakespeare, the aesthetic explicitly reflects on or allegorizes itself as the ground—or the groundless ground—of political being, and in doing so posits law, not as a normative category, but in relation to the more primordial opening that defines man as social being. In *Hamlet*, that aesthetic "solution" is ultimately enlisted in a structure that anticipates something like the modern, rationalized state, even while it suggests the ontological fragility and cost of such a historical ordering.

Chapters 4, 5, and 6 turn to Shakespeare and his central place in the thinking through of proto-modern political aesthetics. *Othello*'s relation to a set of familiarly modern political categories—citizenship, domesticity, the state, and formal law—is directly bound up with the status the play claims for itself as a self-referential literary form. The drama's mixed generic form, a tragedy constructed on a comic structure, reflects its efforts to constitute a version of absolute literariness, to extend the self-referential field of the literary to the point of death without abandoning its status *as* literary. Insofar as such an infinite and cognizable field corresponds to the modern space of aesthetic reflection, the historical limits of the play's construction can't be neatly separated from the unstable horizon of our own speculative relation to the play. That limit—the point where the problem of reference recurs—is also the point where the problem of race is inscribed, I argue; thus the particular insistence of race in the age of the universal citizen-subject.

The Winter's Tale and *The Tempest* focus on sovereignty as a specifically early modern form, that is, sovereignty as it is constituted in the kind of signifying universe implied by *Othello*. The problem of autonomy—the autonomy of the sovereign, the autonomy of the subject—is directly related to the outright way in which these late plays self-consciously present themselves as works whose inclusive aesthetic form incorporates the audience in its unstable, performative effects. In *Winter's Tale*, the focus of chapter 5, the possibility of sovereign agency depends ultimately on an articulation between the categories of aesthetics and law, an articulation necessitated by the illimitable character of both. The close of the play hinges on the possibility of maintaining a ratio between law and art, which also means a space for subjectivity as such.

The very scale or scope of the aesthetic solution articulated in these late works, the fact that it takes in the possibility of speculative history and subjectivity, intimates the abyss against which political aestheticization is staked. *The Tempest*, which is the focus of chapter 6, foregrounds the inextricable relation between aestheticization and alterity, whether that alterity is conceived as the cultural otherness, the otherness of the unconscious drives, or the radical contingency of history. The early modern political aesthetic, the historical process by which sovereignty is recouped through a mechanism that might seem ameliorative—a sublimation of power—in fact brings to view something dire at the ontological core of the political, something more disquieting than the death of kings.

Chapter 7 turns from the creationist aesthetic and the fluidly political space of the Renaissance polis—Shakespeare's world—to the "rationalized" state of Hobbes and the proto-Enlightenment era. The aesthetic is, I argue, what must be foreclosed to establish the encompassing fiction of the modern state—it is what the neutral state as the space of reason poses itself against. At the same time the aesthetic is what returns with a force directly proportionate to that exclusion, not dispersedly, as in the universe of Shakespeare's late works, but as the fixed but unacknowledgeable lining and support of modern political space.

CHAPTER I

Early Modern Political Aesthetics

Aesthetics: Renaissance and Early Modern

D epending on what term one chooses for the era, and thus, perhaps, on critical affiliation, the phrase "political aesthetics *in the time of Shakespeare*" will seem either redundant or merely nonsensical. A pleonasm insofar as the Renaissance—to retain that term for the period—is itself an aesthetic formation, founded as it is on *imitatio*. In Jacob Burckhardt's Hegelian *Kulturgeschichte*, through which the era dialectically constitutes itself as universal form by way of a negation and absorption of the past, the Renaissance becomes itself by becoming an image. Just as the state is realized "as a work of art," so too early modernity is the era in which eras become something like aesthetic forms.

Or else else the phrase is meaningless, insofar as the reference to aesthetics is assumed to be anachronistic. A more recent generation of cultural materialist analysis staked itself in good measure as against what it took to be the political and historical impertinence of the "aestheticization" (to use the term favored by cultural construction theorists) implied by the term *Renaissance*. The fact that the aesthetic does not appear as a philosophical term until the eighteenth century or as a marked ideological operation until the nineteenth century gives the early modern literary critic pride of place in the general materialist project of analyzing the work according to its cultural "embeddedness," which means treating the work as something like an anthropological artifact.[1] Or else, where the aesthetic is admitted, it is with an insistence on its porousness as a category, which is to say as no real category at all.

The curious all-or-nothing status of the aesthetic in the era is worth holding in view, first, because it is not resolvable, and second, because that irresolvability is what makes the aesthetic a political matter. But something of the difficulty of coming to grips with early modern aesthetics may already be evident in the terms of the debate as I have very schematically outlined thus far.

That debate—the difference between the *early modern* and *Renaissance* as appellations—might simply be characterized as an opposition between historicizing and aestheticizing, a recognition of historical difference as counter to the impositions of nineteenth-century models of universalizing aesthetic acculturation. And yet, it may be hard to know on which side to place history in such a conflict. It was precisely through the sense of difference implied by the structure of *imitatio* that humanist history first articulated a self-consciousness of its own historicity.[2] The effect is not confined to the domain of letters; it bears on the process through which the phenomenal world itself becomes "little more than the idea of its own past."[3] Moreover, and to trouble these initial distinctions even further, according to the logic of such a self-separating consciousness, anachronism becomes the very hallmark of historicization. "I am happier," Petrarch writes, "with the dead than with the living."[4]

To the extent that that experience of "historical solitude" or pathos remains within a model of "supercessive history," the temporality it articulates could be said to remain within the Hegelian, that is systematic and speculative, structure that underwrites Burckhardt's understanding of a progressive universal culture.[5] But, as Lisa Frienkel has subtly shown, the foregrounding of literariness—of the "languageness of language," as Joel Fineman puts it—during the era aligns the experience of finitude with a breaking down of the figural, projective/retrogressive logic that sustains such a speculative structure—a revealing of *figura* as pure troping. With Petrarch, where the tropic language of poetry turns "toward the language of turning itself," the erosions of time become inseparable from the limitless movement of its articulation.[6]

At the same time, historically contextualizing critique can be hard to separate from the most seemingly dehistoricizing variants of aestheticization. Louis Montrose's well-known phrase, "the historicity of texts and the textuality of history"—a formulation whose notable critical currency derived from the way it seemed to have finessed the hard relation between representation and history for a generation of early modern literary critics—is notable for the way it determines the relation between language and history by way of a structure that is itself rhetorical. Indeed, Montrose relies on a trope, chiasmus, whose reflective symmetries might seem to place it strongly on the side of a speculative annulment of difference.[7] That Montrose can move unanxiously from such a formulation—which he explicitly describes as a matter of "figur[ing] forth from within discourse" the "reciprocal relationship between discourse and material domains"—to accounts of writing as a historically determinate event "performed *in* the world and *upon* world," where world and history resume their substantive forms, may suggest how lightly intended the engagement with the problem of rhetoric is here.[8] Or it may suggest that rhetoric is doing greater duty than we might suppose; to what extent is the paradoxical operation through which textuality chiastically incorporates itself as a limitable term, even as it thereby exceeds itself, the condition for the production of oppositional categories like *text* and *world*?

Montrose's formulation comes out of a moment when the literary field was still preoccupied with categories such as textuality. But the problem of the aesthetic insinuates itself even into texts with a more unequivocal commitment to the hard-nosed business of empirical analysis; indeed, following a logic that I will explore, the aesthetic may most insinuate itself where it would seem most excluded. Douglas Bruster's recent advocacy of a return to a quantitative, data-driven analysis of culture is sophisticated about the mediated nature of the analytic object. Bruster argues in part that in forsaking a recognition of the complex social mediation of the object as developed in, say, Marxist analysis, the naïve materialism of recent object studies work in the early modern field fails to engage the political and historical dimensions of its undertaking.[9]

The larger aim of Bruster's project is to forward an argument for a broader, aggregative approach to analytical evidence, a technique of "thin description" he sets against the Geertzian "thick description" favored by New Historicist and Cultural Materialist schools of thinking. In Bruster's account, the latter approach is based on a rhetorical figure—the synecdochal *pars pro toto*—that allows the practitioner a rapid-fire passage from anecdotal detail to large cultural claim. The danger of such a technique is explicitly an aesthetic matter, he argues. New Historicist analyses found favor, Bruster argues, because of the seductive force of the tales they tell, a form of "narrative spell" that draws in the listener even as it threatens to blind the analyst herself to a larger frame of reference: "the aesthetic—generally banished as an object of critical inquiry—has returned with ironic but uncanny persistence as a mode of critical inquiry itself" (53, 41).

The "thin description" Bruster proposes to "break the spell" of such narratives entails a more assiduous and expansive aggregation of empirical evidence. Bruster justifies that accretive method by way of the metaphor of sampling. Following their particular narrative threads, the New Historicists do not account for "the size and shape of the web," "the cultural web's circumference" and "design" (47). To know that design, we need a multiplication of samples cut from the bolt of cloth that makes up the culture in its entirety; only then; can we begin to recognize the larger pattern (46–47). The difficulty with the analogy is that a multiplication of samples can only be said to reveal a true pattern if we presuppose in advance the limitable character of the field of analysis. In other words, we presume a posture of externality in relation to that field from which we could view it as a totality. The "convenience" of New Historicists consists in their "never having to represent the culture from outside, or as a whole" (47). And yet, if we are already in a posture to see the culture from the outside, in its entirety, then what is the purpose of the sampling?

The difficulty is not a function of the sampling metaphor; it is inherent to empirical method as such. However one may speak of the cultural field being "open," the aggregative method implies a logic of adequation, that is, the sense that one builds toward a full, or fuller, approximation of the object. With that comes an implied reference to a presupposed totality. Empirical method inevitably entails the positing of a horizon to constitute the space within which its "discoveries" are made.[10] This does not mean that one could do without empirical evidence. The point is rather that evidence cannot be separated from exemplification, and exemplification from the *pars pro toto* of synecdoche, with everything such a trope suggests of rhetoricity and interpretive force. And of the aesthetic; when Bruster speaks of cultures as "open unities"—or of culture as a "totality" that is "full of contradiction and conflict" and operates "dialectically," yet which nevertheless remains a totality—he repeats the work of Burckhardtian *Kulturgeschichte*, the sublating task of negating and translating sheer particularity into unity even while retaining those particulars in all their rich multiplicity.[11]

The matter of rhetorical force bears on the way an argument for the most chasteningly austere modes of data analysis—the thinnest of thin descriptions—can take on the character of an agonistic drama.

For Bruster, the pleasures of the New Historicist turn out to be at once exhibitionistic and solitary. Like all "storytellers," thick descriptors "like to hold the floor," but they do so self-absorbedly: "Because the critics in question typically decline to 'place' their remarks in relationship to an established conversation, what we hear are pleasant solo voices whose echoes soon fade" (52). That these critics tend to be "addicted" to their own tropes, engage in a narrative mode that "has a way of leading critics in directions of its own choosing," and tend to "defer payment" on their "scholarly dues," all suggest the onanistic character of the activities of the aestheticizing critics and their private speculative pleasures (44, 39, 51). Against that scene is set the unglamorous labor of the more traditional researcher, staying out of the limelight, but more willing to take "seriously conversations about a particular topic" (51). Understood thus, the problem with the thick descriptive method is its "reluctance to acknowledge 'otherness' in the critic's own field" (51).

"Otherness" is the title of this section of Bruster's chapter, and the term functions as a rhetorical pay off. Set off in quotes as it is, we are not sure whose voice we hear in the reference to " 'otherness.' " The ambiguity lets the term at once signal an irony even as it genuinely ups the ante of the argument. A matter of scholarly conversation—citing your sources, for example—takes on a political charge. It becomes a question of who speaks for the other: the argument assumes a larger referential claim. Yet it is an ironic turn as well in Bruster's view. For the voice of the other is foreclosed thus precisely by those most likely to invoke "otherness," the New Historicists and "new materialists" who imagine their approach to be "politically liberating" and who speak in terms of "colonialism, class, gender, sexuality."

This is a rhetorical moment through and through insofar as its force depends on a suspension of the referential dimension of language, an unmooring of voice. But it is also a case of a critical method leading the critic "in directions of its own choosing," of its "run[ning] antithetical to the author's own positions," inasmuch as that suspension of voice and reference is serving an argument for the importance of citing one's sources (39). All of which merely bears out Bruster's observation about the way the aesthetic, "generally banished as an object of critical inquiry," tends to return "with ironic but uncanny persistence," in this instance in relation to an argument explicitly staked on the importance of keeping the aesthetic in its place.[12]

The difficulty of placing or contextualizing the aesthetic as a specifically Renaissance matter is connected to the problem of the relation between the aesthetic and historicization generally. Bruster's opposition between aesthetic pleasure and data is itself a historical phenomenon, although one that poses the question of what *historical phenomenon* means. According to a familiar sociological account, the aesthetic emerges during the late eighteenth century as a category of autonomous experience in a doublet with empiricism, as its opposing term with its own versions of truth claims, but also as a function of what an increasingly refined empirical method came to suggest about the possibility of multiple and discrete discursive fields.[13]

One can dispute the claim on historical grounds; as Michael McKeon shows, there are important precursors for the empirical-aesthetic distinction, especially the Renaissance revival of the Aristotelian difference between history and poetry, between the factual or singular and the universal.[14] One could imagine making a case for an earlier appearance of the category based on such antecedents. But the stricter period formulation may actually bring us closer to what is distinctive and problematic about the "early modern aesthetic." The sociological narrative might suggest there simply is no aesthetic before the eighteenth century. And yet, the binding of the aesthetic to the empirical—the fact that they share the same horizon according to such an account—would also compel one to say merely that the aesthetic does not exist as a phenomenon of *empirical history* prior to its eighteenth-century advent. If it existed, it would exist in relation to a different version of historicity.

The paradox is that it is just such a possibility that is first opened in the eighteenth century with Kant's articulation of the aesthetic as a mode of contingent judgment—a matter of *sensus communis*—but one not fully assimilable to norms of cognition and thus to fully realized phenomenal representation. The contingency of such judgment means the aesthetic is not universal (or ahistorical) any more than it is empirically particularizable. The aesthetic is historical, but its historicity is inseparable from the division and ellipsis implicit in its own appearance, the fact that it is a category definitionally out of sync with itself and with its articulation as a cognizable category. In other words, the aesthetic may be most realized or at least in effect when it is not fully realized as a manifest philosophical category.

The problematic relation between the aesthetic and historicization is implicit in the category's fundamental relationship to the problem of autonomy. In one sense, to speak of an "autonomous aesthetic" is re-dundant: as a philosophical matter, the aesthetic is the privileged instance of discourse's capacity to ground itself on principles internal to itself. The aesthetic amounted to the means of thinking autonomy—thus Habermas's claim that "the problem of grounding modernity out of itself first comes into consciousness in the realm of aesthetic criticism."[15] Why the aesthetic and autonomy? As the system of representation always potentially severed from an instrumental function—and thus lending itself to reflection on its own status as representation—art is the domain in which the problem of discourse's self-grounding is brought to the fore.

That self-grounding necessarily implies the sort of irresolvable relation between structure and history encountered whenever one describes a field—for example an epistemological domain, or a social domain—as a discursive field. The historical character of that field cannot be located as extrinsic to it; to do so merely suspends and defers the problem of genesis to an anterior discursive field. Nor can the field's grounds be located within it, insofar as it is the contingency of the field as field that is at issue. Aesthetic foundations assume the form of a breach or division that takes place neither within nor beyond the structure, an effect neither immanent within nor transcendent to it. The historicity of the aesthetic, always in both senses of the genitive, takes the form of a contingent material inscription never fully assimilable to the closed, speculative operations of the structure it constitutes, including the speculative ordering of the forms of narrative historicizing which would place the aesthetic *purely* as a period phenomenon.[16]

That foundational operation suggests the methodological paradoxes that attend the category. The familiar claim that the aesthetic implies closure—and above all a closing off of the work from its historical conditions—is not wrong. Such a claim is certainly borne out in its fully developed ideological forms during the bourgeois era, where the autonomous work analogizes something like possessive individualism—the aesthetic is always invested in the prospect of its own closure.[17] The analytical "solution" to such a trait is contextualization, that is, engaging the determining causes of such an ideological formation. And yet, understood as the appeal to a governing context, historicizing repeats the aesthetic operation it seeks to explain; for the defining operation of the aesthetic, the process by which it seeks to constitute itself as a field, is the procedure by which it would enclose and delimit itself as against a determinable outside.

The aesthetic is, in that sense, the process of its own contextualization; the always failed, because always self-exceeding, story or allegory of its own grounds. Thus the "ironic but uncanny persistence" of the aesthetic. The route "out" of aesthetic ideology—which is also to say the route to imagining our way to its fringes as a phenomenon of our own time—then, is not through contextualization but by way of a passage further in as it were, by absolutizing or radicalizing the claims of autonomy. To take up the aesthetic's own unstable foundational mechanism is to engage historical contingency and specificity as what inscribes itself as something other and less settling than a narrative of extrinsic causes.

Because the aesthetic is in an acute sense inseparable from the problem of its categorization, its historical character becomes inseparable from the problem of interpretive procedure. The aesthetic's intrinsic relation to the problem of boundaries gives early modern aesthetics the status of a formation that can neither be determined as historical adumbration nor as retroactive projection. The value of an epithet like "early modern aesthetic"—straddling uneasily between the *Renaissance*, with all that the term implies about a secure fit between aesthetics and periodization, and the *early modern*, with its presumed antiaesthetic historicism—consists in its ability to keep that relation between history and interpretive irresolution in view. This means keeping the question of interpretive force in view as well.[18]

The Literary and Its Limits: As You Like It, King Lear, *and* Dr. Faustus

The (synecdochic) evidence for a heightened preoccupation with a distinct aesthetic sphere during the era—for a sense that, in Cassirer's formulation, "the feeling for form . . . is advanced beyond the feeling for life"—is manifold. For Cassirer, that autonomization is bound up with historical structures of consciousness, the turn from "homo" to the "homo-homo" of formally reflexive self-identity.[19] Paul Kottman describes such a translation as a passage from classical *poesis* to early modern "*auto-poesis*."[20] That reflexivity is registered equally at the level of the arts as a disciplinary category, in what Robert Williams describes as art's growing reflection on its own systematicity. He associates such a development with "the autonomy of culture as a whole—its emergence as a complex, yet integrated set of codes, a realm defined by the power of representation."[21]

As that last formulation suggests, aesthetic autonomy can be associated with world-gathering totalization, a capacity that is forwarded by Renaissance theorists who claim "nothing less than that art creates culture."[22] But the experience of form advanced "beyond the feeling of life" can equally shape itself as an experience of sheer superfluity, the sense of literate knowledge as "waste," as Robert Matz has shown in his analysis of English literary culture of the era.[23] That conjunction of totalizing encompassment and superfluity has a sociological referent, bound up as it is with the ambiguous, betwixt-and-between status of the humanist man of letters in the emerging class structures of state.[24] But the contradiction—what Clark Hulse nicely describes as literature's "encompassing extraneousness" during the era—may also simply be the surest sign that one is in the throes of the aesthetic as such.[25]

I would like to approach the logic of "encompassing extraneousness" in a preliminary fashion and indicate where such aesthetic concerns assume a political dimension—where aesthetics becomes political aesthetics—by way of two Shakespeare plays: *As You Like It* and *King Lear*. The comedy suggests how the aesthetic is bound up with a developed sense of literariness associated with sexuality and ethics. The reflexive inclusiveness of such a category problematizes New Historicist accounts of the literary aesthetic as one limitable and porous category amongst others. By tracing the literary to its limit—by giving it its due—we will be able, turning to *King Lear,* to recognize how the political emerges precisely at that boundary and in a different ontological register. In *King Lear*, such a limit is the point where questions of aesthetic autonomy and sovereignty intersect. Later, I will return to that political aesthetic conjunction from the vantage point of political theory.

The aesthetic status and stakes of *As You Like It* are most apparent in the way the play addresses us at the close, at the point where Rosalind steps aside from her character and from the play to engage the audience directly. Her power to "conjure" us—to place us under the sway of the work—is directly related to her status as literary and erotic go-between, as a superfluity that nevertheless embodies the work at its most irreducible:

> It is not the fashion to see the lady the epilogue; but it is no more unhandsome than to see the lord the prologue. If it be true that good wine needs no bush, 'tis true that a good play needs no epilogue. Yet to good wine they do use good bushes, and good plays prove the better by the help of good epilogues. What a case am I in then, that am neither a good epilogue nor cannot insinuate with you in the behalf of

a good play! I am not furnished like a beggar, therefore to beg will not become me. My way is to conjure you; and I'll begin with the women. I charge you, O women, for the love you bear to men, to like as much of this play as please you. And I charge you, O men, for the love you bear to women—as I perceive by your simpering, none of you hates them—that between you and the women the play may please. If I were a woman I would kiss as many of you as had beards that pleased me, complexions that liked me, and breaths that I defied not. And I am sure, as many as have good beards, or good faces, or sweet breaths will for my kind offer, when I make curtsy, bid me farewell.[26]

What promised to be a simple enlistment of all parties—once you accrue the women for the love of men, the men for the love of men, you've included everyone, you might think—turns out to be a considerably more ambiguous form of conjuration. Why do we clap at the end? For the manly men—the good-bearded sorts—the impulse might well be aggressive, a matter of bidding farewell indeed to the approaches of the curtsying figure. After all, she had already let the mask drop: "If I were a woman." In that sense, clapping would be of the spell-breaking sort, a matter of drawing the line on what has been a thoroughly ambiguous fiction.[27] But of course she never said she was a man, only "if I were a woman," and thus never stepped aside from the play's infinitely iffy, infinitely conjectural world, where the opposite of "if I were a woman" is only ever "if I were a man." "'If' is the only peace maker," says Touchstone, resolutely (5.4.91–2). If we feel trapped by Rosalind's approach at the close, it is by virtue of our having snared ourselves; it is, in other words, precisely the audience's desire to draw a line on the fiction that renews its inscription within it. We are guilty in defense, as King Henry V says of the encircled citizens of Harfleur.

Here, that ensnarement is expressly a matter of the irreducibility of the relation between fiction and desire. Just as to repudiate the weakly solicitous figure is merely to betray the fact of its threatening power—which is also to say the presence of one's own untoward desire—so forcibly to determine the limit of the fiction is merely to reveal the fact of its illimitability. Just as the figure who "insinuates" or comes between men and women constitutively divides them even as it joins them, so what turns us from what we want shows us the way to our desire, shows us, that is, how such veering is precisely as we like it.

What seemed a primitive ploy—to clap to banish the fiction signifies one's approval—turns out to obey a more intractable logic. In relation to the prospect of illimitable conjecture—a sphere where, as Touchstone puts it, "the truest poesy is the most feigning"—one can only draw the line. Such a demarcation is what lets us call this an effect of fiction at all, and thus claim a space of judgment beyond.[28] And that is what inscribes us, what determines fiction as limitless. The relation between desire and inscription can be felt in the wavering of agency in the epilogue's words. Note the slippage between transitive and intransitive, animate and inanimate, that occurs as we approach the inclusive close where the constitutive boundary between play and epilogue, inside and outside, reaches a vanishing point, and thus the point where enunciating identity becomes indistinguishable from the language of its desiring enunciation: "If I were a woman I would kiss as many of you as had beards that pleased me, complexions that liked me, and breaths that I defied not." Just as desire is inseparable from its prohibition, fiction—the literary, the theatrical—will have been nothing but the reiterated effect of the effort to contextualize it, to know it as fiction. Such an inscriptive effect is for Shakespeare a form of aesthetic knowledge, an express retort to, or perhaps simply an ironizing of, Sidney's remarks in the *Defence of Poetry* about literary "conjuration" as a circumscribed power.[29] The literary is at once nothing—neither this nor that, sheer difference and thus incognizable—and illimitable: the groundless ground of any cognizable form.[30]

This is not just a supplementary turn at play's close. It is what the play has been about. If we miss the ungrounded character of the epilogue's hypothetical—if we are caught presuming a ground—it is only because we chose to forget the thoroughgoing iffyness of the play's resolving "recognition" scene:

DUKE SENIOR   If there be truth in sight, you are my daughter.
ORLANDO   If there be truth in sight, you are my Rosalind.
PHOEBE   If sight and shape are true,
 Why then, my love adieu!

(5.4.107–10)

"[I'll] make conclusion," Hymen, the god of marriage declares, "if truth holds true contents" (115, 119). Hymen's presence is itself of course the most extravagant "if," a point made clear by the remarkable inverse *deus ex machina* of the conclusion: a god imported precisely at the point where all is resolvable. Rosalind has managed everything, pulled all the strings, and would seem merely to have to reveal herself to conclude the play. In that sense, the fictive, mediating god, who arrives to "bar confusion," prompts confusion—a barring of our desire that is, of course, the engine of a desire that never has been in anyone's hands.[31]

And again, we should have known—the conclusion is anticipated. When, with the end approaching, Duke Senior remarks that "this shepherd boy"—disguised Rosalind—recalls to him his "daughter's favor," Orlando replies that when he first saw him, he, too, remarked the family resemblance:

> But, my good lord, this boy is forest-born,
> And hath been tutored in the rudiments
> Of many desperate studies by his uncle,
> Whom he reports to be a great magician
> Obscurèd in the circle of this forest.
>   (5.4.30–34)

The audience takes this fiction as *mere* fiction—a subterfuge—only by virtue of a proprietary assumption of the truth claims of the fiction it has been inhabiting—in other words, by virtue of its having been seduced by the fiction. In fact, if it is a matter of scale—which fiction circumscribes which—the tale of the magician uncle might have the greater claim, whether by virtue of a reference to the circle of the theater itself (the O within which all fictions have transpired), or through the metaphorical association between the forest and the entanglements of illimitable fiction. However, the error and the captivation are not of the corrigible sort. To have pointed there, at the reference to the unseen conjuring circle, as the secret heart of the play, would be to repeat the force of an inscription renewed precisely by the claim to designate it, one in which seduction is an effect of vigilance.

That aesthetic effect amounts to an ethic for Shakespeare, and an ethic that is distinct from whatever might be implied by the familiar *theatrum mundi* trope. The point is made explicit in Jaques's set piece rendition of that motif. As critics have noted, it is hard not to feel that Jaques's "All the world's a stage" speech expresses something other than a neutral representation of the "universal theater" of human existence. The sense that it says as much about the speaker's bitterness and self-regard, that it bears out Duke Senior's claim that his presumption to the fool's license is driven by his own libertinage, might be brought home by the appearance on stage of poor Adam carried on the back of his devoted charge just as Jaques ends with cold reference to the "last scene of all," "second childishness and mere oblivion, / Sans teeth, sans eyes, sans taste, sans everything" (2.7.162, 164–65).

But the problem is not mimetic, the fact that Jaques's emblems of life's stages reduce the richness of human life. Old Man Adam on the back of the young is at least as emblematic. The problem is rather that he has misconstrued the remark that launched him into his panoramic set piece. "Thou seest we are not all alone unhappy," the Duke had said: "This wide and universal theatre / Presents more woeful pageants than the scene / Wherein we play in" (2.7.135–38). The fact that there are other scenes than the one wherein we play is not an empirical point, as if a wider view might bring them into view. It is rather the necessary condition of a supervening and thus always exorbitant scenography: a universal, in the sense of infinite, theater. Whether we read it in relation to the fact of sociality or the fact of the unconscious, the "other scene" as other is a structural condition of the human.[32]

In that sense the scene amounts to Shakespeare's before-the-fact commentary, not just on empirical knowledge but on a certain version of antifoundationalism: the version that imagines the absence of grounds implies pure relativity, a world of equatable meanings, cultures, or "stages." To perceive thus is in fact to presume a posture of exteriority from which one could see the world as a system of equivalence. Relativism is, in that sense, a variant of transcendentalism. Jaques's narcissism, his claim to liberty and autonomy, is precisely a function and an effect of that presumption of transcendence. And, again, it is that presumed externality that inscribes. Jaques is legible in every detail of his "universal theatre" because such a scene is never anything but the reflection of the force involved in the claim to make it knowable. In that sense, the ethics of the other scene is an epistemological ethic founded on the distinction between not knowing and knowing you do not know.

The reference to ethics and knowledge in relation to the aesthetic makes plain that we are engaged with an aesthetic ideology. It is an ideology whose distinction from a later bourgeois equivalency between the aesthetic and autonomous individualism is sufficiently marked to give it the character of a prescient critique: a critique, in fact, of the complicity between notions of equivalency and forcibly claimed autonomy. The aesthetic of other scenes is an ideology nonetheless, and one that is as fragile as it is expansive. For it takes very little for the unseen circle in the forest in *As You Like It*—the unknowable space that reveals or constitutes the human as social being—to become the unspeakable nothing, the zero, of *King Lear*. The distinction is not a function of generic difference per se. It is rather an effect of a signifying structure that lies behind the distinction between comedy and tragedy as modern forms.

In one sense, the shift between the comedy and the tragedy can be described simply: in his status as sovereign, King Lear assumes, or is placed within, the place or the nonplace of the other scene, of the circle as illimitable and empty. This is a claim to sovereign autonomy, but an impossible autonomy distinct from Jaques's unstable narcissism. Instead it is a radical autonomy that can be categorized as neither immanence nor transcendence; it is the mark of a play in which the boundaries between insides and outsides, sexual and familial, ritual and real are endlessly dissolved. From the outset—from the ex nihilo "decision" against which and from which the drama emerges—blindness is identical with an impossible knowledge. Lear's banishment of the daughter he most loves insures her a marriage based on love. More fundamentally, the act through which Cordelia is placed beyond the sovereign's ken—a blind act of rage and an act of love—constitutes the space of the drama itself as a drama of recognition within which the characters as knowing subjects will be constituted.[33] Sovereign ritual is that opaque, autogenerative opening of the space within which sovereignty itself will be formed.[34]

The all and nothing of *King Lear* should be read in relation to the limits of the aesthetic ideology—a form of Montaignian skeptical humanism—manifest in *As You Like It*. The comedy, with its claims for the possibility of forms of rapport based on the knowledge that one does not know, is governed by an understanding of language as groundless and thus illimitable. And yet, that understanding of language as a pure, formal system is founded on a contradiction; based on the banishment of all reference, the structure is nevertheless marked by what it excludes precisely in its own claims to self-referentiality. Phenomenal reference recurs, not as a function of content—that is, not at the level of the signified—but precisely in the form of language's inevitable movement beyond itself, as what Paul de Man describes as an inevitable aberrance inherent in language.[35] The recursive doubling back of language in its self-referential movement means a division or deviation that is the condition of language as language, as a self-riven form that is always at once phenomenal and nonphenomenal.[36] That insistent division and difference represents the aesthetic's engagement with the fact of its own radical contingency and its historicity. History, in that regard, takes the form of a reiterated mark of finitude that is at once inassimilable to and the condition of the aesthetic as a cognitive form.

The inscriptive and destabilizing force of that finitude is apparent at the close of *King Lear* where the play returns to the *ex nihilo* of its self-creation. Lear holds his daughter in his arms:

> Thou'lt come no more,
> Never, never, never, never, never!
> Pray you, undo this button. Thank you, sir.
> Do you see this? Look on her, look, her lips,
> Look there, look there! *Dies*
> EDGAR   He faints! My lord, my lord!
>
> (5.3.306–10)

What the king sees on Cordelia's mute lips is a corrective to his initial presumption: "Nothing will come of nothing: speak again." Nor are we in a position to say he sees nothing—that all is merely an illusion. The recognition—the convergence of father and daughter toward which the play has aimed—occurs by way of a mutual and indeterminate crisscrossing of death's limit that dissolves the boundary between fictive and real, self and other, subject and object. Death reveals itself as what is absolute—the determining limit of consciousness and being—and yet, insofar as it is known as limit, as something compassable, has already been crossed. It is, in that sense, what is infinitely finite.

The delimiting "look there" that at once marks and renews the play of limits is a snare, but one that operates in a different dimension than the forms of reifying objectification that inscribe the audience within the comedy's play of fictions. Rather than a claim *on* fiction, a delusively objectifying claim to know fiction as fiction, Lear's deixis enacts the referential function *of* language, that is, the posited and unstable condition of any phenomenalization whatsoever. What had been in the comedy a cognitive question—a matter of plays and epilogues, of what is known and unknown played out in the relation to the work as signifying system—becomes in the frameless tragedy a matter of being, of the ceaseless *ex nihilo* creation and de-creation of the world as existent.[37]

The ontological character of *King Lear*'s engagement with sovereignty suggests the register in which we might address the relation between aesthetics and politics during the era. I will discuss shortly political sovereignty from the vantage point of political theory, but first, I want to consider what has been the most familiar way in which literary autonomy has been affiliated with social and cultural conditions of the early modern moment: the relation between literature and commodification. Whether understood in terms of the corrosive, ground-dissolving fungibility of a culture of self-fashioning or perceptions of the limitlessly substitutive character of sign and meaning, autonomous literariness has been affiliated with the dizzying supervention of exchange value implied by the commodity: the "all that's solid melts into air" of early modernity as proto-capitalism. This is an accurate association, and certainly one of the stories the era tells itself about the dangers of the literary. "The world is but a word," Flavius says (2.2.147); it is no coincidence the insight is embedded in a work, *Timon*, devoted to the world-dissolving properties of exchange. And yet we can ask if the analogy with economy—whether we take aesthetic autonomy as an extension of or as a mystifying protection against the fact of economic causation—exhausts the question of the aesthetic, or even whether it engages the political dimension of the aesthetic at the right level.

Consider Marlowe's *Dr. Faustus*, a work that has focused attention on the relationship between the autonomy of the signifier and commodification, most extensively in David Hawkes's *Faustus Myth: Religion and the Rise of Representation*.[38] "Lines, circles, signs, letters, and characters—/ Ay, these are those that Faustus most desires" (1.1.53–54).[39] Such captivation, an effect of the autonomous activity of the "efficacious sign," is, by Hawkes's account, a historical phenomenon: "the Faust myth emerged as a response to what the people of early modern Europe believed was a vast and deleterious increase in the practical power of the performative sign," the sign that takes on a life of its own.[40] That deleterious power is a consequence of the scope of exchange in the era, a power of buying and selling that extends in the play right to the contractualization of the soul. An early critique of possessive individualism, *Dr. Faustus* is also, for Hawkes, a fundamentally antitheatrical play, a drama that critiques the seductive and unmoored character of the literary work.[41]

Hawkes's argument crystallizes in relation to Faustus's famous Helen of Troy speech, where the alienability of the soul is directly correlated with the demonic hold of the image.[42]

> Was this the face that launched a thousand ships
> And burnt the topless towers of Ilium?
> Sweet Helen, make me immortal with a kiss.
> [*They kiss*]

Her lips suck forth my soul. See where it flies!
Come, Helen, come give me my soul again.
[*They kiss again*]
Here will I dwell, for heaven be in these lips,
And all is dross that is not Helena.

(5.1. 90–96)

The "forward and backward" of exchange here is correlated with the power of the untethered image, a seduction whose relation to literary autonomy is emphasized in its proximity to autoerotic exchange: Faustus calls forth, or has called forth, the image that seduces him. And yet, any effort to moralize the scene, to see it as a commentary on the dangers of commodification or of the signifier, are complicated by the curiously open-eyed character of the seduction. The fact that Faustus himself, like a chorus to the moment, offers something like a running commentary on the alienation of the soul ("see where it flies!") is of a piece with the self-consciousness of the literary seduction; it is not Helen who seduces, it is a knowing relation to literariness as literariness—"signs, letters and characters"—that draws him in.[43]

Faustus's self-consciousness—that quality of self-exteriority one feels throughout the play—is inseparable from the question of what we mean by literary autonomy, and how that bears on the limitability of the literary. The literary becomes the literary by virtue of a power of self-exemplification, through the turn that lets the Helen scene, for example, figure the experience of playgoing. But because that movement of self-exemplification *is* the literary as such, because the aesthetic is the problem of its own framing, such a turn does not provide a posture of exteriority; in that sense commentary is indistinguishable from inscription, and knowingness is indistinguishable from absorption.

That paradox can be read in the larger, autotelic movement of the play. In one regard, the Helen scene is consistent with the narrowing course of the play itself, its reduction from cosmic flights to slapstick parody, a trajectory that is the measure of Faustus's (and the audience's) reductive absorption within the space of theater. But constriction is equally the sign of a knowingness, the knowledge precisely of what it shores against, and the limit Faustus and the play itself have contracted for themselves: the end of life, the end of theater.

That open and closed, knowing and unknowing, condition becomes the condition of literary subjectivity in the vortex of the play's last

moments. Faustus's final address is governed by its intensifying contradictions: a terror of finality that is also a terror of infinitude, a movement
of aversion "hide me from the heavy wrath of God") that is also an eroti-
cized embrace ("*O lente, lente currite noctis equi!*"), an external constraint
that cannot be distinguished from an internalized check (who, indeed,
"pulls [Faustus] down" when he would "leap up to [his] God"?), a pan-
icked immersion in the moment that is also the experience of self-distance
implied by Faustus's mode of address "That Faustus may repent and save
his soul" (5.2.77, 66, 69, 65). All these tensions represent the increasingly
hystericized and self-divisive enunciation of a work in which description and positing, encunciator and enunciated, have become indistinguishable. The play brings on its own end in a form that nevertheless
remains alien to it, and thus approaches a vanishing point rather than
a closure. In that regard, the B-text's account of dismemberment and
dispersal is neither the final indicator of divine judgment nor its
inverse—a realization of what Mephistopheles had threatened for
Faustus's having forsaken the satanic cause—but the allegorization of
the work as what dissolves in its own movement any prospect of such
normative judgments.

It suspends any neat narrative of its own cause. Accounts of *Dr. Faustus* as a threshold text in the history of representation center on its more
alien moments, for instance, the strange scene in which Faustus hap-
pily gluts himself on the parade of grotesque allegorical vices Lucifer
conjures for him: "O, this feeds my soul!" (2.3.157). One can gluttonously feed, but what does it mean to feed on the *representation* of glut-
tony? One might say that at such moments the play reveals its roots
in a premodern, nonpsychological mode of didactic representation.[44]
And yet, the scene might equally reveal the play at its most "modern"
and psychologizing, showing Faustus's desire as the negational, self-
overreaching, and contentless drive of a sheer relational, literary subjectivity—a Faustus drawn, defiantly, *because* the figures warn against
themselves. The more external and alien the figures, the more ineffable
the depth psychology. The point is not that the scene represents the play's
source as the switch point between historical forms, but that the literariness it sets in motion gluttonously consumes whatever narrative is posited as its extrinsic historical ground.

The question of historicity needs to be situated in a dimension
other than narrated causes. This brings us back to the cultural relation
between literature and commodification, and of what there is of the

literary that may not be subsumed in that analogy. Economy, understood as a calculable system of exchange, is, like narrative history, a
speculative form. Even extended infinitely, commodification remains
a determinate, or closed, speculative operation—as is literature, in a
measure. Faustus can be seduced by an image he himself has conjured
because his desire is caught up within the movement of that speculative loop.

But to describe literature in such speculative terms, and to understand the hold of theater thus, is also to ask what opens the possibility
of such a dialectical structure in the first place. Is the literary *like* an
economic contract—the equivalent of a system of equivalences—or
should it be located at the point where the contractual act does not sustain itself?[45] The point in the play, for instance, where the contractual
act is blocked and suspended, where the blood-ink congeals and another
script forms itself automatically: "Here in this place is writ / '*Homo, fuge!*'"
(2.1.80–81). Is this divine injunction: flee this place, this scene? Is it alienated self-address: flee yourself, the end rebellious Faustus attempts to
accomplish by force of will? Or is the phrase a nominative designator
without grounding or source beyond its own written inscription: "*homo
fuge*," man as flight, the unmotivated emblem of literary subjectivity,
man as the vectorless detouring of allegorization itself?

That account of the literary as inscription beyond and in advance
of speculative exchange can be teased out from a detail in another scene
of conjuring. After Faustus has called up the images of Alexander and
his "beauteous paramour" for the Emperor, the Emperor remarks that
he had heard the "lady while she lived had a wart or mole in her neck":
"Your highness may boldly go and see." He does, leading him to de-
clare, "sure these are no spirits, but the true substantial bodies of those
two deceased princes" (4.1.62–63, 65–66). Why the excrescent detail?
In one regard, it is what punctures the illusion: however absorbed, the
attentive audience member would hear the allusion to the witch's mark,
and thus be reminded of the demonic character of the enterprise. At
the same time, though, the paramour's mole is the fulfillment of the
fantasy as fantasy. The detail persuades the Emperor that these are "substantial bodies," because no one could have anticipated the question—
the flaw is magically already there, a function neither of the speculative
or projective circuit of the creator's act nor of the Emperor's own narcissistic investment in flawless images of rule. It anticipates, in that sense,
the "purposiveness without purpose" of the Kantian aesthetic.

The point is not the simple, ironic correspondence between these readings, a claim, for instance, that real substance turns out to be aesthetic fantasy. What the scene reveals moves outside such a mimetic, correspondent economy. The paramour's flaw shows the referential function, reference itself, as the unstable moebius-like movement through which the real passes beyond itself into fantasy—even as fantasy exceeds itself, passing beyond its own structuring frame. That torsion—the process through which the aesthetic fulfills itself by passing beyond itself—is, again, the unstable, self-differentiating movement of phenomenal reference as such. To situate the hold of theater and the empirical object alike "there" is to locate their grounds beyond exchange, even an infinitely extended exchange, in relation to an operation of phenomenalization prior to commodification, and in relation to a contingency that exceeds and determines the possibility of its empirical historical accounting.[46]

Political Aesthetics: Greenblatt, Lefort, and Agamben

What would it mean to approach the political stakes of early modern literature in these aesthetic terms? Stephen Greenblatt's influential New Historical description of the fungible relation between work and culture in terms of the fluid "circulation" of props, artifacts, energy, charisma—cultural capital in general—can be critiqued for severing economy from actual, material conditions: one can argue it is too "aestheticizing."[47] One might equally address the critique from the other direction, as it were, by arguing that for all its talk of fluid transformations and translations, such an account remains too closed, precisely insofar as it casts the social domain as an economy—a space of circulation—and thus as a determinate system.

What is true of Greenblatt's account is a fortiori true of those more familiar analyses that understand the imperative to historicize as a matter of understanding the work in terms of its embeddedness within a given culture, with what such formulations imply of the social sphere as an already given space, as the space, precisely, within which the work is embedded. Criticism that describes cultural causation in such terms— that speaks of the social fabrication of identity, for instance—merely replaces an essentializing account of the subject with an implicitly totalizing account of the social.

Such observations have special pertinence for the analysis of early modernity. In an extended reading of Carl Schmitt, the Italian political theorist Carlo Galli has argued that the early modern moment consists in the reversal through which a structure in which space (understood as a given, onto-theological form) determines politics becomes one in which the political determines space, that is, the space of the social as such. Galli's point is not simply that modern society is divided and conflictual, and thus open to a multiplicity of interpretations. The argument is rather that society is deontologized—that it does not exist except as a function of the force that totalizes it and thus grant it the fiction of an immanent form.[48] Without transcendent reference, the social becomes the unstable drama of its auto-foundation, the divisive, self-exclusive movement through which it constitutes itself in a form that does not escape, in Claude Lefort's phrase, the "enigma" of its "external/internal articulation."[49] "The social," Lefort writes, "can't be dissociated from the problem of its institution."[50]

A function of its divisions—constituted on division—the *ordini nuovi* of political society is a society definitionally open to its own historicity. Irreducibly relational, without being or essence, the social is constitutively overdetermined—incapable of totalization and structured in relation to the limit or void that opens it, Lefort argues. Understood thus, the empirical divisions that make up the social domain as a factual domain—the division of classes, the division between civil society and state—are irresolvable as divisions insofar as they are a function of a prior, only ever retroactively apprehensible division that opens the space or interval of the social as such and marks it as irreducibly political.[51]

The divisive self-institution of political society articulates human personhood as that which "opens onto itself by being held in an opening it does not create."[52] That inhuman sociality can be read in different registers. It is the insistence of the political-theological dimension in early modernity, but a political theology that does not accede to a transcendent source or reference, one whose opening is the agentless *translatio* of its own definition.[53] It is also law, not positive or instrumental law, but law as the intractable, permeable and impermeable limit that opens the relational space within which the human is inscribed, and without which any notion of human freedom would be inconceivable. The inhuman, however, is also the register of the aesthetic, particularly in its character as technè, in so far as the aesthetic is the operation by which that division and historicity assumes phenomenal form, and thus becomes figurable as a story of origins, including political-theological origins.[54]

To frame the political aesthetic in relation to the *mise en forme*, or primordial shaping of early modern sociality itself, helps us specify its ideological contours. It also helps us distinguish it from a later bourgeois conception in which the aesthetic is understood as the symmetrical counter to a rationalized state.

As a political formation, early modern aesthetics retains the creationist emphasis of *poesis*, but a *poesis* become untethered from transcendent reference, or one that reflects back on and thus problematizes the analogy with divine creation that governs it. And yet, it is a creationism not (yet) translatable into the terms of an elevated authorial function, whether understood as the controlling hand of the artist or, in Burckhardt's version of political aesthetics, the shaping hand of the ruler; it is the autonomy or autogenesis of the work, not the autonomy of the artist, that is at stake in the interval of concern here.

That autogenetic aspect of the work is deducible from the most strongly marked paradox of the era's aesthetic conception: the relation between the work as imitation and the work as autonomous, or *ex nihilo*, creation. That tension can be understood in terms of the competing Greek and Christian provenance of Renaissance conceptions. However, such a genealogical account risks missing the paradox's status as founding antimony rather than simple contradiction, a fact evident in what makes the Renaissance aesthetic conceptions most alien to us. For *imitatio* as it was understood in the era did not imply derivativeness. That the imitated could, indeed, be "more present than anything that belongs to the universe immediately given as present" is a function of the relation between imitation and the temporal character of the work as event character of the work.[55]

Lefort speaks of the distinctly early modern character of Machiavelli's discursive communion with the long dead in terms of a particular experience of the art work: "the idea that works of art are contemporaneous *within* a time-difference; the idea of a conjunction between something that no longer exists and something that does not yet exist."[56] Lefort is not describing a simple, syncretistic correspondence between an already given past and an already given present. The contemporaneity Lefort evokes entails a "singularity" that "cannot be broken down into a 'once' and a 'now'" because it is a matter of the image as unlimited *imitatio*, that is, without presence except in the material dialectic of its temporal coming forth; the image manifests itself, not then or now, but in the self-differentiating event of its conjunction, and thus as what is at once momentous and beyond time.[57] The social logic of the early modern aesthetic is a function of the work's capacity to sustain itself in that simultaneously immanent and transcendent condition. By virtue of such a formative operation, the aesthetic becomes not simply an ideological subset of the cultural field, what underwrites, for instance, an idea of possessive individualism or divine authorship. Rather, it partakes of and sustains the fiction through which the social would constitute itself from within itself as a phenomenal space.

Lefort's reference to the early modern work's singular "transcendence within the world" brings us back to the question of the relation between the aesthetic and the political incarnationism represented by the figure of the sovereign, a being at once "man-made" and "sempiternal" in Kantorowicz's well-known analysis.[58] It is certainly in relation to the sovereign that autonomy as a specifically political problem is most explicitly engaged during early modernity.[59] That association between sovereignty and autonomy is a modern one; it is related to the shift from genealogical conceptions toward a conception of legitimacy based on the legislative act—thus the critical importance of the indivisibility character of sovereign authority for a theorist like Jean Bodin, and thus too the importance of Bodin to Carl Schmitt, with his account of the authority of early modern sovereignty as a function of the sovereign decision.[60]

However, that account, which presupposes the agency of the sovereign, is subordinate to the more primordial question of the relation between autonomy and political origination as such, that is, sovereignty as self-authorizing and self-founding condition.[61] Whatever sovereignty's empirical status as a mixed form during the era, it is the formal relation between sovereignty and autonomy that brings the category closest to the problems of foundations effecting early modern society as an irreducibly political society. In relation to the problem of foundations, or the problem of nonfoundations, the sovereign and the representation of the sovereign become inseparable. For that reason, the literary sphere, and a work like *King Lear*, to become a privileged site for enacting what sovereignty means.[62]

In one regard, the autonomy of the sovereign can be read as a stay against the divisions of historical society, a recovery of the "organic" social body of another era. In fact, however, the autonomy of the sovereign as a distinctly modern formation has a more ironic relation to the political society within which it is bound. Insofar as it claims its authority in terms of its unity as a supervening formal concern, sovereign autonomy necessarily carries the signs of the relational society within which it is inscribed; sovereignty in the time of absolutism particularly is a sovereignty that cannot separate itself from its unspoken political alternatives.[63] At the same time, as the figure of self-identity as such, sovereignty is bound up with the process through which political society as a whole becomes conceivable at all.

Such a dialectic—the sovereign's contingent and absolute condition—is apparent in Lefort's analysis of the structural role of the modern Prince as articulated by Machiavelli. For Lefort, the emergence of "class" society, that is, a constitutively divided socius, cannot be conceived as a function of the opposition between positive or already defined terms; those identities—the people, the Grandees—are rather a function of social division as such, so the question becomes how they are consolidated in relation to such a division (297–98). In Lefort's reading of Machiavelli, the people amount to a purely negative term, as insistent and corrosive nonidentity vis-à-vis the Grandees. As a political third term, the sovereign is what opens the possibility of political identity as such precisely insofar as he figures the fact of its founding difference. On the one hand, the sovereign is a purely mediating function. A relational figure, he is what "only has his being for others, and has his being outside" (164). On the other hand, insofar as he *embodies* that difference, the sovereign is also the very locus of any possible identification; the delusion by which the people are caught by the charisma of the Prince and locate their prospects in him is not an easily dismissible one, for it is the delusion of political identity and imaginary community as such (170). The Prince thus has a founding relation to sociality insofar as he enables a relation to the void around which it is structured. That mediating operation remains, for Lefort, a dialectical one. Because the separation that constitutes the Prince as third reproduces the division it embodies, he remains caught up within the very operations of social difference and desire he makes legible, within and beyond the social, within and beyond history (188–90).

Lefort's account is in many ways classically psychoanalytic, if not oedipal. It is a description of the passage into symbolization by way of the mediating third term of the paternal function as what gives form to the founding division of signification. As such, it is vulnerable to the difficulties encountered by all such genetic narratives. If the sovereign function is indeed constitutive, it cannot be articulated in terms of a narrative of anteriority. On the one hand, that prior ground will already be a sovereign ground—the Grandees must have already fulfilled the sovereign operation. On the other, the sovereign merely reiterates the divisions of the social in his own self-divided condition without attaining to a mediating or embodying status at all.

The challenge of sovereign autonomy reappears in a somewhat different form in more recent claims for the biopolitical dimensions of the modern political dispensation, claims that have equal pertinence for the study of early modern power. Giorgio Agamben's analysis of the grounds of sovereignty in *Homo Sacer* develops out of a radicalization of Carl Schmitt's decisionist account of the sovereign power where the sovereign is he who decides on the state of exception.[64] In the biopolitical analysis, that process is brought to bear on creatural existence: the sovereign exception in Agamben becomes that mechanism through which sovereign law at once appropriates and abandons life, constituting—and constituting itself in relation to—the politically liminal category of "bare life" as that which belongs neither to nature nor to polis.[65] The state of exception thus becomes that authorizing process by which sovereignty, in Samuel Weber's formulation, "suspends the rule of law only to totalize it in and as its other."[66]

Much of the productive tension in Agamben's analysis consists in the ambiguity of the "in" and the "as" of Weber's formulation. For to speak of bare life—the "homo sacer," the figure that can be killed but not sacrificed—as the object of sovereign force is a misnomer, according to Agamben's own account. In its originary form—insofar as it is originative—the sovereign exclusion or ban does not function according to an agonistic or even a predicative logic. It amounts instead to the self-exception through which sovereignty constitutes itself in the first instance as what remains at once within and beyond the symbolic field, as the included exception that opens that field. Insofar as such an operation does constitute sovereignty, it would be more accurate to say that the sovereign is a function of the ban.[67] In that regard, the foundational instance—what opens the domain of the political—concerns neither object nor agent but the banning movement of the ban itself, the exception's capacity to constitute itself. In Agamben's citation of Kiergegaard, "The exception explains the general *and itself*" (16; my italics). And if the exception is able to explain itself—to "think itself" as Schmitt says—it is through the movement of a negating self-exempting by which it posits itself as figure or example. Founding law—the *Grundnorm* that opens social formation—is law that exceeds itself, disappears in its appearing, and thus is a law that cannot be separated from the movement of its figuration.[68]

Agamben's ability to hold together the two elements that define his project—the "dialectical" argument related to sovereign foundations on the one hand and the Foucauldian, biopolitical claims on the other—depends on the relatively fluid way in which he moves from such an account of the figurative status of the sovereign ban—the sovereign ban as what problematizes "the structure of reference in general" (29)—to bare-life as the object, the correlate, or, precisely, "the first and immediate referent" of such a ban (29, 107).[69] The tension between those strands threatens to expose the category of bare life as a hypostasization that repeats the "materialization of the state of exception" that marks, by Agamben's account, the most egregious moments in the epochal history he narrates: the grounding horror of the death camps, for instance.

The problem of reference in Agamben is managed by way of a critical shift in his account of sovereignty, a splitting or doubling of the category. Prompted by Walter Benjamin's enigmatic call at the end of "Theses on the Philosophy of History" for a revolutionary transformation of the current state of emergency, Agamben comes to posit a distinction between "virtual" and "real" states of exception: the possibility of an affirmative political recourse will depend for him on that distinction. The difference consists less in the virtual/real opposition as such—after all, it was the logic of exception that established the possibility of reference according to Agamben's argument—than in the way the doubling of categories allows a re-articulation of the relation between law and life within each.

The virtual state of exception amounts to the structure of the sovereign exception as he has articulated it thus far, as a law constituted on its own exception, its own beyond, and thus a law capable of inscribing itself indefinitely. This is Kantian law as a law "in force without signification," all the more in force for its purely formal, contentless character (51). At the same time, posed against "real exception," that purely formal effect now takes on a negatively predicated form. What had been a pure indetermination of law and life becomes law as a force capable, in Agamben's phrase, of "capturing life."[70] With that, an infinite structure also becomes an instrumental structure, law in force without signification becomes the very ground of modern disciplinary culture. And from there, Agamben's rapid-fire (and forced) passage from Kant to the death camps (52).

What then is the "real state of exception"? It also entails a condition in which one is "no longer able to distinguish exception and rule," but in a form in which law and life are united. If the solution feels hard to distinguish from its alternative, that is not far from the point, for the important element winds up being the inverted symmetry of the forms. Agamben writes:

> Law that becomes indistinguishable from life in a real state of exception is confronted by life that, in a symmetrical but inverse gesture, is entirely transformed into law. The absolute intelligibility of a life wholly resolved into writing corresponds to the impenetrability of a writing that, having become indecipherable, now appears as life. Only at this point do the two terms distinguished and kept united by the relation of ban (bare life and the form of law) abolish each other and enter into a new dimension (55).

For Agamben, that new dimension amounts to the passage beyond relationality as such, and thus beyond law altogether.

What is notable about such a formulation of the passage beyond law and relation—notable particularly given Agamben's usually vigilant anti-Hegelianism—is its recourse to a classic dialectical structure of sublation. The apparently insuperable logic of the sovereign ban finds itself inversely mirrored within a symmetrical, self-canceling relation that in this instance annuls the structure of the relation as such and thus yields "a new dimension." The movement beyond law, toward "a politics freed from every ban" (5), thus winds up reiterating at another level the logic of the sovereign ban in its most dialectical form, as a movement of self-conserving negation. "The ban," Agamben had written, "is essentially the power of delivering something over to itself, which is to say, the power of maintaining itself in relation to something presupposed as non-relational" (109–10).

Whether it is a matter of conceiving sovereignty as the embodiment of the founding void of the social or in relation to bare life as its coalescent ground, Lefort's and Agamben's accounts ultimately run up against sovereignty's impossible task of instituting a relation to nonrelation, that is, the problem of autonomy as such. That task is not a matter of making the division of the social knowable, which implies the prior existence of such a void. Like the existent/in-existent nothing in *King Lear*, it is a matter of the movement through which that void constitutes itself: the opening of relationality and difference as such. Sovereignty in that sense is an aesthetic, not a cognitive, form, situated at the level of its phenomenalization.

This brings us back to Burckhardt's political aesthetics—the state as created form—but with a difference. For understood thus, sovereignty is not a matter of a shaping hand in relation to the given matter of the political, nor even of what is constructed in or out of a presupposed emptiness, but of an *ex nihilo* creation around which political and aesthetic agencies must seek to structure themselves. As the singular emergence of illimitable relation, the sovereign—whether the sovereign ruler, the sovereign state, or the sovereign people—bears the problem of history as such in the finite infinitude of its condition.[71] The aesthetic is the mechanism within which that condition is articulated.

CHAPTER 2

Leonardo's Hand: Mimesis, Sexuality, and the Polis

Ⓘn their introduction to *Renaissance Florence: A Social History*, the editors offer a reflection on their own methodological moment, a crossroads that can be taken to represent the promise of a new era of Renaissance cultural studies:

> We are poised at an exciting moment in the history of our disciplines when we can with profit consider the ways in which the two heretofore distinct academic fields have learned from one another and whether we should be moving toward a single academic enterprise, or whether there is still more that can be learned from maintaining the distinctions in training and approach between history and art history.[1]

Although they pose this as a question, there is little doubt about where the authors' investments lie, judging from the interdisciplinary mix of the collection and by the tenor of their own introductory essay— "The Dynamics of Space in a Renaissance City"—which attends in equal measure to the dialectic of representation and to the protocols of sociological history. However, what strikes one most about the passage is how unproblematic such a prospective mingling of the disciplines feels, as if disciplinary knowledge were purely accretive and thus available to being pooled when the time is ripe, and as if history and representation could be conjoined in a single descriptive space, the space, precisely, of culture. What vanishes in such an account—and vanishes as if it had never been there—is the entire problem of the aesthetic, the aesthetic as a problem. In that sense, the passage can be read as one terminus in the arc of modern Renaissance studies running from Burckhardt's conception of the early modern state as artwork to the contemporary ascendancy of the work as a subset of material culture.

In one regard, Burckhardt aside, there is nothing surprising about that ascendancy in the context of early modern studies. Emerging as it does before the philosophical elaboration of the aesthetic as an episte-mological category—before Kant, and even before a fully developed sep-aration between the mechanical and the liberal arts—the Quattrocento work would seem particularly suited to the norms and procedures of cultural materialism. Indeed, the claim that the early modern art is not yet conceived as an autonomous formation has amounted to a critical doxa—whatever else may be uncertain about the status of the Renais-sance work, we can at least say that.[2] In part, such a conviction is un-derwritten by an assumption about the ideological implications of the emergence of the aesthetic as a full-fledged category, the way in which it is seen to disaffiliate the work from the fact of its cultural and mate-rial conditions.[3]

And yet it is worth putting some pressure on the claim that the Re-naissance work is not engaged with something like an aesthetic dimen-sion. Recent critical literature has noted in the era marking the transition from "the cult image to the cult of the image" an increased self-reflexiveness of the image and an increased consciousness of its status as representation.[4] Such a transformation is inextricable from the trait that Robert Williams locates at the core of the Renaissance image's mo-dernity, its "engagement with the systematicity of representation."[5] That systematicity is evident, according to Williams, at every level of the Renaissance artistic endeavor, from the development of perspective as a relational structure to a self-conscious awareness of the relationally de-fined categories of genre, style and decorum—all those elements that suggest a new awareness of representation as a field of contingent and differentially defined meaning.

How do we reconcile such an emphasis on systematicity—art as ex-tensive referential system—with the more familiar claim that the aes-thetic emerges in relation to a conception of the work as self-creative form? I refer to the argument that the "language of aesthetics was de-veloped in response to the artistic autonomy realized by Renaissance works" such as Leonardo's sfumato-shrouded images, which seem to bring themselves forth out of nothing.[6] The later might be construed as a theologically inflected throwback, even a counter to awareness of the image as signifying structure.[7] The singularity of the Renaissance aes-thetic becomes apparent when we recognize that these two conceptions are, in fact, coterminous.

That congruence can be understood in terms of the relation between systematicity and the question of grounds. Although Williams emphasizes the representational domain's character as an encompassing system of clarifying correspondences with art assuming a "superintending" function, systematicity, as he describes it, troubles the claim for art's totalizing role.[8] Insofar as it is determined for the first time explicitly in relation to the domain of representation as such—in that domain's character as "radically contingent," differential, and thus open—meaning will be subject to the illimitability of such a field, and the work to the problem of how it constitutes itself as discrete instance in relation to that openness.[9] To the extent that early modernity is the point at which the work assumes the status of a "meta-signifier" (to borrow a term from Claire Farago), it is also the moment where the work necessarily confronts the question of the field's constitution as a field, a question reiterated at the most intimate level of the image's own reflexive formation.[10] Understood in these terms, far from severing the work from historical conditions, the *ex nihilo* of the Renaissance image engages the problem of contingency and thus the fact of its historicity in its most radical form.

The problem of the constituting grounds of the Renaissance image is, I argue, broached in an explicit way in representations of the incarnation. I will focus on two Leonardo images that take on that miraculous phenomenon and its relation to the status of the image in a particularly outright way: the London cartoon of the Virgin and Child with Saint Anne and John the Baptist, and the late Louvre portrait of St. John. I am not making a claim for the theological foundations of Renaissance aesthetic form. Instead, I will suggest the thematic concern with incarnation provokes the work's engagement with the more radical and supervening question of its own grounds as image, and with the problems of referentiality that attend the work's attempt to figure or allegorize grounds in the deracinating break implied by art as indefinite representational field.[11] With such images, the *ex nihilo* of divine creation transits into the no less opaque contradiction that characterizes the Renaissance image: the necessity and the impossibility of its autogenetic constitution. At the same time, in engaging their own self-constituting grounds, these works also crystallize the problem of mimesis in its distinctly Renaissance form. The apparent contradiction of that conception—mimesis as *imitatio*, mimesis as affective presence—reveals, not competing and negotiable traditions, but the irresolvably antinomic character of the Renaissance image's coming forth as image. From that antinomy, the modern notion of immediacy is invented.[12]

Even as it can be described as distinctively modern, in its engagement with problems of reference and foundation the work that aspires to autonomy inevitably broaches the problematic character of the relation between aesthetics and history. In one regard, the Leonardo images I will consider exemplify the transition between what Walter Benjamin terms ritual and exhibition values, and suggest the historical process through which the locus of theological mystery shifts from the limits of the world to the opaque origins of the work.[13] That genealogical claim will be crucial in what follows. At the same time, the difficulty of such a genetic formulation is apparent when we recognize that it describes the appearance of the work precisely as contingent, historical form. For that reason the history of the Renaissance image is always also an allegory of its own origins.

The trenchancy with which these images pose the question of their own historicity is precisely a function of the scope of their claims to autogenesis. The problem of autonomy such images pose is something distinct from what will come with the era of the artist as originative genius: it is the autonomy of the work, not of the artist, that is at stake. The Renaissance incarnationist image suggests the conditions for the possibility of that construction of the artist, and thus the degree to which such a phenomenon is itself an effect of the work. Indeed, as I will show, the foundational character of the incarnate image makes itself felt most directly through its formative or inscriptive powers. More than merely soliciting a subjective response, as if such a response were ready and waiting, the works constitute an aesthetic subject and the ratios that sustain it.[14]

Understanding the incarnational image in terms of its constitutive effects makes evident how deeply it is bound up with the political domain more broadly—for all their obvious meditative dimensions, these images are fundamentally political forms. The transformations in the representational domain implied by the Leonardo works crystallize a shift that can be traced across the cultural field, from the inherent sociality of late medieval and Renaissance devotional image, to Machiavelli's own essentially performative conception of the political, to the nascent category of the state, that partial, inchoate and as yet undefined space of mediation that constitutes the political domain of the Quattrocento.

My argument, however, is not that the aesthetic—or proto-aesthetic—amounts to one instance in an array of social instances. I suggest instead that aestheticization needs to be understood in relation to the way the social field constitutes itself at all. In that sense, recovering the category of the aesthetic means countering the received constructionist notion that understanding the work politically means recognizing its cultural and material "embeddedness."[15] Embeddedness in what, we need to ask. How does the social field—which is itself necessarily a relational domain—constitute itself as a determinate space, as a totality, in the first instance, and thus as a field capable of determinable meanings? How, in other words, does early modern culture *incarnate* itself and establish the fiction of its own self-immanence?[16] The aesthetic's engagement with the problem of autogenesis has its fullest significance in relation to that problem of social formation. To approach the work in these terms means recuperating something of the force of Burckhardt's insight about the fundamental relation between the aesthetic and the Renaissance political domain, perhaps even reviving the claim that culture itself is an aesthetic form, while countering the implied individualism and decisionism of his affiliation of the aesthetic with the creative hand of the Prince. Indeed, the political consequence of the early modern aesthetic is apparent, I will suggest, only at the point where it is divorced from an instrumental account of its function.[17] Engaged at that point, where the work becomes inseparable from the operation of phenomenalization as such, and where it suspends recourse to causal accounting, the problem of the incarnate image is the problem of historicization itself.

Mimesis

Leonardo's cartoon or preparatory drawing, *The Virgin and Child with St. Anne and John the Baptist*, is well rehearsed in the critical literature (Figure 2-1). It figures significantly in Freud's famous—or infamous—psychobiography of Leonardo, and in the French psychoanalytic tradition has been the subject of a monograph by André Green.[18] I want to begin by considering the cartoon according to its aesthetic logic, by tracing out the image's formal and thematic preoccupation with self-creation. The "creationist" dimension of the work is most directly evident in the peculiarly undifferentiated, emergent quality of the central figures of the composition. The parthenogenetic implications of the doubling of

Figure 2-1. Leonardo da Vinci, *Virgin and Child with St. Anne and John the Baptist.*
National Gallery, London. (© National Gallery / Art Resource.)

the maternal figure are of a piece with the undifferentiated way in which the central figures seem to emerge from one another: St. Anne's splitting off from her daughter's body, the confusing, slightly monstrous multiplication of legs below, the Christ child's swimming emergence from the Virgin's body, as if he were the barely differentiated continuation of her arm. Such details suggest, as critics have noted, an allusion to the Virgin Birth, and perhaps as well to the Immaculate Conception: Leonardo produced the image at the height of the doctrinal debates over the miraculous character of Mary's own birth.[19] The self-sufficient, self-inclusive character of the scene is emphasized formally as well in the central compositional circle running from the women's heads through Mary's arm and curving back through the child, the spiral through which the central portion of the image completes itself. Or almost does so. What to make of the spectral, upward-pointing hand that appears where the Christ child gestures beyond the sacred circuit toward St. John?

That hand is a signature motif for Leonardo. It appears in similarly hieratic, disembodied form in the *Last Supper* (Figure 2-2)—the hand of St. Thomas, the doubter—and reappears with a kind of disquieting prominence in the late paintings of *St. John the Baptist* (Figure 2-3) and the *Annunciating Angel* (Figure 2-4) and.[20] The St. Anne cartoon suggests the theological underpinnings of the referential gesture. If the sacred group is able to appear in such a self-creative form, as a Virgin Birth,

Figure 2-2. Leonardo da Vinci, *Last Supper* (detail). S. Maria dele Grazie, Milan. (Erich Lessing / Art Resource, NY.)

it is because the paternal function has located itself in the space of an absolute beyond, the space of the divine Other. Indeed, read according to the classic psychoanalytic account, insofar as it breaks the closed maternal circuit, the indicating hand amounts to the paternal signifier of the division that inaugurates the very function of sign, of culture, of interpretable meaning.

What is significant, theologically speaking, is the placement of that sign, its appearance in the interval between Christ's benedictory gesture offered from within the sacred circuit and St. John beyond—the hand seems to appear out of the V formed by the infant's extended arms. That compositional placement sorts with the Baptist's role as the figure who foretells Christ's earthly coming and, in the iconographic tradition, mediates between our human lives and the divine. The ghostly hand thus at once emerges from and fills the gap of Christ's passage into human, passional history. By virtue of that double status—a sign that, like every sign, arises from the opening of time and historicity, and yet seals the breach of historical, creatural existence—the hand underwrites the miracle of Christ's incarnate human and divine existence. Such a guarantee informs the consoling gaze St. Anne directs to Mary just as the child presses outward beyond the closed, maternal space toward his sacrificial destiny.[21]

And yet, none of this explains the calculatedly effaced character of the hand. To understand that peculiar dimension of the form, we need to consider how the thematic concerns with self-generation bear on the image's status as image, which means reading the image not thematically but as pure form, not as a matter of *istoria*, but as *designo*.[22] At that level, the form appears just at the point where the Christ child's fingers do indeed complete the compositional circuit by touching the line of St. Anne's shoulder. The upward pointing hand appears as what remains beyond the perfect completion of the image. At the same time, Christ's fingers seem to be in the process of marking out, or about to mark out, that other hand. Those suggestions of both formal totalization and reflexiveness can be understood in relation to the aesthetic logic of the self-generative image. Can the absolutely self-creative and inclusive work incorporate everything, including its own ground and origin? Yes, except for a remainder—the trace of the hand that recursively inscribes itself there, at once ghostly cause and residue of the image. In that sense, the spectral hand amounts to a signature gesture indeed, but the mark of a vestige as much as a source.[23]

That ambiguous formal condition is sustained through the mode of perception the image solicits from us, an ambiguous attention that reiterates at the level of aesthetic reception the doubleness that characterizes the hand's placement within the image. For insofar as we are able to apprehend the image as at once *istoria* and inscription—as if Christ's hand were blessing that form *as* form—the unmoored, reflexively self-divisive hand of the maker coincides with the hand that indicates the image's true, securing source in the transcendent otherness of the divine. By means of that mode of aesthetic attention, the image fulfills itself as autonomous form; through the recursive, self-inclusive sweep of its compositional movement, the drawing can be seen to incorporate the division that institutes it, and thus constitute itself as what it was from the outset: a sacred sign and image.

The recursive, self-inclusive logic of the *St. Anne* cartoon (Figure 2-1) takes us to the heart of what constitutes the Renaissance image as a specifically Renaissance image.[24] Consider a paradox about the drawing I have yet to comment on. An image preoccupied in an especially intensive way with the *ex nihilo* of its own creation, the *St. Anne* drawing is also the most classicizing of Leonardo's major compositions, and thus the most governed by the laws of *imitatio*. Leonardo had visited Tivoli in 1501 and the cartoon clearly bears the marks of the Roman sculptures of the muses that had recently been unearthed there.[25] According to the thinking of the era, there was less tension than we might suppose in such an apparent contradiction. *Invenzione*, for example, meant both invention, in our sense of the term, and the discovery of what was already there.[26]

This is a testament to how thoroughly the Renaissance falls outside the orbit of our received conceptions of originality. But the cartoon suggests the aesthetic coherence of that earlier understanding. According to the logic of the recursively self-constituting image, the created object is also from the outset a returning object: an image. What is important in relation to the Renaissance is the way the drawing structures that recursive division and return as a sacralizing passage. The point is not simply that the gesturing hand offers up the classical form toward a sacred end. Rather, through the recursive movement of the image's self-creation as image and sign, the pagan past is shown also to have been from the outset divine. At the same time, whatever its explicit or implicit theological support, that movement through which the image at once splits off from its ground and in doing so constitutes that ground as ground amounts to the paradigmatic form of the Renaissance image as such.[27]

For a sharper sense of that relation between the internal logic of the incarnational image and its mimetic status as image, and to begin to engage the relation between such images and the aesthetic, I will take a closer look at Leonardo's late *St. John the Baptist* (Figure 2-3), a work that has historically provoked not just critical misgivings but an outright desire to wish it from the canon. Here, I want to emphasize the painting's status as exemplum of an emerging valorization of immediacy.[28] That mimetic character—the *incarnate* character of its presence—is indissociable from the way the image reiterates and reorients the structural logic of the *St. Anne* cartoon.

Freud's emphasis on narcissism and homoerotic doubling—the relation of like to like he places at the center of his account of Leonardo's homosexuality—would certainly seem to be borne out by the androgyny of the *St. John* figure, as well as its mirroring relation to the artist's own, earlier *Annunciating Angel* (Figure 2-4). Indeed, the viewer as well is located within such a dyadic structure. Both paintings—and this is their strangeness—situate us within the circuit of their sacred, annunciatory address, as if we were incorporated within that inner loop of the *St. Anne* image. At the same time, the signifying hand again opens out that imaginary circuit, insofar as it points beyond, and insofar as it is a sign and thus aligned with the status of these images as annunciatory forms, that is, associated with the symbolic dimension of word and law. The Angel Gabriel, of course, hails Mary into her sacred narrative, and in the gospel of John, it is the Baptist who pronounces, "And the Word was made flesh."

In its compositional logic, *St. John* articulates the conditions for that organizing ratio between imaginary and symbolic, between gaze and sign. As a thought experiment, one might read the image against the prospect of pure self-relation intimated by the sculpture of St. John produced by Leonardo's pupil, Rustici, under the guiding hand of the master (Figure 2-5). The sculpture approximates the mystery of the self-enclosed infinity of hand and eye that, as I will show, Leonardo describes in the notebooks. It also suggests the perfect, stupefying inscrutability of that prospect of the mind absorbed by its own gesture. Imagined from such a starting point, the painting amounts to a constitutive unfolding. The turn of the head that opens the initiatory gap between gaze and signifying hand is the turn that incorporates the viewer into the circuit of the image. At the same time, the sweep of the right arm that delineates the continuity between thought and sign in the contraposal rotation of the figure simultaneously breaks the dyad of our relation to the image, just as it visually breaks the self-completing loop of the arm behind. At its various concatenated levels, the image figures the play of division and union that

Figure 2-3. Leonardo da Vinci, *St. John the Baptist.* Louvre, Paris. (© RMN–Grand Palais / Art Resource, NY.)

Figure 2-4. Anonymous, after Leonardo, *The Angel of the Annunciation*. Kunstmuseum, Basel. (© Kunstmuseum Basel / Martin P. Bühler.)

constitutes its status as signifying form, all organizing along the continuum of its spiraled composition.

The faint, vestigial staff-like crucifix John holds within his arm bears on that structure. Marking the interval between the gaze and signifying hand, the crucifix aligns that initiating break with the event with which the cartoon aligns it: Christ's sacrificial passage into human

Figure 2-5. Giovanni Francesco Rustici, *St. John the Baptist Preaching to a Levite and a Pharasee.* Baptistery, Florence, Italy. (Scala / Art Resource, NY.)

history. At the same time, the image also encompasses and includes that sign of loss in the spiral of the arm, even as it points toward the image's true source in a now transcendent beyond. The ambiguous quality of the crucifix, its simultaneous appearance as support and mere trace, is connected with the movement through which the image in its recursive turning at once effaces and retains the breach that founds it.

The retroversive quality of the gesture, and its relation to the image's status as image, are more apparent when we keep in mind, as contemporary viewers would have, St. John's announcing words: "There is one who cometh after me."[29] The over-the-shoulder arc of the gesturing arm alludes to that coming after: compare, on this score, the alternate version in the arm of the *Annunciating Angel.* At the same time, the figure that will follow is in another sense a figure still to come: John is, of course, a harbinger. That forward allusion is evident in a later version of the Baptist, subsequently converted to a Bacchus (Figure 2-6). The ambiguity about where the saint points is intimately related to the temporality of the image itself. While within the diegesis of the image, that is, for the "historical" figure, the reference is forward to an event still to come, the image as image in the here and now of its apprehension alludes back to a prior event. The phantom crucifix is integral to this temporal crux. What is still to come and already past, the crucifix is not

Figure 2-6. Leonardo da Vinci, *St. John the Baptist/Bacchus*. Louvre, Paris. (© RMN–Grand Palais / Art Resource, NY.)

simply an iconographic anachronism; it is an index of the mysterious status, even the knowingness, of the image as image and autonomous form.

The peculiar, emergent character of the figure is bound up with the irreducible character of these temporal ambiguities. If the hand finally points neither forward nor back but upward in its oddly suspended form to an absolute beyond, it is because the image is located neither then nor now but within the ellipses implied by its ambiguous temporality, as a form that conjures itself from the outset as what was already there and in that sense as a truly *ex nihilo* form. The luminous disembodiment of the sfumato-shrouded figure—the quality that likens it to the emergent figures in the London drawing—should be understood in terms of that form of coming forth, a function not of the timelessness of the icon, but of a dehiscence within time and an *ekstasis* particular to the mimetic image as image.[30]

How does the forthright hand in this painting relate to the ghost-form in the *St. Anne* drawing? To see their connection, we need to take the sacred image's formative status seriously. For to experience the *St. John* image as constitutive is to find oneself within its mirroring gaze, to experience one's own gaze from that originative locus. And to see one's seeing from there, from the Saint's viewpoint, is to see the signifying hand in the phantom form it assumes in the cartoon, as an apparition at the peripheries of sight. The image in that sense has the logic of a visual lure: to force the hand from view in the name of specular self-completion—to realize the promise of narcissistic closure the image seems to afford—is merely to renew the distractive power of that unmoored form.[31] The painting fulfills itself as aesthetic form insofar as it sustains the viewer within its vortical structure somewhere between such radical absorption, where the image's self-sufficiency is realized at the cost of ground and reference, and an exteriority from which the referential meaning of the gesture, the arc of arm and hand, is retained at the cost of the image's reduction to mere image and derived form. Such doubleness is the condition for the incarnational image; indeed, through that mode of suspended apprehension, the viewer, as much as the artist, becomes John, the inscribed onlooker at once within and outside the sacred drama.[32] That simultaneous apprehension of the image as *istoria* and as inscription, as mere image and as constitutive effect, is also the condition for the mimetic work as such, as it is for the aesthetic subject sustained in the interval such an image opens.

The Speculating Hand

The creative, referential hand provides the clue to the relation between the aesthetic logic of these works and the historical and representational moment to which they belong. I spoke of the way the hand appears by virtue of the distinction between *istoria* (or narrative content) and *designo* (or inscribed line), and through the mode of attention such a divided form demands. That condition lets the ungrounded hand find its support in a sacred beyond. More fundamentally, it is that double condition and suspended attention that lets the ghostly cause come to view at all, that lets the division that constitutes the image as a totality appear within that totality as content and as locus of identification. With that, the infinitely self-divisive movement of the hand becomes a self-reflective turning and the hand itself a speculative instrument.

And that's what the hand was. Robert Zwijnenberg associates Leonardo's innovative advocacy of the *componimento inculto*, the rapid and exploratory sketch, with Nicholas Cusanus's account of the "pasturing of the mind" (*mentem depascere*) that the craftsman/philosopher allows himself in the process of making: "The groping movement of the hand that leaves *pentimenti* behind on the paper is also a pasturing movement—*manum depascere*—in which the hand grants itself a respite by a self-reflecting movement that does not seek the definitive line."[33] None of Leonardo's remaining sketches suggests the out-of-nothing quality of the procedure as vividly as the notebook draft for the *St. Anne* cartoon, where the dim form emerges out of the thicket of *pentimenti* (Figure 2-7). As speculative interval, the "reverie of the hand," as Gombrich terms it, opens up the infinitude within which man secures his divinity. For Cicero, the locus classicus on these matters, the hand is at once the source of all human culture and what opens the "ratio that is capable of penetrating the vault of heaven."[34] Indeed, when Leonardo looks for the measure of infinitude, he finds it within the interval opened between the hand and the eye, the infinitely divisible arc of the hand as it moves, the infinitely divisible turning of the eye as it traces that movement.[35]

Such an account can be approached in terms of the place the speculative hand holds within the history of technology, after the elevation of techne during the era of artisanal capitalism and before the emergence of an oppositional distinction between the sphere of mechanical reproduction and a fully distinct aesthetic domain.[36] Within that interim, the artist creates through an *ars productio* in which the hand does not so much reflectively copy as continue the world according to the infinitely permuting ratios of a *mathesis* inherent within the phenomenal world and man alike.[37] According to such a conception, the aesthetic entails a passage, not through the supersensible, but through the infinity opened by the hand's own movement.[38]

The hand's speculative, securing burden is equally evident when we consider its accented role in relation to the early modern representational system *tout court*. That Leonardo's images reflect on the problem of aesthetic grounds in quite self-conscious ways is apparent when we consider the upwardly pointed hand in relation to the era's emerging articulations of visual space. The gesture can be read as Leonardo's turn on Alberti's injunction in *della Pittura* that the painter should incorpo-

Figure 2-7. Leonardo da Vinci, preparatory sketch, *Virgin and Child with St. Anne and John the Baptist*. British Museum, London. (© Trustees of the British Museum.)

rate within the image a "pointer" directing attention to the locus of the drama within the scene, a call picked up almost universally among painters of the era.[39] The proliferation of the gesture has been read in terms of the way in which Renaissance painted images seek to implicate their viewers, and thus in relation to emerging demands of visual immediacy.[40] However, such an account does not get at the riddle of the directive.

Given the tremendous focalizing quality of the newly devised perspective construction, why is such pointing necessary, a pointing that in fact provokes a kind of splitting of attention between indicator and object? And, given the gathering mimetic intensities of the artwork, why at this moment the necessity of a model for the viewer's affective response? Something of the strangeness of the device is apparent in the sheer redundancy of Mary's directive gesture in Masaccio's *Trinity* (Figure 2-8). In other instances, the gesture can feel vastly overdetermined. One can trace out the logic of the allusive gestures in Raphael's *Transfiguration*, but it is hard to escape the impression that what we are looking at here is a scene of . . . pointing, of pointing to pointing (Figure 2-9).

The connection between the pointer and Alberti's elaboration of the era's more famous pictorial innovation, the perspective device, becomes apparent in relation to such problems of reference. For the infinity of the perspective construction is directly bound up with the problem of grounds, insofar as that device entails an image that creates a space within which it is at the same time inscribed, a mirror or window within the world it constitutes.[41] If a modeling figure is called for in relation to the absorptive infinitude of that construction (Figure 2-10), it is not just to mediate but also to posit a viewing subject. One must identify with identification, point to the condition of one's pointing, to reference as such. And that is a necessary and an impossible condition.

The problematic character of pictorial reference is intimated by the notably unstable status of the hand in Leonardo's work, where the anatomical extremity is by turns unrealized (it is the one unfinished element in the London *Madonna of the Rocks*) and obsessively realized (the forty drawings of the hand depicted from systematically varied angles in the Windsor manuscript were part of a projected plan which would have run to hundreds of pages).[42] Leonardo's equivocations around "the pointer" are more directly apparent in the two versions of the *Madonna of the Rocks*. In the Louvre painting, the hand of the angelic mediator already assumes that peculiarly floating condition, levitated between Mary's hand and the infant John, as if the mystery were suspended there, not in the holy referent, but in the act of referring itself (Figure 2-11). In the London variant, the hand simply vanishes (Figure 2-12), as if the two images together played out the contradiction that will be resolved in the spectral, there-and-not-there hand in the later cartoon.

Figure 2-8. Masaccio, *Trinity*. S. Maria Novella, Florence, Italy. (Alinari / Art Resource, NY.)

Figure 2-9. Raphael, *Transfiguration*. Pinacoteca, Vatican Museums, Vatican State. (Scala / Art Resource, NY.)

Figure 2-10. Bartolomeo della Gatta, *Annunciation*. Musée du Petit Palais, Avignon. (© RMN–Grand Palais / Art Resource, NY.)

In one regard, the upwardly turned hand "solves" the problem of reference simply by breaking the signifying chain of allusive hands, pointing us to an absolute beyond of the image. At the same time, and *as if by the same gesture*, the disembodied, hieratic hand signals itself precisely as a sign, or a signifier of its own signifying, and thus figures reference in that groundless ground.[43] The recursive device by which the *St. Anne* cartoon systematically articulates those two elements together, thus granting that nonground its invisible "transcendental" support, amounts to the condition for phenomenal reference as such.

The very sophistication of the aesthetic solution Leonardo articulates draws the work into relation with the tradition from which it breaks. For through it—and this is perhaps what is most obvious about the upward-pointing hand—the image recalls the *per se facta* of the iconic form, the image without human origins.[44] And yet, precisely in likening itself thus, Leonardo's work signals the radical nature of the transformation it embodies. For the originless character of the premodern icon is a function of the fact that it was not an aesthetic work at all, but an immanent manifestation of the divine.[45] In these terms, Leonardo's hand indexes, not a shift in the instrumental causes of the aesthetic work, but the appearance of the work of art as such, that is, the work constituted around the vertiginous character of its own *ex nihilo* condition. Leonardo is an effect of that emergence, even as his work cannily reflects on its conditions.

If there is an origin of the aesthetic understood in these terms, it would be at the point where what appears within the work of art is . . . art,

Figure 2-11. Leonardo da Vinci, *Madonna of the Rocks*. Louvre, Paris. (© RMN–Grand Palais / Art Resource, NY.)

Figure 2-12. Leonardo da Vinci, *Madonna of the Rocks*. National Gallery, London. (© National Gallery, London / Art Resource, NY.)

through the reflexive turn by which the work at once depletes itself and opens itself as a speculative space. Hans Belting and Joseph Koerner have pointed to the historical significance of the appearance of Veronica images such as Hans Memling's, where the iconic seems to fold back on itself, offering itself up in the mode of display.[46] And yet, the difficulty lies just in this act of historical pointing, for it is exactly the problem of designation—of reference—that appears with the aesthetic. Whether any account of its prehistory amounts to empirical history or retroactive construction is the very question that the aesthetic opens and suspends. At the same time, with that problematization of reference, the modern conception of historicity—history as ceaseless ungrounding and self-difference—has already figured itself forth.[47] In that regard, far from severing itself from its historical context, the autogenetic work—the work that systematically articulates itself in relation to the problem of its own constitution—is a work staked in an irreducible way on its own historicity: it is an essentially political form.

Image and Polis

The claim for the political character of these devotional images would have been less surprising than one might assume. St. John was the main patron saint of Florence and the one most strongly affiliated with the city's distinctive civil character; through his feast day, the city annually reaffirmed itself as a self-governing, consensual society.[48] Moreover, St. Anne was the patron saint most directly associated with the city's status as a republic, for it was on St. Anne's day that the citizens of Florence rose up against the foreign tyrant who had governed them as absolute ruler for ten months in the mid-fourteenth century: the main altar in the Florence council hall was the altar to St. Anne.[49] Commissioned during a time when the city was again at risk, the drawing would have been charged with civic meaning.

But the social meaning of Leonardo's images extends beyond their thematic concerns. In the case of the *St. Anne* drawing, that further dimension is evident in what we know of the history of its reception. Vasari gives an account of the artwork's public presentation—or rather, the presentation of one of its variants—which reads like a textbook example of Walter Benjamin's analysis of the artwork's transition from cult to exhibition value. Having been commissioned by the Servite Friars in Florence to produce an altar,

> [Leonardo] kept them waiting for a long time, without ever beginning anything. Finally, he did a cartoon showing Our Lady, St. Anne, and the Christ Child, which not only caused astonishment [*fece maravigliare*] in all the artists, but once completed and set up in a room brought men, women, young and old, to see it for two days as if they were going to a solemn festival to gaze upon the marvels [*le maraviglie*] of Leonardo, which stupefied the entire populace. . . . This cartoon, as will be explained, was subsequently taken to France.[50]

The point is not simply that the work was exhibited expressly for the gaze of the polis. The social nature of the work is equally evident in the presumably calculated economy of withdrawal and display through which the contingent form takes on its marvelous surplus meaning. The locus of wonder shifts from the borders of the world to the creative origins of the work and its mysterious inscriptive powers. Ripa defines "maraviglia"—Vasari's term for the work's effect—as that "stupor of the mind that occurs when something new is represented," creating "a suspension of the senses in that new thing."[51]

The *Lives of the Artists* is, of course, the hagiography that announces the painter's life as the structuring term for art historical understanding. And yet, it would be a mistake to read reception accounts such as this simply as manifestations of an incipient author function. Indeed, the social and formative character of the Leonardo images becomes more apparent when we consider them in relation to the structural logic of the late medieval and Renaissance Florentine devotional image in general, a logic already suggestive of the implicit sociality of such forms. According to Michael Baxandall's well-known dictum, the Quattrocento work is the "deposit of a social relationship."[52] Insofar as it conceives art as a social precipitate, such a formulation leaves open the question of its active, constitutive role vis-à-vis the field of social-symbolic relations.

Taken most broadly, the sacred image in the context of the emerging civium is marked by a contradiction. On the one hand, such images with their allusion to pure sacrifice functioned to underwrite the potentially unstable systems of exchange that made up the social network of the city; contracts were literally performed in their sacralizing presence. At the same time, the images were themselves subject to deracinating exchange, their value measured, for instance, by the fact of their expropriation from beyond the bounds of the city. Indeed, auratic force was renewed on occasion by the destruction and substitution of sacred images.[53]

That relation between the image and the system of social exchange is evident at the most concrete level of its mise-en-scène, in what Richard Trexler refers to as the sacred image's "triadic" structure. Trexler's term refers variously to the relation between image, frame, and viewer, and to the relation between image, donor, and devotee; the two formulations can be mapped onto one another insofar as the image of the donors was inscribed chorically within the image during the era—its internal frame, as it were—and insofar as the material frame was itself the visible index of the community's investment in the image. Trexler describes the latter as the work's "social frame." Such relations are not merely accretive, a matter of borrowing from the legitimizing force of the sacred form. They are dialectical: "In Leonardo's terms, the honor due the *virtù* of the object was the frame: The more honorable the materials, the more valuable the object was to the patron whose arms stood on the frame, the more valuable the object to those who viewed it."[54]

That relational configuration was not simply a matter of enhancing the value of its various terms: it had a structuring force: "In order to keep the image, the frame, and the devotees together, it was necessary to keep them apart. These views were . . . a prescription for maintaining the life of the image, and thus of the commune."[55] Beyond the social hierarchies they imply, the image participates in establishing the fundamental divisions that structure the polis as polis. At that level, the image's triadic form amounts to the very figure of its sociality, for it is only through such a triangulation—again, a viewing of viewing—that the ratio that constitutes the *socius* as a relational field is brought into view.[56] Trexler intimates how thoroughly that condition inhabits the object as such when he speaks of the "triadic sensation of the holy presence."[57] Leonardo's devotional images simply realize that sensation and the splitting it implies as their own constitutive grounds.

By recognizing how irreducibly it is bound up with its own mediated condition, we can also see how implicated the *ex nihilo* image is with shifts in the mediated structure of the social domain at its largest level during the era, including the appearance of the state. Or rather, with the *problem* of the emergence of the state—that "event" has been the object of particularly intensive historical debate. On the one hand, scholars recognize that something shifts during the era; in the Italian context particularly, the "theory that harmonically combined the unity of the Christian world and the pluralism of autonomous political entities" had begun to dissolve; the political unit had begun to constitute itself from below, as it were, at the level of its particularity.[58] On the other, whatever it was that did emerge was not the state in its modern centralized form. Such a formation—neither feudal nor bureaucratic—could, at best, be described, in Chittolini's phrase, as an "arena of mediation," experienced in the generalized intuition that the political dimension had become "more than the sum of its parts."[59]

The problem of designating the origins of the city-state amounts to something more than a descriptive issue, of course. At the largest level, what is mediated in such an "arena of mediation" is the relation between private and public domains. And yet, those categories—private, public—are themselves coterminus with and are effects of the emergence of the state form.[60] In other words, the problem of determining the historical origins of the state is inseparable from the problems of ground implicit in the coming to the fore of the political dimension as at once purely mediative and determinative; the state as it appeared in the interval before its inherently problematic character is resolved, or seemingly resolved, in its later, rationalized form.

The significance, as Pierangelo Schiera describes it, of the "vicariate" in relation to proto-state foundations bears directly on such problems of figuring a totalized social sphere. For Schiera, the imperial vicar should be seen as "a stage in the evolution of local particularism toward the acquisition of sovereignty through the addition of a significant trace of 'superior' power, even if delegated." But one can equally argue that the appearance of that supplementary, vicarious, and largely symbolic figure, with its suggestion that "more is required to assure the presence of a 'state' than simple civitates," is an index of the problem of grounds implied by the indeterminate universal particularism of the emerging domain of the state.[61] The significant relation between the state and fictitiousness—the fact that the state was marked in a defining way by its capacity "to assume the trappings of its own fictive personality"—should be understood in terms of the unfounded, even phantasmatic, character of that new domain.[62]

That relation between the state and fiction lies at the heart of the very conception of the political, as Machiavelli's theorization of the state—or proto-state—suggests. For Schieri, Machiavelli's originative role in "granting the title of autonomous 'discourse' to political thought and the title of autonomous 'institution' to the practical reality this thought expressed—namely, the state"—is a function of his absolute valorization of pragmatic effectiveness in the political realm.[63] But to recognize its relation to the autonomy of those domains, we need to understand that emphasis on effectiveness in its most radical sense, as something beyond a preoccupation with strategic ends, and to see it especially in relation to Machiavelli's antinomic conception of the political act.

Nothing preoccupied Machiavelli more profoundly than the problem of the unity and origin of the state; political sovereignty is the condition of self-origination. At the same time, for Machiavelli the political domain is profoundly historical; it is a contingent space within which action is always inscribed and strategic.[64] The fully political character of the sovereign act is realized in relation to that paradox. Divorced from any supervening ethos or frame, the act of governance becomes purely conditional, a matter of sovereign will and choice, even a matter of willing the mode of governance within which one's choice will have had its meaning. In other words, insofar as it is political, the act is at once constitutive and already inscribed; for Machiavelli, *virtù* is characterized by just that metaleptic structure. It is, as Victoria Kahn notes, at once "cause and effect," the "attempt to control fortune," but at the same time the source of the fortuitous effects that prompt such acts.[65] Insofar as it entails that self-inscribing conception of the act, the political becomes illimitable; henceforth, even to choose against the political—to choose "nature"—is a political choice.[66]

In its broadest terms, the art's function can be understood in relation to that emergence of the political as at once autonomous and illimitable. Here is Leonardo's own account of *homo aestheticus*:

> Man does not vary from the animals except in accidental things
> [*accidentale*] and it is in this that he shows himself to be a divine
> thing; for where nature finishes its production with its species, there
> man begins with natural things to make with the aid of this nature
> infinite species of things, which ability is not necessary for him who
> governs himself adequately as do the animals and for which it is not
> the custom of these animals to seek.[67]

What defines man is the accidental thing, that which remains beyond the completeness of what is finished. Insofar as it opens him to infinity, that accident shows him to be divine. At the same time, man's capacity as maker is the index of an inadequacy, the prosthesis required of a creature incapable of natural self-governance.[68]

Measure of a fundamental inadequacy of man's being, a failure of self-relation that makes him something less than natural, art is at the same time what allows for the possibility of human self-governance. And it does so according to the contradiction that marks its own formation. The aesthetic is a remainder, what goes beyond what is already complete—in that regard, the image is, as it is for modernity, a mere image. At the same time, that inessential *accidentale* is what completes man in his self-governing self-relation, completes him insofar as he is an irreducibly political and historical being. The infinitude of man's relational existence assumes a totalizable, and thus an identifiable, form—it becomes a polis—by virtue of such a constitutive remainder, the ghost hand of the aesthetic. The power of a mere image, a pointedly unfinished image, to hold its citizenry should be imagined in relation to that contradiction.[69]

Flesh and the Stones of the City

Or at least the image would seem to fulfill that consolidating function. In fact, the distinctiveness of the Renaissance political aesthetic may be most evident in its fragility. I noted the way the speculative logic of Leonardo's *St. Anne* drawing centered on the distinction between *istoria* and *designo*, and the mode of suspended attention such a divided form enables; sustaining the work in its miraculously self-completing form, that aesthetic logic underwrites the work's formative relation to the subject as well as its totalizing relation to the political/symbolic domain. And yet the tenuousness of that opposition between content and form, the fact that it is itself a purely formal distinction and thus a function of inscription, would have been particularly evident in the dispensation of *ars productio*, where speculative difference is sustained by the movement of the inscribing hand alone. With the undoing of that ratio and interval, the recursive turn that sustains the aesthetic and theological economy of the image veers toward what the auto-mimetic hand and the self-completing work perhaps inevitably threaten to veer toward: sheer auto-affection. With that speculative collapse, the materiality of the image troubles any attempt to place it as a cognizable, and thus narrativizable, form. At such a point, where aesthetics disengages from mimesis, we encounter first intimations of the problem of the aesthetic as such.

This more troubling version of self-relation is hardly subterranean in Leonardo. Auto-affection is implicit in the famous mirror writing. It is present in the torqued and spectral mirroring of the twinned female figures of the cartoon, the differentiated/undifferentiated space in relation to which the securing hand is explicitly staged. And it is present, of course, in the relation of like to like implied by the *St. John* painting, where the referential hand functions as a minimal stay against the prospect of desubjectifying absorption. The erotic underpinnings of that appeal are made outright in the remarkable sketch that appears in the margins of the notebooks in which the Word turned flesh is literalized in the form of the annunciating angel's flamboyant erection, a matter of divine afflatus as tumescence (Figure 2-13).[70]

Figure 2-13. Leonardo da Vinci, *Angel in the Flesh*. Private collection, Germany.
(© Pedretti Foundation Trust.)

That sketch bears, of course, on the homoerotic dimensions of the painting; no doubt those elements of the painting have played a role in the history of its equivocal modern reception, nor would they have been far from the surface for its contemporary audience, given the explicit affiliation between homoerotic bonding and fantasies of autonomous creation in both the aesthetic and, in relation to the Baptist particularly, civic domains.[71] But the more untoward aspects of the painted image, and those affiliated with autoeroticism particularly, extend beyond its identificatory erotics to the more fundamental level where it engages the symbolic lineaments of subject and civium, a level at which the aesthetic's structuring and destructuring effects become indissociable.

How is that limit manifested in the *St. John* painting? However comprehensive its transferential effects, something of the erotic force of the painting is not assimilated to the speculative economy of the image as I have explored it—the image takes hold in another register. I mentioned the hand and the eye, but what to make of the lambent intensification around the mouth, in this painting and in others? Many have made much of the Leonardo smile, of course, including Freud, who found in it the returning trace of an infantile oral eroticism. Sarah Kofman, on the other hand, associates the permanent mystery of the Leonardo smile precisely with its contentlessness, with what is "always already lost" in representation.[72] But the mouth in this instance hardly suggests lack—if anything, it is too much. André Green may get us closer to that overdetermined quality when—noting the correspondence between the Baptist's smile and St. Anne's, and suggesting Leonardo's own infantile identification with John—he argues the smile intimates an incestuous fulfillment prior to and unmarked by paternal prohibition and the organizing function of the paternal signifier.[73]

And yet, the smile is not simply outside the structuring forms of the image. The curl of the lips mimics the arc of the arm—indeed, read precisely, the curve of the arm and shoulder draws the attention, not to the gaze, but to the lips as that point of fascination where the structure blindly and enigmatically reduplicates itself. The smile condenses the structuring components of the image, the arc and the divide, but now as indistinguishable terms: an arc that simultaneously divides. That divisive conjunction amounts here to an inscription within the flesh prior to the articulating interval of the sign. The mouth in that sense evokes the point where the interval that sustains the viewer's speculative relation to the image wavers, not in the form of an incestuous fulfillment outside paternal law, but in a more troubling undoing of the distinction between the imaginary body and law. It thus suggests an eroticism at the core of form and law where desire becomes inextricable from prohibition.

Understood in this way, the image suggests the source of the often-remarked intimations of fatality in the famous, recurrent smile. For the eroticism of the mouth unsettles the sacrificial logic of the image, the internalizing, subject-forming dialectic of Christian self-annulment at the center of its structure, insofar as it suggests the blind erotic drive underpinning the image's embrace of loss.[74] Consider in this light—and in relation to the problem of auto-affection—the gesture through which the Christ child grasps his sacrificial destiny in the Louvre version of *St. Anne* (Figure 2-14).

The limits of the image's speculative logic can be understood in relation to the pictorial conventions of the era. The opposition I have been exploring in Leonardo's painting between eye and hand, gaze and sign would have been familiar to the Renaissance spectator within the theological context to which the image alludes, for it forms the axis on which the Annunciation drama was quite explicitly played out. Consider the form such representations almost universally assume during the era, where the Angel's hailing address to Mary laterally across the image is intersected by the viewer's own gaze inward toward the visual infinity of the image's vanishing point (Figure 2-10). Much is staked on the chiasmus or crossing through which those modes of interpellation are at once mirrored and distinguished. For the subjectivity implied by such images is constituted and sustained between those twin prospects of absorptive infinitude, a state reflected in the recurrent motif of Mary's distracted gaze as she turns from one scene of inscription to another, from the old dispensation Book of Psalms she reads to the angel's call: again, the subject finds its opening in that interval (Figure 2-15).[75]

The ambition and the risk of Leonardo's image consist in the way it draws those axes together by turning the sacred address toward the viewer. For Leonardo, the mystery of the incarnation—its sacred scandal—and thus, too, the riddle of mimesis, lies in its vertiginous approach to that point of convergence where the sustaining ratio between body and word nears a dissolve. The *ekstasis* of the mimetic form—the marvel of its emergent, self-sustaining being—forms itself on a continuum with that opaque vanishing point, the abyss of the artwork's aesthetic formation.

For Leonardo, that abyss is where the recursive turn of the image, and the turn of his own hand in its most intimate and distinctive form, becomes something inhuman. Consider one of Leonardo's late apocalyptic drawings showing the destructive effect of a deluge on

Figure 2-14. Leonardo da Vinci, *Virgin and Child with St. Anne*. Louvre, Paris. (© RMN–Grand Palais / Art Resource, NY.)

Figure 2-15. Roger van der Weyden, *Annunciation*. Louvre, Paris. (© RMN–Grand Palais / Art Resource, NY.)

the walls of the city, an image whose preoccupation with fatality is inseparable from its character as a wildly condensed manifestation of the motif of the coiled line—the *figura serpentinata*—that appears at every level of his work (Figure 2-16).[76] It is an image of chaos. But the force of the drawing consists in the almost psychotic formalization of the scene. In that sense, it might be seen as a reflection on the relation between art and negation: art as stay against suffering and annihilation, or even art as what begins where the world is abolished: *Fiat ars—pereat mundus.*

And yet, such a reading does not explain the most striking feature of the image, not that the layered curls negate their ground, but that they seem to become their ground even as they shear away from it. Indeed, the integration of the fragmenting stones into the spiraling vortices of the water gives the sense that the curls are becoming "substantified,"

Figure 2-16. Leonardo da Vinci, *Deluge*. Royal Castle, Windsor. (Royal Collection Trust / © Her Majesty Queen Elizabeth II 2014.)

that they are assuming petrified form. In that sense, the image suggests the "grounds" of the aesthetic in the autonomic turn through which it ceaselessly constitutes and undoes its ground, abolishing the distinction between form and matter, law and substance.[77]

That scene is a civic one—it is the walls of the city that are at stake. And the dissolution of the sacrificial economy that structures these images as speculative forms bears directly on polis and civium. In Renaissance Florence, the relation between art and sacrifice was in plain view in the Piazza Signoria, the space where "the sovereign citizen body came together in its guise as the universitas civium." The definition of the citizen as citizen is, as Stephen Milner goes on to remark, explicitly a matter of "the triumph of sacrifice over contract in the conscious sacralization of civic space," a triumph that, we might add, gives economic contract its structuring limit.[78] Such civic sacrifices were there for all to see in the symmetrically arrayed statues of Judith and Holofernes on one side, Perseus and the Gorgon on the other: two scenes of beheadings. These are images of conquest; they are also images of division suggestive of

that something that must be sacrificed to attain to the supervening totality of universal citizenship. The notably self-mutilating character of
such images as images might equally suggest art's own self-sacrificial role
in that political/aesthetic formation.

What is most striking, however, is the effect claimed for these works.
John Shearman notes the remarkable proliferation, even before the in-
stallation of Cellini's *Perseus*, of accounts describing the civic works' pet-
rifying capacity: even as such images seem to come to life, they assume
the power to turn their viewers to stone, the laudatory sonnets claimed—to
fixate and "astonish" the citizen.[79] That transformation participates in
the ambiguity that always marks such Medusa effects. They can be read
in relation to castration—a connection borne out by the thematic concerns of the statues—and thus in terms of a logic of sacrifice: such is
the price the subject pays for symbolic accession. At the same time they
undo sacrificial logic insofar as they abolish the distinction between living and dead on which that logic is staked. In that sense, the aesthetic
is most directly realized by the epitaph on the painter Francia's tomb,
where the performative force of the image derives from the indeterminacy of the relation between life and death that it enacts in its own
eerie voice:

> While the painter fastens his eyes on his work
> Too fixed in his gaze he becomes pale and dies.
> I am therefore living death, not a lifeless image of death
> If I perform death's task.[80]

Taken in these terms, the aesthetic is associated with a conception
of the polis unacknowledgeable within the humanist understanding of
man's political existence. People, Brunetto Latini declares, "are not
called fellow citizens of a commune on account of their being gathered
within a wall . . . but rather due to their being drawn together to live
according to a shared rationale [*ad una ragione*]."[81] But the slide in Vasari's account of aesthetic foundations from prosopopoeia to something
more extravagant suggests a more intimate, less humanistic, relation between the citizen and the stones of the city. It is wrong, he asserts, to
draw images of the republic on walls that "had not been witness to the
valor of the Florentines as these old ones were," stones that, "despite many
travails and changes in government, population, money, laws, and
customs . . . have nonetheless honorably made war on their enemies
and subdued the surrounding towns and cities."[82]

The slippage that turns citizens into stone—a matter of being caught up in one's own trope, of forgetting foundations even while asserting foundations—enacts a small allegory of the aesthetic grounds of the polis. The citizen-turned-to-stone conveys that foundation not as a function of internalization, guilt, and debt, but as a radically arbitrary and unstable rhetorical positing that inscribes the subject in a form at once internal and alien to it.[83] In these terms, aestheticization is associated with the materiality of the polis not as a function of human relations or instrumental laws of governance, but as the reiterated division that opens the possibility of sociality and history in the first place—the polis in Heidegger's definition, as "the historical place, the there, in which, out of which and for which history happens."[84]

In its most extensive form, the form, for instance, of Leonardo's spiral where totalization is indistinguishable from division and noncoincidence, the Renaissance aesthetic is tied to the complex, contradictory opening of historical time. In that sense, its historical designation is necessarily a problematic matter. Yet, one can identify from our vantage point what gives the Renaissance aesthetic its disquieting character. In one sense, its power is of a piece with its apparent naïveté. Obeying an immanent aesthetic, the Renaissance work realizes its speculative claims in the material movement of the hand without recourse to a distinct supersensible domain even as it claims an autonomy indistinguishable from the totality of the world. That implied passage to the limits of subject and world means the early modern aesthetic realizes its truth on a seamless continuum with the inhuman. In relation to that uncanny continuum Kant's division of faculties can seem as prophylactic as it is revealing.

And yet, strange as it appears, that continuum reveals the condition of modern mimetic form, the occluded grounds of its luminous mystery. In that sense, the proto-aesthetic also exposes the relation between mimesis and sexuality in the continuity between the work's speculative claims—its status as a cognitive form—and the more incalculable level at which it infracts and takes hold; the early modern image's vocation as autonomous form draws it into proximity with the inhuman, autonomic operation that underpins it. That hold bears, I have argued, on the subject's condition as a political being insofar as we conceive of the polis as a genuinely aesthetic form, beyond and in advance of the forms of exchange, economic and otherwise, that constitute the space of culture. Indeed, the spiral of the aesthetic may be

legible in the broadest contours of the state-form during the Quattrocento, not in the fulfillment of the city-state, of course, but in its
notable untimeliness: no moment was so precociously committed to
the state as aesthetic totality and none pursued its dissolutions with
such unwavering consistency.[85]

CHAPTER 3

Shakespeare Distracted: Political Aesthetics from *Spanish Tragedy* to *Hamlet*

At this point we turn from painting to literature, and from Quattrocento Italy to post-Reformation England. A leap across faiths, but not a leap of faith, I believe, as there are continuities across media with regard to the autonomy of the work as work. Whereas the "incarnationist" focus of the previous chapter draws from an obvious theological context, I now turn to questions of state in a less mediated way. The confessional crises of the later era if anything bring the problem of society's deontologized condition more starkly into view; with that the artwork's phenomenalizing vocation becomes more outright. Among other things, this chapter will suggest Shakespeare's role in the turn by which the aesthetic's foundational status becomes explicit and negotiable. In the process, the relation between art and history will be rearticulated.

In the context of English drama of the period, the argument for a relation between representation and sociality has been richly engaged, most familiarly in the New Historicist claims for the improvisatory and theatrical character of early modern identity. Insofar as that conception remains an instrumental one—a matter, precisely, of improvisation— it's fair to ask if it is colored by a later era's understanding of the originating self as locus of meaning. But in its most sophisticated formulations, such as that forwarded by Stephen Greenblatt in his well-known essay on Martin Guerre, the theatricality of early modern identity would seem to shift us away from our anachronistically modern construal of the subject as organizing principle to the truth the era knew about itself, the fact of "the social fabrication of identity."[1] In that orientation, at least, New Historicism is of a piece with the cultural materialist approaches that have dominated the field of Renaissance studies.

But what does "the social fabrication of identity" mean, exactly? For Greenblatt, it means understanding the subject in relation to "the network of lived and narrated stories, practices, strategies, representations, fantasies, negotiations, and exchanges that, along with the surviving aural, tactile, and visual traces, fashion our experience of the past, of others, and of ourselves."[2] The flurry of determining elements in such an account—an invocation of multiplicitousness characteristic of much Foucault-inspired cultural critique—has a rhetorical purpose: it is meant to counter the "totalizing vision" of a master narrative, including the one that enlists identity as a universal point of reference.[3]

And yet, is multiplicity opposed to totality? Insofar as such multiple terms are conceived accretively, as a cumulation of discrete categories or phenomena, they operate by way of reference to an implied horizon—without such a reference, the terms would lose their status as positively determined and self-consistent elements, that is, they would not be collectible at all. That reference to totality is evident in Greenblatt's familiar reference to culture as system—the network of lived stories and practices, or, in other contexts, the "circulation" of social energies, with that term's implicit allusion to economy as an organizing metaphor. This is the idiom of New Historicism, but it simply makes outright what is implicit in all social construction accounts—the reference to the social domain as an already given point of reference, as cause. What such accounts foreclose, paradoxically, is the problem of the political, understanding the political, not as a collection of social practices, but as what forcibly constitutes the social field in the first instance as an immanent if unstable domain, and thus as a point of reference.

This is a general claim about what's implied by the contingency of the social. But it has particular force in relation to early modernity, or, more precisely, the interim between theocratic institutions and the establishment of a fully formed or rationalized state structure. For that interim corresponds to a deontologizing of political space, a shift from the social field secured by a transcendental referent and thus by a precedent idea—the idea, precisely, of society as incarnate—to the dissolution of such a reference and the emergence of the very space of the social as antagonistically constituted.[4] Provoked by the multiplication of belief structures, the post-Reformation interim in particular is characterized, in Walter Benjamin's account, by a political-symbolic order without transcendental recourse, a domain that is at once emptied out—a matter of pure theatricality—and illimitable.[5]

Such a condition amounts, in Benjamin's turn on Carl Schmitt's analysis of the primordial dimension of the sovereign decision, to a permanent state of emergency, but one in which no decision is possible because no external posture is available from which such a decision could be made.[6] Understood thus, the social field becomes at once radically immanent and exorbitant, permanently incapable of coinciding with and thus completing itself.[7] The early modern aesthetic forms itself in relation to that social contradiction—society's constitutive overdetermination—and answers to it according to its own aporetic logic. Purely supplementary *vis-à-vis* the genuine stuff of social life to which it refers and self-divisive in its own operations, the aesthetic also amounts to a condition for the manifestation of the social field as autonomous and phenomenally realized form.

I will address post-Reformation political aesthetics in the English context by looking at revenge drama, particularly Thomas Kyd's *The Spanish Tragedy*, the ur-play of the genre, and *Hamlet*. The association between aesthetics and revenge may be less than self-evident. The clue to the affiliation can be traced in the apparently paradoxical terms by which Kyd's play is given pride of place in literary historical narratives. On the one hand, *The Spanish Tragedy* is the first modern work to realize drama in its fully realized Aristotelian dimension, as a drama structured according to human causality and motivation.[8] In other words, it is a fully mimetic work. On the other, it is the first to introduce a metatheatrical—that is, a critically and formally self-conscious—element into English drama, a feature that distinguishes the modern variant of the genre from its classical forebears.[9] Those dimensions of the play are in fact inseparable. The mechanism through which the drama would reflexively constitute itself as literary form is the very condition for the play's assuming its stable mimetic possibilities. In that regard, the play confirms the inherent relation between the recursive recoils of revenge— the act's imitative character—and revenge's relation to the problem of mimesis as such. The social stakes of that representational preoccupation are suggested by the way the drama articulates its formal status through the relation between emerging conceptions of literariness and law, the two offices embodied in the primordial revenger, Hieronimo. The play's status as stable speculative form ultimately depends on the possibility of that symmetrical rapport between law and literariness.

Tracing out the representational logic of the revenge form will bring into relief the force and significance of Shakespeare's intervention in

aesthetic history. Reading revenge, taking it for the interpretive operation it always was, *Hamlet* translates the impasse of the revenge act into
its very ground—or groundless ground—as literary formation. With
that, we move from metatheatricality to the appearance of the aesthetic
as such. That aesthetic turn has contradictory consequences. On the
one hand, it amounts to a deepening and radicalization of the relation
between history and literary form. Through the reflexive turn by which
the play reiteratively inscribes its own historical interim—the interval
of early modernity—the play constitutes itself by way of a *translatio* in
which aesthetics, history, and political foundations show themselves to
be radically coterminous. On the other hand, precisely in producing such
an allegory of aesthetic origins—in producing the aesthetic as the story
of its own grounds—*Hamlet* creates the possibility of the management
and, indeed, abrogation of the aesthetic that will underwrite the homo-
geneous political space of a coming era. In that regard, the play articulates the entire trajectory of the current project from creationist to
instrumental aesthetics, and from polis to the fully developed abstract
state. The play also suggests the costs and the fragility of that modern
political narrative.

Revenge and Political Society

The relation between revenge and metatheatricality can be understood
broadly in terms of the mimetic crisis that animates the genre. The limitless, inescapable and nontranscendable condition Benjamin describes
is explicitly realized in the reinscriptive mechanisms of the revenge cycle.
In the act that would bring him into his own, the revenger becomes
indistinguishable from the figure he sets himself against, and revenge
becomes a matter of boundless surrogacy and substitution—of theatricality through and through. "Brother, that's I; that sits for me; do you
mark it? And I must stand ready here to make away myself yonder. I
must sit to be killed, and stand to kill myself," Vindice declares.[10]

In the early modern context, a representational crisis of this type is
a function of the relation between the work and the unstable constitution of the socius as immanent form.[11] Benjamin's argument that the
open, infinitized political space of the early modern era amounts to a
domain in which no decision is possible is borne out from the outset in
The Spanish Tragedy. According to the play, revenge originates not from
any fateful act, but from the impossibility of deciding. In the play's pro-

logue, the avenging ghost, Don Andrea, explains his returned presence. Cast into the afterlife to meet his judgment after his defeat on the field of battle, the dead hero finds himself confronted with a sequence of non-decisions about the terms of his judgment, whether he belongs in the underworld with the lovers or the martialists. In the place of decision, he is issued a series of passports sending him up the Stygian chain of command—death itself amounts to a notably inconsequent passport office—until it is Pluto's paramour, Prosperpina herself, drolly enough, who sends him back to the land of the living with the injunction to revenge. The preoccupation with delay which we associate with *Hamlet*'s finer-tuned psychologizations are already at work from the start, as it were, for revenge itself—the fateful act—amounts to nothing more than a stand-in and a postponement. The illimitability of such delays is borne out at the close of the drama, where the ghost finally finds satisfaction in the opportunity the play-ending slaughter opens to continue his revenges in the afterlife.

The particular horns of the dilemma on which Don Andrea's fate is suspended are sign enough that we are within the traces of "mimetic crisis." According to the logic of such a condition as René Girard characterizes it, the distinction between love and war, friend and enemy, what consolidates and what opposes is no distinction at all. Insofar as identity is purely and from the outset differential, the process of difference is infinitized, without originative ground or object. And because it is infinite, every act of difference becomes limitlessly equivalent: the more rivalrously opposed, the more equivalent; the more the same, the more self-divided—revenge drama's familiar impasse.[12] Thus, the impossible identifications between revenger and his object; Hieronimo turns Don Lorenzo into a version of himself, a figure of mournful, suicidal conscience, in his projective imaginings of the murderous adversary he must overcome.[13]

Thus, too, the peculiar erotic tenor of the revenge play, where love becomes inextricable from "sweet revenge." After her paramour Don Antonio is cheated of life on the battlefield by Balthazaar, Bel-Imperia—the name tells its own story—turns her affections to Antonio's defender, Horatio, the figure who recovered the beloved's corpse:

> Aye, go, Horatio, leave me here alone;
> For solitude best fits my cheerless mood.
> Yet what avails to wail Andrea's death,
> From whence Horatio proves my second love?
> Had he not loved Andrea as he did,

He could not sit in Bel-Imperia's thoughts.
But how can love find harbour in my breast
Till I revenge the death of my beloved?
Yes, second love shall further my revenge.
I'll love Horatio, my Andrea's friend,
The more to spite the prince that wrought his end.

(1.4.58–69)

Horatio can be loved in his own right precisely because he stands in for another love. There's nothing secondary or inauthentic about such second love; Bel-Imperia will love Horatio to the death. Constituted within the circuits of rivalrous displacement, love is surrogacy, a standing in the place of a prior love, in the place of another rival. "Whom loves my sister, Bel-Imperia," Lorenzo declares, "I mean, whom loves she in Andrea's place" (2.1.60, 63). Someone stands "where I should stand" says Balthazaar (2.2.129).

Indeed, love is inextricable from what would annul it: death. The familiar Renaissance conceit of love-as-war is given piquancy in the play by its proximity to—its indistinguishability from—actual threat. The murderous rivals eavesdrop on the lovers:

BEL-IMPERIA	Why stands Horatio speechless all this while?
HORATIO	The less I speak, the more I meditate.
BEL-IMPERIA	But wheron dost thou chiefly meditate?
HORATIO	On dangers past, and pleasures to ensue.
BALTHAZAR [*above*]	On pleasures past, and dangers to ensue.
BEL-IMPERIA	What dangers and what pleasures dost thou mean?
HORATIO	Dangers of war, and pleasures of our love.
LORENZO [*above*]	Dangers of death, but pleasures none at all.
BEL-IMPERIA	Let dangers go, thy war shall be with me,

But such a war as breaks no bonds of peace.

(2.2.24–33)

The familiar Renaissance literary effect through which extended rhetorical ornament effaces individual agency as an organizing locus is heightened here when the reechoing passes between fatally opposed figures. The lovers' reference to war can fall under the heading of dramatic irony, except that the love itself is shot through with foreboding and the animating threat of dangers still to come. As Katherine Maus notes, Bel-Imperia's invocation at the close of the scene of the "gentle nightingale" "with the prickle at her breast" picks up the Renaissance association

between beauty and violence, in this instance a specifically masochistic violence: transformed Philomela prods herself to song with an
endlessly self-inflicted wound. In that regard, the conceit's frisson,
and its relation to aesthetic violence, consists precisely in the way it suspends itself indeterminately between characterological knowingness and
subject-eliding irony.

The dissolution of the distinction between desire and its negation
makes vengeance hard to distinguish from the endlessly self-depleting
propulsions of the death drive. For Hieronimo, as for Hamlet, the thought
of revenge means thoughts of suicide. Death is at once the sole satisfaction for revenge—Hades's judge will "do thee justice for Horatio's
death," Hieronimo declares as he contemplates his own passage to the
underworld—and what the revenger must abjure to accomplish the act—
"Who will avenge Horatio's murder then?" And, just as the boundary
between self and adversary wavers, the choice of death itself divides
and suspends itself: poniard or halter? Horatio asks; having cast the
undecidable instruments of self-violence aside, he instantly picks them
up again, now refigured as tools of vengeance (3.12.13, 18, 20).[14] So the
cycle continues.

Those perturbations of identity and desire reflect the political entailments of the drama. The social antagonism that energizes the drama—
the split Hieronimo suffers between an older aristocratic formation based
on lineage and blood loyalty and an emergent meritocratic dispensation
affiliated with a new legal, bureaucratic and literary caste—comes to a
head with the dissolution of the distinction between friend and enemy
that, at least in the Schmittian account, constitutes the political dimension.[15] When the Spanish King attempts to resolve the breach with Portugal by converting his Portugese war prisoner, Prince Balthazaar, into
his heir by marriage to his niece, Bel-Imperia, the martial act which had
conferred status on Hieronimo's son—his victory over the prince—is
annulled. "External" political resolution translates directly into "internal" dissolution; indeed, Hieronimo's madness coincides with the
destructuring of the social field.[16]

Such antagonistic division is not merely circumstantial. It's a function
of the social domain insofar as it has become a political, that is, contingent, domain. In the play, the distinction between friend and enemy
never was quite that. Portugal, the defining adversary, was already the
representative of a dependent state, a viceroy to the Spanish imperial
sovereign, and the breach that initiates martial confrontation consisted

of the nonpayment of tribute money. That fact would seem to bear out Schmitt's claim that the dilution of the founding friend-enemy distinction amounts to a passage into the depoliticized domain of economy. More fundamentally, though, the structure of fealty engages the question Schmitt's account waives. If the friend-enemy distinction is foundational, who—what agency—institutes that divide in the first instance, given that friend and enemy are already social forms? To imagine sovereignty as originative one would need to imagine it in just the sort of supplementary terms the play posits, according to the internal alien structure of vice-regency and in the form of a divided identification: "Spain is Portugal / And Portugal is Spain," the King declares (1.4.132–33). Sovereignty is, in that sense, an economic operation, constituted through a breach internal to economy, understanding that term in its original sense as the exchange that establishes the very space of the *oikos* or home.[17]

The relation between such a divided condition and the play's formal status is most legible in the figure of the ghost. In early modern revenge, the ghost's return—the event that sets the revenge mechanism in motion—is something more than the mnemonic expedient it is in Senecan tragedy. Insofar as the social domain is radically contingent, the prospect of its totalization as a signifying field will depend on its capacity to exceed and inscribe its own limit; to accomplish what a ghost alone can accomplish: the narration of one's own death. That is the specter's ontological definition—the one being that can complete its own narrative—and the feat Hamlet's ghost does and does not manage, to hair-raising effect.[18] The difficulty of such an act is not the empirical one. It derives from the more fundamental because anterior formal impasse. To compass death is at the same time to bypass it as limit, and thus to deplete it as a constitutive boundary. Revenge drama transpires in that space beyond—what Lacan terms the "between-two-deaths."[19] Hieronio inhabits such an interval, a state of mourning in which the choice between life and death constantly yields to a third term, the condition of unburiedness—his dead son's actual condition for the duration of the play.[20] The point is not that death's limit is abolished. In revenge, death is absolute, but infinitely absolute. It is, in fact, a revolving door. Hieronimo's mimicry of the ghost's process in his own passage out one stage door and in the next signifies madness insofar as it obeys the logic of the absolute and porous limit, a real and reiterated subjective annulment.[21]

This subjective condition extends beyond the bounds of the play. When the ghost returns with his allegorical companion, Revenge, it does so to occupy the position of chorus, that is, our own posture as audience: they remain its spectators, above and to the side of the drama throughout. The ghostly bypass of every limit is the condition for the possibility of any totalizing encompassment of the play as play, and that cognition—what lets us know fiction as fiction and thus site ourselves beyond—is a condition of subjectifying knowledge; like the ghost, the subject is the site of an included exemption from the signifying field.

The instability of that posture is evident in the vagaries of the revenants' own disposition toward events. The moment where Revenge falls asleep and must be roused reflects those points where the audience itself forgets his presence at the choral margins of the drama; it figures the fact of the audience's own self-forgetful theatrical absorption. Like Hieronimo, and like Hamlet, one looses the ends of revenge in the enactments of revenge. At the same time, as much as our exteriority, that forgetting and absorption is no less a condition of subjectification, for it is precisely the falling away of the revenge frame, with it's providential, *de casibus* claim on the course of events, that opens the space of a newly intentionalist form of theater—modern tragedy.[22] Ultimately, the subjectifying dimension of the play inheres neither in the one posture nor in the other but in the unstable movement between them. Like the ghost's and like Hieronimo's departures and returns, understood as sheer contingency, the spectatorial subjectivity consists in nothing more than such a reiterated border-crossing and *aphansis*, its disappearance and reappearance to itself. Theatrical subjectivity amounts to a consciousness energized solely by its repeated failure, just as vengeful judgment is driven solely by its reiterated impossibility.

In these terms, the play offers its own critique of the terms of recent debates on whether the early modern stage amounted to a proto-public sphere.[23] Is the disappearance of the chorus in early modern drama what opens the novel place of audience as locus of judgment?[24] Or is the presence of the extrinsic vantage point necessary to index the space of such an audience? It would be most accurate to say that the very possibility of judgment is opened in the vacillation between those possibilities, in the ceaseless opening and foreclosure of an audience function. Occasioned in the interval between judgment understood as transcendentally providential locus and the later constitution of a public sphere as a space of normative judgment, early modern theater reveals judgment as definitionally riven, that is, as irresolvably political—no space at all.

The volatility of the play's definitional boundaries suggests what's at stake in the metatheatrical impulse in revenge drama. Metatheatricality is something more than a supplementary device or motif. It bears on the possibility of the play as a play. The specter's returns give thematic form to the larger reflexive, metatheatrical movement through which the play establishes itself as what it is: a revenge drama. That such metatheatricality in *The Spanish Tragedy* is related to the possibility of translating experience into phenomenal and narratable form is apparent in the revenger's own staging of the act.

Hieronimo's decision to enact the fateful event as a play, to turn the drama into a revenge drama and inscribe himself in that turning, responds to the intractable singularity of what he mourns, the son whose death is, in the language of the play, "incomparable," beyond any structure of ransom, exchange and symbolization. "O my son, my son! / My son, whom naught can ransom or redeem!" (3.12.65–66). To be without compare is not to be individual or particularized, for what is fully present thus would be available to exchange. More radically, to be beyond compare is, according to the play, to be in a condition of contingency or relationality without prospect of return or redemption—a form of substitutability that does not resole into equivalence.[25] That form of relation is the madness the son's death provokes. Hieronimo's exchange with his alter ego, the Old Man who seeks him in his role as legal advocate to redeem the murder of his own son, sets off an unstable transference:

HIERONIMO   What's here? The humble supplication
   Of Don Bazulto for his murdered son.
OLD MAN   Aye, sir.
HIERONIMO   No, sir, it was my murdered son:
   O my son, my son, O my son Horatio!

(3.13.78–81)

What cannot be compared to his son, the Old Man also *is* the returned child—"Horatio, thou art older than thy father," Hieronimo declares, addressing the aged interlocutor (3.14.149).

Stability is managed through the conversion of such transference into a specular equivalency, a turn accomplished—fleetingly—through mourning's translation to an image:[26]

HIERONIMO   Aye, now I know thee, now thou namest thy son:
Thou art the lively image of my grief;
Within the face my sorrows I may see.
. . . .
And all this sorrow riseth for thy son:
And selfsame sorrow feel I for my son.

(3.13.160–68)

That movement into image figures in small the larger metatheatrical trajectory of the play. The drama's resolution consists in the turn through which Hieronimo translates the dead body, which has remained unburied and inassimilable throughout, into a narrative denouement; the body is staged in the final play within the play. Given the illimitable mimetic extension of the revenge cycle, the very possibility of the work as totalizable form will depend on that reflexive self-inclusion[27]: thus the indissolubility of the relation between revenge and metadrama, and thus too the intimate relation between revenge and a certain version of literariness. "O where's the author of this endless woe?" Horatio's mother, Isabella, exclaims (2.4.101). Revenge is a matter of determining the authorship of the crime—who did the act. But it's more than that, for in its self-inclusive turning, revenge drama constitutes an author function. "And, princes, now behold Hieronimo, / Author and actor in this tragedy" (4.4.145–46).

And yet, that reflex through which the act is made compassable and thus cognizable is also necessarily the self-exceeding, self-mutilating movement through which the revenger reiteratively inscribes his own death. Commanded to explain his motives for the revenges he has enacted, Hieronimo bites out his own tongue, a gesture, as Carla Mazzio has shown, associated with the playlet's own fragmentary, multitongued form; at least according to Hieronimo's directions, each participant is to speak his part in a different language. "Now to express the rupture of my part," the 1602 edition adds.

For Mazzio, that polyglottism—an intensification of the condition of the play as a whole—bears on the era's anxiety concerning the multiple and self-divided condition of vernacular language, and thus, too, anxiety about the possibilities of a national tongue.[28] But to understand the association between such intensified sundering of language and the reflexive turn of the play—between revenge and metatheatricality generally—that fragmentation must be seen in terms of what's involved whenever it's a matter of language reflecting on itself: the play's self-incorporation exposes the indissociability of the constitutive and dissolvative effects of language, a political and linguistic fact enacted, more than reflected, in the work. In that sense, revenge drama aspires—and this may be its aim—to translate itself into an allegory of its own condition.

The mute, supplementary space that opens beyond Hieronimo's self-mutilating act—an interval of death's "lively image" (3.13.162)—is in one regard a space beyond revenge, in another, the space of the fulfillment of revenge. It is also a space associated with writing. Pressed to inscribe what he cannot speak, Hieronimo agrees and asks for a knife to sharpen his pen, and with that implement performs two final acts—he kills Castile, the King's brother, and then himself.

Castile's killing has been read in ethical and developmental terms—here, if not before, Hieronimo moves beyond revenge as reciprocal justice: Castile has done no injury to Hieronimo, he is innocent.[29] But to decipher the otherwise peculiar affiliation between that seemingly gratuitous death and Hieronimo's climactic suicide we need to understand that gratuity in terms of what has been revenge's deepest stake all along: totalizing completion, that is, autonomy. In killing Castile, Hieronimo severs the Spanish King from any lineal expectation—"My brother, and the whole succeeding hope / That Spain expected after my decease!" (4.4.203–4). With Castile's death, the King stands radically alone. "I am the next, the nearest, last of all" (4.4.208). And that disastrous standing alone is also, paradoxically, sovereignty's fulfillment. According to a familiar historical narrative, with the shift from feudal conceptions of suzerainty to modern sovereignty, sovereign power separates itself from its organic basis or any relation to the legitimizing bonds of fealty, instead locating itself in its novel claims to autonomy.[30]

Castile's death represents the irreducible antinomy of such a conception: the fact that sovereign autonomy, that is, sovereignty *per se*, will be founded on the iterable divisions of its pure self-relation, the condition of being one's own next and nearest. The equation at the close between Castile's murder and the revenger's suicide—the drama's critical remainders—should be understood in terms of that question of autonomy, insofar as suicide duplicates sovereignty in the self-exceeding, self-completing gesture of a self-authorizing subjectivity.

That completion, such as it is, allows revenge even as it passes beyond revenge. For the accomplished act does not emerge out of an already established system of exchanges, the seemingly limitless economy of revenge. It entails the leap—the blind act—that constitutes the very space and possibility of such a system of reciprocity and exchange, the act that establishes revenge and economy alike as organizing structures. It is no surprise that during the era of early market capitalism justice should be conceived in economic terms, as an issue of reciprocal returns, of debts accrued and repaid. Linda Woodridge argues convincingly that revenge drama answers to a specifically economic experience of injustice during the era.[31] But the exorbitance of revenge—its gratuity—does not just reflect economy: it bears on the constitution of economy as an organizing structure, as it bears on the possibility of the social field's constituting itself as a system.

The space of that constitutive beyond is the space of writing. Self-silenced, Hieronimo commits his final outrages under the injunction to write. The turn from speech to script coincides with the movement from the play within the play—the thematized representation of the play as its own self-reflection—to the supplementary interval of pure form in which play and play-within-play become indistinguishable. With that loss of distinction, the literary becomes nothing but the movement of its autogenetic self-divisions. In that sense it recalls the limitless turnings of Leonardo's self-inscribing hand. Such turning is the element of the play's final acts insofar as those acts entail the primacy of sheer form in relation to content, the blind and contentless positing that constitutes the signifying system as a system. That posited condition is sovereignty's condition insofar as the self-severed self-relation of its autonomy supersedes and swallows—like "Scylla's barking and untamed gulf" the Viceroy evokes at the close—all ground or relation, including the story that would cast such a calamity developmentally, as a determinable transition from lineal descent to formal autonomy (4.4.214).

The passage to writing is bound up with Hieronimo's literary role as the figure that oversees court entertainments, and is thus charged with the supplementary and central task of presenting the sovereign's self-image.[32] But it is equally related to his legal office, his position as *corregidor* and court martial of law; the play will work itself out through the relation between those literary and legal functions.

Law is explicitly aligned with script in the court scene where the citizens petition Hieronimo with their papers—a declaration, a band, and a writ of lease (3.13.65–67). In one regard, the call of blood revenge is measured against the mere form of such writs. Once "Proserpine may grant / Revenge on them that murderèd my son," mad Hieronimo declares, "Then will I rent and tear them, thus and thus, / Shivering their limbs in pieces with my teeth. / *Tear[s] the papers.*" "O, sir, my declaration . . . Save my bond!" the citizens exclaim.

> THIRD CITIZEN   Alas, my lease! It cost me ten pound,
>   And you, my lord, have torn the same.
> HIERONIMO   That cannot be; I gave it never a wound.
>   Show me one drop of blood fall from the same!
>   How is it possible I should slay it then?
>
> (3.13.120–30)

Again, psychic stability is a function of the conversion to image, and here it is law that is reduced to the status of mere writ.

But we know from the senex's petition that what is written can have an affiliation with the claims of blood beyond any spoken word.

> HIERONIMO   Say, father, tell me what's thy suit?
> OLD MAN   No, sir, could my woes
>   Give way unto my most distressed words,
>   Then I should not in paper, as you see,
>   With ink bewray what blood began in me.
>
> (3.13.73–76)

And if Hieronimo attacks the writs it may be because they can, in fact, draw blood. Hieronimo receives his first petition in the play— the writ that first names his son's murderers and calls on him to seek vengeance—as a blood script from out of the blue:

> The cloudy day my discontents records,
> Early begins to register my dreams
> And drive me forth to seek the murderer.
> Eyes, life, world, heavens, hell, night, and day,
> See, search, show, send some man, some mean, that may—
> *A letter falleth*
> What's here? A letter? Tush, it is not so!—
> A letter written to Hieronimo!
> *Red ink*
> [*Reads*] For want of ink, receive this bloody writ.
>
> (3.2.19–26)

We have good reason to believe the letter is from Bel-Imperia—she will confirm it latter. But the play highlights the letter's apparent sourcelessness: even as it drops from above, Hieronimo seems to invoke the missive as an answering call from his own state of projective dreaming. In that sense, the writ seems to arrive from some phantasmatic site in and beyond the thematic logic of the play.

Hieronimo's own suspicion that the letter may be a fatal snare—"thou art betrayed, / And to entrap thy life this train is laid" (3.2.37–38)—will turn out to be true in the long run, of course—revenge is a fatal trap, and not the less so for Hieronimo's attempts to evade its call. In that regard, the letter falling from above might be read as something like a disruptive—and fatal—bleeding of the play's frame, where revenge has the force of providential injunction, into the diegetic drama. But the letter's ambiguous formal status is more accurately understood in relation to the status of script at the close. For what blood writing reveals at the outset of revenge, as it does at the finale, is what at the heart of revenge has always exceeded and enabled revenge's authoring conditions. The bloody writ has the inscriptive force of law insofar as it calls forth the revenger absolutely, as self-defining self-address, but as what nevertheless arrives from elsewhere and could just as well not be for him. The most intimate of forms—the stuff of dreaming—the writ is also alien to the subject and to the speculative and reciprocal logic of revenge that might seem to propel it, an inward alien condition figured in the scene of Hieronimo physically consuming the petitioner's writs.[33]

The scene suggests the contradiction Samuel Weber argues the law necessarily entails in the burgeoning era of the individual; what is inwardly bound to the intentions of the subject—a matter of guilt—the law is at the same time definitionally indifferent to the subject: ignorance before the law is no excuse.[34] The wound of law's intimate misaddress, what vacates the subject even as it calls it into being, opens the substitutive movement of revenge and theater alike. Law, then, is neither the equivalent of vengeance nor is it imposed on revenge from without, a corrective to what Francis Bacon terms its "wild justice."[35] It mysteriously precipitates from reciprocal justice, at once its effect and its precedent cause.

What's the significance, then, of the revenger's mixed office? Literature and law share a similar place within the body politic. Like the avenger himself, both have a marginal, even adversarial, relation to the court culture they inhabit. And yet they are also the supplementary terms that constitute the sovereign's form and being within a new dispensation. However, that does not address the question of their relation to one another. With all the play's problematized equivalencies, that correspondence between law and literariness remains intact, and much is staked on it. In one regard, the convergence brings to view the paradoxical features inherent in both terms: positive law is shown to have the phantasmatic dimensions of imagination, literature the intractable and prevenient hold of law. By the same token, however, the unmarked continuum between law and literature allows a silent maintenance of the normative associations of both. It is the ambiguities of that chiasmic separation and conjunction that allow revenge its constitutive exorbitance without it quite passing beyond the orbit of condign punishment. At the same time, the conjunctive disjunction between literature and law reflects another, more profound organizing continuity at the level of the play itself: that between theater and script, speech and writing. We move from one *to* the other according to a thematic progression in the play. Through that structuring logic, the radical impasse and blind leap of speculative judgment retains a narratable form.

Speculating on Revenge

The claims I am forwarding about the law's constitutive and disruptive relation to drama's speculative logic can be set in relation to recent arguments for the enabling relation between law and theater's new-found mimetic capacities. Lorna Hutson argues persuasively that the emergence of that mimetic dimension in English drama is bound up with early modern theater's self-conscious deployment of forms of forensic rhetoric and logic derived both from Roman New Comedy intrigue and from emerging juridical concerns with the evidentiary basis of justice. Forensic conjecture becomes the model for those forms of inference that open drama to imaginary prehistories—the stuff of what will come to be depth characterization—and establish drama according to the causal, motivational logic Aristotle established as its ideal form. Insofar as such effects are a function of narrative conjecture, as opposed to the immediacy of theatrical enactment, they conduce to early modern drama's new inward dimension, and insofar as they are temporalizing, they "imitat[e] life as we experience it."[36]

The very self-consciousness with which the new drama represents the constructed character of its conjectural plots reinforces its mimetic force, Hutson argues, insofar as hermeneutic uncertainty evokes the "sense of reality" that attends "an expansive horizon of interpretive contingency."[37] *The Spanish Tragedy* can be seen to have an exemplary place in such an account because it was the first publicly performed play to represent "human causality" on stage, and because its engagement of the afterlife gives the broadest historic perspective on the forensic turn. With the post Reformation dissolution of Purgatory as a space of judgment, justice becomes a matter of this-worldly evidentiary determinations—Hieronimo's delays are a function of that forensic process.[38]

Such a version of narrative mimesis derives, Hutson argues, from Aristotle, or more precisely, from that philosopher's (surreptitious) equation of mimesis with *muthos* or emplotment: dramatic mimesis conceived as "the composition of events into an intelligible yet apparently natural sequence."[39] Even in its most skeptical moments, early modern drama remains within the terms of that initial transposition to the dispositional function of plotting, in Huston's account. In other words, early modern drama is concerned with a second-order mimesis: a question of the conjectured, falsifiable, often undecidable, relation between events, but not a question of the status of the event as such. By the same token, the subjectivity to which such mimetic effects appeals is a subject given in advance, already inclined by "mimetic prejudice."[40] Whatever questions the plays may pose about the construction of causal form or the invention of inwardness do not extend beyond the frame of the dramas, for the viewing subject is already an intending subject—one given, precisely, to mimetic prejudgment—and the mimetic force of the drama derives from its reflective, rather than constitutive, relation to an audience; its success is a function of its evocation of "the spatial and temporal contingency that we experience in our lives."[41]

By contrast, I have argued that, precisely insofar as it fulfills the mimetic logic of early modern drama, revenge drama problematizes that logic well beyond the level of narrative emplotment. Rather than being a matter of judging between potentially undecidable events, revenge drama troubles judgment and event as such, and rather than simply enlisting powers of conjecture, it vexes even as it constitutes the possibility of speculation, including the audience's own speculative relation to the play. According to the dictates of the genre, revenge is no revenge if the victim does not know why he is being punished. However, revenge is an epistemological concern in a more thoroughgoing sense. The reciprocal violence of the act of revenge is the violence of speculative thought.[42] According to the leveling, differential logic of the revenge cycle, all is staked ultimately not on the confrontation with the adversary, but on the prior and more fundamental confrontation with and encompassment of limits: for the avenger and victim alike, the face-to-face with one's own death. In the reflexive divide of that impossible encounter, the avenger violently reiterates the violent event he would comprehend. In that regard, revenge is always a matter of the missed encounter, the absolute end that does not end. Such misfires are not merely the undoing of revenge, they are also the source of revenge drama's frisson.[43]

Understood in these terms, the almost parodically pure revenge act is the one through which Vindice "answers" the Duke in *The Revenger's Drama*. In the scene, the unwitting Duke kisses the poisoned lips of the adorned skull of Vindice's beloved, the figure the Duke had raped and murdered, and the figure who for Vindice has long since—from the outset—been nothing more than a prop in the machinery of revenge. The force of the scene derives precisely from its status as missed event. The Duke discovers too late that death has already passed the gates. Through poison's invisible migrations—the revenger's favored device— the villain's fatal end is made to coincide with the revenger's words announcing it as such. The formative, subjectivizing force of the "event" consists entirely in the minimal delay through which the limit—death as such—is internalized, becoming the image of theater's own inscribing properties. And what the Duke recognizes in this recognition scene is that death is what he has desired all along. With that, the revenger momentarily occupies the ideal posture: he becomes a spectator to a redounding mechanism that functions without him. Ideal and fatal: at play's close, Vindice will give himself away with the perfect indifference of an onlooker.

Shakespeare gives this speculative logic its exemplary form in the "mousetrap," *Hamlet*'s play within the play. Sheer diversion—an opportunity, not for forensic judgment, but for Hamlet to prove what he already knows and to put himself at risk in the process—the scene is also the closest the play will come to revenge's fulfillment. For insofar as it does transfix, what the dumb-show's mute scene of ear poisoning conveys to sovereignty is nothing but the fatally dividing image of its own speculative absorption, a figure that equally conveys Hamlet's own suicidal absorption in the machinery of enactment.[44] The scene fulfils theater's new-formed mimetic function as well as its relation to judicial knowledge just insofar as it bypasses the event and the act of judgment itself. Understood in its larger historical frame, revenge embodies early modern drama's political theological moment, and the grounds of its *energia* as theater, in terms, not of the Reformation shift that make this-worldly deliberation available, but as the impossibility of decision attending the depletion of judgment's transcendental reserve, whether we understand that reserve temporally as the deferred time of purgatory or spatially as the secure external ground of divine authority.

The logic of such disarticulated judgment is embodied in *The Spanish Tragedy's* condensation of two central tropes: the pass or passport—"To whom no sooner 'gan I make approach / To crave a passport for my wand' ring ghost" (1.1.34–35); "my passport straight was drawn" (1.1.34); "Sir, here is his passport" (3.7.23)—and the intercept—"I stood betwixt thee and thy punishment" (2.1.49); "My noble lord / Will stand between me and ensuing harms" (3.3.13–14); "Who is he that interrupts our business?" (3.12.30); "'tis he that intercepts your suits" (3.14.133); he "intercepts our passage to revenge" (3.15.15). By the close, the play enacts the indissociability of those conceits: what opens the way to revenge and speculation alike is what blocks it. Mazzio notes the extravagant repetition of a term in the ghost's final speech: "let me be judge . . ."; "Let loose poor Tityus . . ."; "let Don Cyprian supply his room"; "let . . . let . . . Let . . . Let" (4.5.30–42).[45] That stammering reiteration—the very motor of revenge and mimesis—can be understood in terms of the radical identity of the meanings "let" condenses as the undisclosed kernel of revenge's mechanism: to allow and that which impedes.

To the extent it can be figured or allegorized, the open and closed operation of the *let* crystallizes the political economy of the play, embodying the condition of subject and sovereign alike. At drama's end, Hieronimo stakes all on his one subjectivizing claim *vis-à-vis* the force of the King: his claim to secrecy. You torture me, "But never shalt thou force me to reveal / The thing which I have vowed inviolate" (4.4.187–88). With that, Hieronimo bites out his tongue. The oddity, as critics have pointed out, is that he's already revealed everything—he's explained the crime and its perpetrators to the assembled court. In that sense, political subjectivity assumes the form of that most inscrutable phenomenon, the open secret, what is absolutely visible and absolutely sealed.[46] Early modern subjectivity *tout court* has something of that lucid opacity, as is evident enough from the recent history of scholarly debates on the status of the subject: early modern drama predates modern conceptions of the internalized subject; early modern drama embodies the emergence of a newfound inwardness.[47]

The open secret is the mark of sovereignty as well. The notable fact that for all his declarations about the inaccessibility of sovereign judgment, Hieronimo only once actually approaches the King, and there self-thwartingly, muting himself before he addresses the King, might be psychologized: he is a proto-Hamlet. But it would be more accurate to say that the revenger's impasse is the ontological condition of the sovereign law he would approach. "Justice and revenge," Hieronomo declares, "are placed in those empyreal heights, / Where, countermured with walls of diamond, / I find the place impregnable; . . . they . . . give my words no way" (3.7.14–18). Sovereignty is what is absolutely resistant and as transparent as the sky.

That inscrutable transparency bears on revenge drama's distinctive—and distinctly modern—relation to its own ideological function: its capacity to place its interpellative or subject-forming machinery in plain sight without that in the least diminishing the hold of the mechanism. In the middle scene of the play, Pedringano, the play's comic machiavel, stands on the gallows accused of murder, a crime to which he readily confesses. Knowing that the prince's pardon is contained in a box held by the pageboy standing nearby, Pedringano laughs at the calls for spiritual repentance. What we know, because the page has told us, is that the box is empty—we watch a character "jest himself to death" (3.5.15). The thrill of the scene lies in the combined sense of vacuity and illimitability: the fact that a character can be caught up by an empty, or pure, mechanism—a "gear," to use the scene's reiterated term—that extends beyond death, to the point, as Pedringano himself puts it, where he is to be "turned off" (3.6.55).

But that is also to say the scene shows theater's own status as open secret. For the only distinction between Pedringano and the audience is that the audience sees the device as a device and still remains theatrically absorbed. Unlike us, the villain dies, of course. Then again, he does not actually, and it is Pedringano's own language that tends to expose the mechanism as mechanism. By the same token, insofar as theatrical inscription is illimitable, the distinction between real and imagined self-loss dissolves. The frisson of the play consists in its asymptotic approach to that condition of seeing blindness. The scene's significance in relation to such a reflexive condition is evident from the anecdote contemporaries repeated to evoke the scandal of an emerging theater's powers. A woman on her death bed enjoined to turn her mind to her spiritual needs cries out instead, "*Hieronimo, Hieronimo*; O let me see *Hieronimo* acted!"[48]

The black box scene emblematizes what revenge drama shows generally: that the social functions without precedent idea, that society is political precisely to the extent that it is contentless. Revenge drama's historical moment coincides with the point where a definitionally overdetermined and deontologized social dimension translates itself into the opaque hold of a sovereign condition. The emergence of literariness and law not just as empirical but as formal or structural categories—literature and law "as such"—is directly related to the possibility of that translation. Through their disjunctive conjunctive rapport, literature and law exceed the mimetic operation even while remaining on a phenomenological continuum with it. In doing so, literary law translates the impasse of the social into its point of suture, a crystallized impossibility variously termed sovereign or subject.[49]

This is not to say that nothing in revenge drama passes beyond such an organizing structure. At the beginning of the play within the play— that is, just at the point where the play allegorizes its own literary status— the King designates his brother as the performance's bookkeeper:

KING   Here, brother, you shall be the bookkeeper:
This is the argument of that they show.
He giveth him a book
Gentlemen, this play of Hieronimo, in sundry languages, was thought
*   good to be set down in English, more largely, for the easier understanding*
*   to every public reader.*
Enter Balthazar [as Soliman] . . . .

(4.4.8–10)

Maus's note suggests the ambiguity of the moment: "possibly the 'play in sundry languages' was actually staged in a variety of foreign languages, or perhaps it was performed in English, and this stage direction is adapted from an introduction by Hieronimo."[50] At the point where the book is introduced into the play, where the text incorporates itself, we enter a textual no man's land. Is the unassigned address spoken or written? Does it derive from Kyd or is it a subsequent staged or editorial interpolation? Did the playlet ever exist in "sundry languages"? As a stage direction, it would remain mute, unstaged. And yet, if the address is to have any explanatory force in terms of the otherwise unexplained contradiction between Hieronimo's assertion that his play would be in foreign tongues (as are many of the larger play's speeches) and the fact it is delivered in English, it would need to be voiced, that anomalous presence of a stage direction within the play somehow affiliated with the seemingly gratuitous presence of the book itself on stage. But what is the strange status of a stage direction within a purely imaginary play, a play that has no scripted form? If, as the modern editorial interpolation suggests, the address is adapted from Hieronimo's own nonexistent play, what is the status of those, present or past, readers or auditors, who feel themselves directly addressed by and incorporated within that purely virtual form?

The important point is the timing of this moment where, mad Hieronimo-like, the text moves in and out of its own space and time. Textual perturbation occurs at the point where the book appears, that is, at the point of the play's self-incorporative divison. In that regard, the "moment"—unlocatable as it is—is of a piece with the thematized division of tongues presented by the play within the play; but with a difference. For here that fragmentation dissolves the phenomenal being of the play itself, just as the body politic is momentarily dissolved by the ambiguous reference to "Gentlemen" and "every public reader" who may be the same or socially divided, who may be truly or fictitiously interpellated at some present, past or future point.

At the point of their coming into being, text, as well as socius, are realized, not as a determinate passage from speech to script, nor as a reciprocal interchange between literature and law, but as a movement of *translatio* without ground or reference. That is, in one regard, the fulfillment of mimesis; the play's capacity to petition us from a point within and beyond itself in the form of a kind of mute speaking is the secret condition of theater's inscriptive force—recall the inscribing hold of the Leonardo image beyond its speculative logic. But it also means mimesis accomplishes itself through the very dissolution of its mimetic, phenomenal form. With that shift, we move from the problematic of Aristotelian mimetics, even in its exacerbated metatheatrical form, into another domain: the aesthetic as such. And we move to Shakespeare.

Senseless Ilium: Shakespeare and the Aesthetic Turn

One consequence of the account of early modern revenge drama I have pursued thus far is to rob *Hamlet* of many of its claims to originality. Indecision, delay, artistic self-reflexiveness are already very much at the heart of the revenge genre itself and its relation to its political moment.

And yet, critics have not been wrong to feel that something shifts with Shakespeare's play, and to recognize that shift at the level of the subject. But to say that subjectivity deepens or becomes more self-reflective does not explain how such a change is possible, given the signifying logic of the era. Hamlet recasts the revenge act, bringing to light its neutral, even inhuman, grounds. That shift, a transformation in the status and temporality of the political event as such, corresponds with a shift from the headlong captivations of metatheatricality to the emergence of aesthetics proper. The play's allegorization of such an aesthetic turn bears directly on its anticipation of modern political representation.

I will sketch that turn by zeroing in on a familiar—perhaps overly familiar—moment in *Hamlet*: the First Player's speech. "The rugged Pyrrhus," "horridly tricked / With blood of fathers, mothers, daughters, sons," discovers Troy's ancient king:

> Anon he finds him
> Striking too short at Greeks. His antique sword,
> Rebellious to his arm, lies where it falls,
> Repugnant to command. Unequal matched,
> Pyrrhus at Priam drives, in rage strikes wide;
> But with the whiff and wind of his fell sword
> Th' unnerved father falls. Then senseless Ilium,
> Seeming to feel this blow, with flaming top
> Stoops to his base, and with a hideous crash
> Takes prisoner Pyrrhus' ear. For lo! his sword,
> Which was declining on the milky head
> Of reverend Priam, seemed i' th' air to stick.
> So, as a painted tyrant, Pyrrhus stood,
> And, like a neutral to his will and matter,
> Did nothing.[51]

Pyrrhus's pause—the moment that would seem to crystallize the mystery of Hamlet's own hesitation—entails a mystery of its own. What checks the revenger in the face of his already felled victim? Not conscience—Pyrrhus is caked in gore. Rather, the suspension is a function of an elision of distinctions; "a neutral to his will and matter," the revenger becomes indistinguishable from the "unnerved" figure he opposes, an equivalency that reflects the sheer oedipal redundancies of a mechanism in which usurper usurps usurper to come into his own. In that sense, Pyrrhus's pause represents the caesura through which sovereign force constitutes itself, not agonistically, but out of and against itself, its exorbitancy a function of the impasse at its source. Like the lull before a storm,

> so, after Pyrrhus' pause,
> A rousèd vengeance sets him new a-work;
> And never did the Cyclops' hammers fall
> . . . .
> With less remorse than Pyrrhus' bleeding sword
> Now falls on Priam.
>
> (2.2.478–83)

The sovereign act is generated on its own failure, a recursive force against the failure of force.

Read thus, the passage places *Hamlet* squarely within the mimetic frame of revenge drama, its conception of sovereignty structured on the same reiterated impasse. But to read thus is also to misread. For what arrests Pyrrhus is not the encounter with Priam, the object or nonobject, but something from elsewhere, the intervening sound of "senseless Ilium['s]" crashing towers—that sound captures Pyrrhus's ear. In other words, at the fateful moment, the tyrant is distracted.

Distraction is no small matter in Shakespeare. It recurs everywhere, from the fly-buzzing-at-the ear presence of Lear's Fool, to Desdemona's self-beguilements in the face of that drama's murderously tightening grip, to the repeated moments of coming to in the comedies. Distraction is an ethical—perhaps the ethical—category in Shakespeare; threatening madness, distraction is also what saves, unbinding the self from object-fixation on the one hand and solipsism on the other. More fundamentally, though indissociably, distraction bears on the groundless, betwixt-and-between status of the work itself—the work as representational go-between between world and subject. In that sense, distraction indexes the appearance of an explicitly aesthetic subjectivity.[52]

Pyrrhus's pause, what translates the avenger into a "painted tyrant," bears out the foundational character of that aesthetic turn. Insofar as mimesis is a function of the illimitable differential movement that determines it, the inaugurating moment, such as it is, amounts to the moment where the subject is posited in relation to that very fact of difference, not as inscribed within an already determined mimetic cycle. That is an aesthetic instance insofar as the mechanism through which sheer difference assumes phenomenal form corresponds to the contradictory, self-differentiating operation through which the work would reflexively cognize its own groundlessness. Situated at the limit of cognition and beyond language understood as a human means, that blindly posited phenomenalization takes the form, as Paul de Man has shown, of an unstable wavering between sensible and insensate: an ekphrastic tyrant, a city whose animacy is intimated precisely in the language of its denial—"senseless Illium."[53]

The scene locates the aesthetic beyond oedipal agonism—that is, beyond law in any normative sense—and beyond the structures of correspondence or exchange that would situate it as an analogue of normative law or economy. Conceived foundationally, the aesthetic posits subjectivity in a direct relation to the event that marks the origin as well as the end of polis, nation, and empire: Ilium's fall. The tyrant's translation is mapped onto the *translatio imperii*. Jane Bellamy associates the traumatic character of Troy's collapse within that myth of Europe's political origins with its metaleptic, always missed status. Aeneas encounters Troy's fall as if for the first time in Carthage's memorial murals. And what is always missed is endlessly repeated: burning Carthage, burning Laurentium, Rome's end. Thus, "senseless Illium" represents Europe's political foundation as, in Virgil's term, *eremia,* the place "where man is not," as apolis.[54]

Pyrrhus's response is an effect of the elliptical temporality of that founding event. The tyrant's translation into something inanimate echoes Marlowe's translation of the moment in *Dido, Queen of Carthage* where Pyrrhus "[stands] stone still, / Viewing the fire wherewith rich Ilion burnt," even as, moments earlier, Jove's marble statue seems brought to life by horror at Priam's slaughter.[55] Marlowe in turn echoes Virgil's own account of Aeneas's response to the images in Dido's temple, where he stands "fastened in a stare, astonished"[56]—that is, like the citizens in Florence's city square, turned to stone. That scene anticipates the close of the epic, where it is Aeneas's rival Turnus who is benumbed: "an eerie numbness unnerved him head to toe."[57] Turnus, in turn, hearkens back to the epic's first description of Aeneas frozen in horror during the storm at sea.[58] The temporal displacement implied by Troy's reiterated fall, a repetition that places the event ahead and behind itself, is figured in the response it occasions, where sovereign force realizes itself as what is already inscribed, already the ekphrastic figure it will have been. In that sense, what Pyrrhus hears, what arrests and suspends him, is Shakespeare.

By what logic is that elliptical temporal and aesthetic effect a specifically political effect? More precisely, why is the cause of Pyrrhus's arrest represented as the inscribing and apparently unmediated force of a purely material manifestation of the polis—the city's collapsing towers? The answer may lie in the relation between such material markers and law as such. "The people must fight for the law as for their city wall," Heraclitis writes. As Andrew Benjamin observes in his analysis of the fragment, that association needs to be understood in its foundational dimension, in terms of law, not as regulative principle, but as *nomos*, that is, the primordial cut which, in Schmitt's analysis, constitutes the space of the political.[59] Rather than a division between determinable spaces—the inside and the outside of the polis—the demarcating cut or interval of *nomos* opens the very possibility of spacing, even as it divides space. In doing so, *nomos* institutes man as a function of the unstable constitutive/dissolvative interval of such spacing, as *ab initio* a contingent being and a being in common. *Nomos*, in that sense, implies what the scene implies: a constitutive sociality beyond and in advance of the subjectivities it constitutes—the paradox of immediate mediation. Thus the political condition of man is inextricable from the impossibility of thought's speculative self-completion, consisting in the division that manifests itself foundationally as an aesthetic, rather than cognitive, phenomenon.[60]

The scene brings us back to Carl Schmitt in more than one regard. Pyrrhus's pause, with its suspension of the normative functioning of law and signification, corresponds to Schmitt's account of political grounds in the state of exception, that act through which the sovereign asserts his constitutive decision from beyond law and state as if by divine fiat. The scene bears out and vexes Schmitt's account. It suggests, on the one hand, that that founding interruption unbinds as much as it provides the occasion for the sovereign act; the drama of political foundations is enacted in the sovereign's self-exemption, which is also his self-exemplifying translation into the allegorical form of the painted tyrant.[61] On the other, it confirms the truth of Schmitt's account of political emergence at the most radical level of the divisions and suspensions of *nomos*, at the level of law's own autonomic normative/extra-normative operation.[62]

The passage equally brings to mind Schmitt's analysis of the relation between political foundations and aesthetics. The scene complicates in obvious ways the schematic opposition forwarded in *Political Theol-*

ogy between the authentic act and mere aesthetics. It bears more interestingly on the suppler version of the aesthetic Schmitt offers in his own reading of *Hamlet*, for there, the relation between work and history explicitly exceeds a structure of mimetic correspondence. History is not merely a topical matter, Schmitt argues. Instead, history manifests itself in the form of a disturbance or distortion of the work's signifying structures, precisely as interruption.[63] It is just its status as unrepresentable—as taboo material which, in the case of *Hamlet*, Schmitt associates with the contemporary succession crisis—that gives history the status of *Einbruch*, as that which breaks into the drama as normative signifying field. *Translatio*'s suspension might be understood similarly insofar as history is conceived as contingent, non-narratable cause.

And yet, that conception of history as extrinsic cause, and thus of the aesthetic as secondary formation, fails to recognize the scene's force as an account of the derivation of law and norm. For to conceive history as intrusion from without, however divided or unrepresentable, is merely to reinforce—indeed, to establish in the first instance—the illusion of the aesthetic as enclosed domain, and of the norm as norm, those conceptions Schmitt derogates. Interruption or distraction as Shakespeare conceives it, the point where text and event overtake themselves temporally, is not a disturbance from without or within; it is a suspension of cause that opens, even as it breaches, the movement of history as a phenomenal and thus a determinable form. In that sense, history, political foundation, and aestheticization are radically coterminous.[64]

Hamlet, then, figures the aesthetic not simply as the inescapable limit point of dramatic mimesis, but at the core of the drama as a scene of political and historical foundations. What is the consequence of that explicit, even stagy allegorization of aesthetic origins? What is figurable is available to negotiation. In *Hamlet*'s case, that means a historically significant recasting of subjective and political grounds. I have suggested in other contexts the way the resolution of the play can be understood in terms of the mechanism through which Hamlet converts the reiterated division of the revenger's act into the defining measure of his life.[65] "The interim is mine," Hamlet says, and it becomes his by means of the violence directed against Rosencrantz and Guildenstern that converts the internal fatality of the act into the anticipated and enabling deadline imposed by his own returning message from England. That sacrificial act, which converts the ambiguous friend/enemy into a mere go-between—a messenger—even as it abjects them in that role, thus consolidates the prince in relation to a now lucidly specular and exteriorized sovereign adversary. Speaking of the meddling go-betweens, Hamlet announces to Horatio, "'Tis dangerous when the baser nature comes / Between the pass and fell incensèd points / Of mighty opposites" (5.2.61–63). Because it is constitutive, that exterior limit is always beyond the subject—"I cannot live to hear the news from England" Hamlet says in his dying speech—but it nevertheless establishes the subject *vis-à-vis* a horizon, precisely as an *intending* subject (5.2.307).

That instrumental being cannot be separated from its political dimensions, for the subjectivizing interim also implies a reconfigured political space. The message announcing the death of Rosencrantz and Guildenstern coincides with the appearance of the ambassadors to announce the approach of Fortinbras. The interim through which Hamlet engages his death as a projective limit is, I've argued, the space across which Hamlet casts his "dying voice" for the new Prince.[66] Julia Lupton has suggestively read that invocation of the elective voice as marking a turn from hierarchic sovereignty to the anticipation of a new, horizontally configured democratic polis.[67] And yet that political space is not instituted by the elective voice, whether conceived in individual or collective terms; it is rather the interim that constitutes the space of the political as a representational field, as well as the deliberative subject such a field implies, and that interval is staked on sacrificial violence. In that sense, it would be more accurate to read such a transformation in relation to the space-clearing force through which Hobbes will institute a newly formalized political domain, a contractual and instrumental domain within which sovereign and subject alike are inscribed. Politically, then, the play allegorizes the transition from the alterior and relativized space of the early modern polis, where the act is inseparable from the political domain it ceaselessly opens, to the forcibly rationalized space of the state.[68]

That representational dispensation emerges out of the aesthetic. More precisely, it emerges from even as it constitutes itself as against the aesthetic, a contradiction the modern political domain will retain. For with the appearance of the political as representation, the aesthetic is recast precisely as the threatened collapse of representation's interval. At the close, Hamlet's stammering movement across every limit—"I am dead, Horatio. . . . Horatio, I am dead. . . . O, I die, Horatio" (5.2.286, 291, 305)—is picked up as a troubling of the boundary that governs our roles as witnesses and auditors: "You that look pale and tremble at this chance, / That are but mutes or audience to this act," Hamlet says to the audience within and beyond (5.2.287–88). The exorbitancy that translates Hamlet's fateful act into nothing but its belated witnessing translates the audience into the role of fatally inscribed actants.

The distinction between a governable representational economy and the contagion of theatrical effect should be familiar: it amounts, one is tempted to say, to the Kantian divide, the separating out of reason's law, or the formal operations of the categorical imperative, from the aesthetic as autonomous domain—in Kant's terms, the distinction between determinate and reflective judgments. For all the profound differences between Hobbesian instrumentalism and Kant's articulation of the conditions of perception, the two converge in the articulation of a new space, in figuring the transition from vertical theological transcendence to what Jean-Luc Nancy describes as Kant's "horizontal transcendence"— the world as horizon.[69]

The risks of such an assertion—of the claim that Shakespeare reveals the aesthetic origins of the enlightenment political/representational order—become evident when we recognize what is at stake in *Hamlet*'s "interim." That interval is the space between the prince and his own death, the interval in relation to which the dying voice becomes a representative voice. It is the interim between reigns, a space reinforced, rather than threatened, according to a new political economy, by the discontinuity of Fortinbras's rule.[70] But it is also the interval between the play and ourselves, the representational interim that structures the possibility of an ordered reading, including the one that construes the play as a story of aesthetic origins.

However, the self-inclusive, self-inscribing character of that dispensation does not prevent it from conjuring an alternative as the inevitable shadow of its own ordering. Unsurprisingly, that counteraesthetic is gendered. The queen recounts Ophelia's death. She holds herself aloft from the willow "that shows his hoar leaves in the glassy stream" until the bough breaks:

> Her clothes spread wide,
> And mermaid-like awhile they bore her up;
> Which time she chanted snatches of old tunes,
> As one incapable of her own distress,
> Or like a creature native and endued
> Unto that element. But long it could not be
> Till that her garments, heavy with their drink,

Pulled the poor wretch from her melodious lay
To muddy death.

(4.7.142, 150–58)

The moment in which Ophelia is briefly suspended in the reflective waters—the space of a divided self-knowledge—should be read in relation to the painted tyrant's pause and Hamlet's defining interim. Here, that interim is not claimed or mastered because it does not take the form of a threat; it sustains like a native element: Ophelia inhabits it, just as she inhabits her distractedness, "incapable of her own distress." Nor does the interim in this instance entail blockage or fixating arrest because it functions outside any act of inaugural determination. In order to recognize the scene as an account of political aesthetics, we need to translate it out of its derogated form as a tale of madness and suicide. Recast thus, the scene articulates a speculative space that—while it cannot be long allowed by the narrative pressures of the play—is not itself staked on exclusionary and consolidating violence, a space in which subjectivity's self-separation is given in advance.

Insofar as that figure sustained in the mirroring brook is no less an other, Ophelia's interval implies the space of a potential aesthetic *communitas*, one in which narcissism, a narcissism prior to ego, becomes indistinguishable from sociality: a community in suspension. We might think of Nancy's description of the world as a mode of coexistence sustained entirely within the constitutive interval of relationality as such:

> Coexistence is that which coheres without being "one" and without being sustained by anything else, or rather being sustained by *nothing*: by the nothing of the *co*—that is indeed nothing but the in-between or the with of the being-together of singularities. That nothing-with is the non-cause of the world, material, efficient, formal, and final. This means both that the world is simply there (it is or it permeates its "there," its spacing) and that it is the coexistence that it does not contain but that on the contrary "makes" it.[71]

Hamlet evokes that political aesthetic possibility—a world that is neither a polis nor a state—even in its abrogation of it.

CHAPTER 4

"To throw out our eyes for brave Othello"

Thus far, my consideration of Shakespearean aesthetics has focused on a pivotal moment that can be read in relation to one of the contexts—the revenge genre—from and against which it can be said to arise. I turn now to *Othello* to suggest, in part, how the logic of the aesthetic underpins Shakespeare's conception of the literary work more broadly. This will entail tracing elements or motifs that recur throughout his oeuvre: the psychic phenomenon of distraction, the structuring operation of the vanishing point. But in turning to this particular play—Shakespeare's domestic tragedy—I also mean to bring to view aestheticization's relation to a specifically modern or anticipatory constellation of issues: the emergence of the "universal" citizen-subject, formal law, and the developing state form.

Regarding Othello

I will begin to consider the relation between *Othello*'s aesthetic status and its political entailments by focusing on a moment in the play that has received a lot of critical scrutiny: Desdemona's behavior as she awaits the arrival of Othello's storm-tossed ship in Cyprus.[1] It's easy enough for us to dissociate ourselves from Iago's forced and prurient habits of reading as he watches Desdemona and Cassio exchanging pleasantries. And yet, why is Desdemona dallying with Cassio when Othello is still out in the storm? Desdemona herself seems to betray a sense of the impropriety of her behavior. "What wouldst write of me, if thou shouldst praise me?" she says to Iago.

DESDEMONA   Come on, essay—there's one gone to the harbor?
IAGO   Ay, madam.
DESDEMONA   I am not merry; but I do beguile
  The thing I am by seeming otherwise.
  Come, how wouldst thou praise me?

$$(2.1.124, 123-26)^2$$

Compare the response of Montano, a more or less inconsequential character, to Othello's plight:

  Let's to the sea-side, ho!—
  As well to see the vessel that's come in
  As to throw out our eyes for brave Othello,
  Even till we make the main and th'aerial blue
  An indistinct regard.

$$(2.1.37-41)$$

But Montano's words are telling. The fact is, you can look so fixedly that all becomes "an indistinct regard." You can lose the object by being too fastened on it, as Othello will do in his killing desire for "the ocular proof," and lose oneself—"throw out [one's] eyes"—in the process (3.3.365). And if fixity ends up beguiling one of oneself, a certain capacity to beguile oneself, as Desdemona does at dockside, can be saving.

Such instances of distractedness recur in the play. Think, for instance, of the peculiar moment when, with the murderous intensities of the drama coming to a head, Desdemona's thoughts turn in the midst of the Willow Song to . . . Lodovico.

EMILIA   Shall I go fetch your nightgown?
DESDEMONA   No. Unpin me here.
  This Lodovico is a proper man.

$$(4.3.34-35)$$

The apparent impropriety of the thought has led at least one modern editor to reassign the line to Emilia on purely characterological grounds, that is, out of an impulse to preserve Desdemona's purity.[3] But Desdemona is neither innocent nor guilty, she is distracted, and it is that by now impossibly fragile prospect of the stray thought that alone stands against the killing force of such fixed, determinative judgments within and beyond the play—"unpin me here," she says (4.3.35). Such moments are not confined to *Othello*. Distraction is, as I have suggested, at the center of a subjective and interpretive ethic for Shakespeare. One thinks of the unbinding effects of the Fool's babble in *King Lear*, or the saving character of the boundary moments in the comedies, the moments of coming to from dreams and from plays, where we fleetingly comprehend what we would possess as what had always been, in Helena's words, "mine own and not mine own."[4]

The scene of Othello's vanishing suggests the opposition that would seem to underwrite such an ethic, the distinction between the saving indirections of fictiveness—Desdemona seeks to beguile herself through impromptu verse—and the mastering, implicitly male, claims of the eye. Montano's call for us to "throw out our eyes for brave Othello" is associated with the play's general preoccupation with castration understood as a threat to the eye of speculative reason as such. "No, when light-winged toys / Of feathered Cupid seel with wanton dullness / My speculative and officed instruments / . . . / Let housewives make a skillet of my helm," Othello exclaims (1.3.267–71). "That's with watching," Desdemona says of Othello's aching forehead, the familiar symptom of the unmanned cuckold (3.3.289). "Watching" is lack of sleep, but it's also simply watching—"give me the ocular proof"—and in that regard it's a line that addresses itself to the spectators beyond (3.3.365).

The encompassments of the aesthetic operation the play articulates become apparent when we recognize that such moments of specular captivation are themselves equally nothing more than instances of distraction. Whether we fix ourselves in the mode of identification or objectification "black Othello" appears, like the Turkish ships in their feinted approach toward Rhodes, as a "pageant" "to keep us in false gaze" (2.3.28, 1.3.19–20). What at once saves and imperils, distraction is illimitable; to imagine oneself on secure ground is to be all the more blindly caught up. The question—and this is the distinctly literary ethic of the play—is only whether one can comprehend the fact of one's own distracted condition. That knowing distraction, a knowledge of the fact of one's inevitable inscription, is the psychic correlative of the emerging condition of aesthetic subjectivity.

That the aesthetic is nevertheless more than an ethical or characterological matter is apparent when we consider the dockside scene in terms of its larger structural function. Montano's enjoining our gaze at the point where Othello momentarily disappears mid-drama recalls the interval during which Hamlet disappears in the midst of his drama—his transformative sea-journey to England—drawing all eyes to him on his return. We should think too of the sublime limit that appears midway through *King Lear*, Edgar's riveting account of the view down from Dover's imagined cliffs where sight again exceeds itself: "I'll look no more, / Lest my brain turn, and the deficient sight / Topple down headlong" (4.6.22–24). These moments are proleptic of tragedy's end. And they all have the structure of a specular trap: to fix oneself upon such a point is to be all the more ensnared. But they have a larger import as well, for they signal Shakespearean tragedy as a tragedy constituted in relation to its ability to incorporate its own formal limit and vanishing point.

More than a mimetic effect, such limit structures correspond to the aesthetic work's capacity to figure from within itself its own illimitability as a purely self-referential representational form, to ground itself on its own groundlessness. In that sense, the absorptive vanishing point represents, not the autonomy of authorship—a later formation—but the autogenetic character of the work, its capacity to constitute itself as self-grounding and limitlessly inscribing form. That turn brings with it its own subjectivity. The founding association in Greek tragedy between negation and speculative dialectic—the relation, that is, between tragedy and subjectivization—is recast in modernity, and in Shakespeare particularly, as an explicitly aesthetic formation, a function of the reflexive, self-compassing, and illimitable work.[5]

What is distinctive about Othello's relation to such an aesthetic transformation? The antinomy that condenses at its vanishing point, I would argue. On the one hand, Othello himself is posited as the play's structuring vanishing point; the heroic subject is that negation and limit. On the other, the entire dockside scene is notable for its gratuity: Othello's momentary disappearance amounts to a theatrical caesura implying no characterological transformation—it is, that is, a pure distraction in the course of the drama. With that conjunction, the play's aesthetic character becomes the basis of its subjectifying effects; Othello becomes our "indistinct regard," becomes the abyss of the play's own reception. That coincidence between subjectivity and illimitable form amounts to the appearance of aesthetic ideology as such.

Such an advent is of a piece with the play's distinctive social and political lineaments as bourgeois—or proto-bourgeois—tragedy. Whatever its generalized relation to castration and the threat to male speculative reason, negation in the drama is ultimately less affiliated with the hierarchical impasses of the oedipal drama, the vertical structure through which prohibition is internalized as the ground of the equivocal sovereign-subject, than it is with the movement of lateral similitudes or substitutions associated, as Julia Lupton has argued, with the emerging category of the citizen.[6] That shift is apparent in the play's concern with bureaucratic substitutability—with "place," "office," "occupation"—and with surrogacy generally, a preoccupation that underwrites the entire drama of projective jealousy.[7] "For that I do suspect the lusty Moor / Hath leapt into my seat; the thought whereof / Doth, like a poisonous mineral, gnaw my inwards," Iago declaims (2.1.282–84): the anality of the line suggests well enough the relation between the prospects of equivalency in the play and the instabilities of the lateral male homosocial bond.[8]

Jealousy itself should be understood in relation to such a political/symbolic ordering, in ways that extend beyond a merely thematic association with bourgeois domestic drama. Self-begotten and borne out of nothing, jealousy converts tragedy's grounding in the mysterious *ex nihilo* of sovereign being and act into the equally opaque workings of an illimitable relational mechanism—an inscribing mechanism. That empty and supervening mechanism intimates the peculiar powers of the state, that phantasmatic ordering force that comes more starkly to view with the dissolution of hierarchical structuring. At the same time, in its groundless character, jealousy also amounts to the psychic and thematic equivalent of the aesthetic as self-constituting, self-perpetuating effect. Thus the complicity between the aesthetic as explicit ideological formation and the modern state form.

Those transformations can be felt at the deepest levels of the play as an epistemological structure. If *Hamlet* is propelled by mystery—what lies beyond—*Othello* poses the perhaps more inscrutable question of what holds us in a play in which we know too much. In such a context, tragic pleasure, ordered around catharsis and sublimation, gives way to sheer masochism, and the internalization of death and negation associated with classical tragedy is replaced by a rivening, self-depleting theatricality in which absorption is merely intensified by the drive for absolute evidentiary certainty. "Make me to see't"; "be sure thou prove my love a whore" (3.3.369, 364). "Go to, well said, well said," Othello declaims from the sidelines, a prompter to the scene in which Iago prompts Cassio to speak of what Othello takes to be his cuckolding (4.1.113); Othello's self-annihilating captivation at such a moment figures the audience's own masochistic absorption in a drama whose trajectory is agonizingly clear, in which we already compass all.[9] The point is not the vast epistemological space between the audience and the hero. At some level, all know and all are captivated precisely because everything functions within a field that inscribes audience and characters alike.

If that infinite field nevertheless harbors a mystery, it is not of the epistemological sort. One can understand what *Othello* is up to with a look back at the distinction I drew in the introduction between *As You Like It* and *King Lear*, comedy and tragedy. As Susan Snyder points out, the play amounts to a tragedy founded on a "comic matrix."[10] That hybridized form is more than a matter of incorporating the thematic preoccupations of the bourgeois world—citizenship, jealousy, and so on—into tragedy. It entails, I would argue, an *absolutizing* of the self-referential literariness of comedy, the attempt to extend the literary through death's limit without abandoning its character as literary. This formal logic can be seen at the end in Othello's death scene—death as a story of death—and, as I will show, in the status of the play's own close which is neither framed by epilogue nor frameless, but entails a conversion of the diegetical drama into a reiterated framing operation. The stakes of those formal peculiarities are more than formal. For that possibility of an infinite extension of pure literary self-referentiality is the condition for the possibility of a comprehensible speculative system. In that sense, the play reveals the relation between aesthetic ideology and the possibility of ideology as such. But in that extravagant absolutizing of its form, the play also necessarily conjures the limits of such a self-referential operation, the point where the very logic of infinitude understood as an apprehensible vanishing point or horizon falters.

That limit coincides with the issue that has been the point of fixed regard for modern readings of the play. It is hard not to read the dockside scene as a story about race, even a relatively progressive story. To fixate on this—as a way of authorizing by way of contrast one's own subjective agency—is merely to enact one's own eclipse; it is to be inscribed within a structure to which one had been blind. In that sense, race is a particular instance of the play's larger critique of empirical knowledge. Empirical proof in the play is not literature's symmetrical counter-term; it is inscribed within fictiveness, amounting to nothing more than a forgetfulness about the fact of one's own literariness. To seek empirical grounds as the way out of fiction is to be all the more inscribed within, the play suggests. In that sense, the play shows that race is a fictitious construct: a modern insight.

But to leave the matter there is to miss the larger force of the scene. For it is precisely that annulment of the subject, its reduction to a punctiform vanishing point, that underwrites the aesthetic formation and the infinite, and thus universal, subjectivity it articulates. In that sense, blindness is complicit with knowingness, for the entire epistemological drama around "black Othello" merely energizes the speculative structure it inhabits. To look *there* at all, to speculate, is to energize the play's force as aesthetic ideology. In that sense, "to throw out our eyes for brave Othello" is not a mistake—it's the sacrifice we perform to sustain him and ourselves as (aesthetic) subjects. The play does not just reveal the fallacy of race understood as an empirical phenomenon, then. It exposes the limits of race conceived as a purely fictional or discursive construct, that is, the limits of the "solution" we have tended to offer to the falsehood of racialization.[11]

To understand race in relation to the play as speculative structure is to recast the familiar debate about the historical status of race in the era. The familiar historical debate as to whether race is or is not present in the play is complicated by the fact that the problem of race *is* the problem of its designation or regard. Race is posited not in relation to fiction but in relation to those problems of reference that trouble the ability of work and culture to constitute themselves as systems at all. That disturbance helps us understand the virulent insistence of race in the new era of "universal" subjectivity. It also situates the question of the play's historicity in relation to the vanishing point of our speculative relation to it. In the following section, I will look at how the play sustains itself as a speculative, self-referential form, focusing particularly on the central role of the historical opposition between law and literariness. In the last section, I will return to the question of race, focusing on the way it manifests itself at the end of the play and in relation to the boundaries of its aesthetic condition.

Cannibal Narratives

To consider the play's reflections on its own grounds, I want to begin with what I take to be the ur-scene of the tragedy, Othello's account of his wooing of Desdemona. Brabantio has accused Othello before the Venetian senate of seducing his daughter by "indirect and forced courses," that is, by witchcraft (1.3.111). The tale of seduction Othello tells is in fact one of "indirect . . . courses"—triangulated addresses, voyeuristic auditions—although who's bewitching whom remains unresolved. Desdemona is drawn in because of the exotic content of the tale of anthropophagi and "hair-breadth scapes" (1.3.135). It is everything she is not, and for that reason it is captivating, it beguiles her of herself: "She wished she had not heard it, yet she wished / That heaven had made her such a man" (1.3.161–62). But Othello's story also seduces simply because it is a tale not *for* her; it is an overheard tale between men. "Her father loved me, oft invited me; / Still questioned me the story of my life / From year to year" (1.3.127–29). And while the men tell it in their manly way from start to finish, apparently without loss or remainder—"even from my boyish days / To th' very moment he bade me tell it" (1.3.131–32)—for Desdemona, it is a tale in "parcels" or fragments heard in passing: "These things to hear / Would Desdemona seriously incline, / But still the house affairs would draw her thence, / Which ever as she could with haste dispatch, / She'd come again, and with a greedy ear / Devour up my discourse" (1.3.153, 144–49). In the elusiveness of that fragmentary over-hearing desire's space opens.

Insofar as it is not the tale told to you and for you but the tale aimed elsewhere that seduces, Desdemona's remark about a friend to speak Othello's story has a kind of weight. "She thanked me, / And bade me, if I had a friend that loved her, / I should but teach him how to tell my story, / And that would woo her" (1.3.162–65). There will, of course, be such a friend. He "went between us oft," Othello later remarks, describing Cassio's role in the early stages of their courtship (3.3.102). Desdemona's call for a go-between can be read as a sidelong invitation for something more direct, or as a sign of Desdemona's inconstancy. But in a more fundamental way it suggests how proximate the tragedy is to the springs of desire in the play, how impossibly close the structures that open desire are to the obliterating workings of what will foreclose it.

That suggestion of the primacy of the go-between is consistent with what the passage suggests about the role of language as such in the working of seduction. As critics have observed, with her "devour[ing] ear," Desdemona—apparently so pliant—takes on the voracious aspects of the cannibals she hears of, as if listening to the tale of monsters she becomes one.[12] Further, though, the idea of a devouring ear is strange. Mouths devour. Even the consuming eye is a familiar enough trope. But the devouring ear is arresting because hearing is not supposed to entail agency. And yet, because language prompts desire, including the desire for meaning, precisely when it is unmoored from any source—told as a tale passed on—it's as true to say that meaning derives from the ear as from the mouth.

To the extent that the tale she hears is also hers—her fantasy, her construction, the image of her own desire—Desdemona can be said, like the anthropophagite, to be consuming "her own"; that reflexive conception of the cannibal—the anthropophagite as autophage—recurs in Shakespeare, as it does in Montaigne and others of the era.[13] Understood thus, Desdemona is not the only one in the scene who might be likened to the cannibal. We have spoken of the opposition between the totalizing narrative Othello speaks to the father and the fragmentary tale Desdemona hears. But there's an extravagance particular to the inclusive story, the one told from the teller's "boyish days / To the very moment he made [him] tell it," that ultimately dissolves such an opposition. The sense that we are on the brink, as Stephen Greenblatt puts it, of "a narrative in which the storyteller is constantly swallowed up by the narrative" is evident in the phrases conflating content and telling: "—the battles, sieges, fortunes, / That I have passed. / I ran it through . . ."; "It was my hint to speak. Such was my process"—and in the ambiguous references or switch points that suggest the story has begun incorporating itself (1.3.130–32, 142).[14] When Othello speaks of the story "wherein [he] spoke . . . / . . . of [his] redemption thence, / And portance in [his] traveller's history," he refers to his conduct during his adventures, but also hints at being carried, ported, by the history he tells (1.3.133, 137–38).

The consuming properties of the tale are most apparent, however, in its effects. "I think this tale would win my daughter, too," the Duke remarks at the close (1.3.170). We might take this to mean what the Duke cannot quite say: that it has beguiled him. Then again, even to conceive the story as addressed elsewhere is, as I have shown, to be caught up within its seductive circuit. Far from judging the story of love from outside, the Duke, speaking for state and law, merely brings to view the scene of paternal seduction with which it began. "Her father loved me, oft invited me, / Still questioned me the story of my life," Othello began (1.3.127–28). Indeed, who's to say the prohibitory father—the very figure of law—was not the go-between and instrument of the seduction that so unmans him? "This accident is not unlike my dream," Brabantio says on hearing of the terrible betrayal (1.1.143).[15] To have "still questioned" Othello from the outset is to have questioned him continuously, but the phrase also suggests the unbounded character of a telling that incorporates its own reception.

Self-consuming, self-producing, a tale that inscribes teller and addressee alike, Othello's oral history is a cannibal narrative, and also, like "the men whose heads / Do grow beneath their shoulders," an acephalic one, a narrative without head or source (1.3.143–44). In that regard, it anticipates much that makes the play monstrous: jealousy, the condition "begot upon itself, born on itself" (3.4.157); Iago's seductions, monstrous for the way they turn their victims back upon themselves ("So will I turn her virtue into pitch, / And out of her own goodness make the net / That shall enmesh them all" [2.3.334–36]); and the literally "preposterous" character of the drama, all the forms of temporal reversal that Patricia Parker has subtly analyzed at work in the play.[16] Iago's strategies of imaginative capture, his oscillations between reticence ("Think, my lord?") and precipitance ("O, beware, my lord, of jealousy!"), his abrupt passages from outsides ("Are your doors locked") to insides ("Your heart is burst")—all simply give form to an inherently elliptical—belated, anticipatory—story, one which from the moment it is known was already there. Such boundary-passing contagiousness—a power to possess—is what aligns the tale with witchcraft.[17]

Something of the scope of that effect, and of the interpretive ethic it implies, is apparent when we turn back on our own reading. We began by noting what many have noted, the correspondence between the cannibals and Desdemona's "devour[ing] ear." But there's nothing automatic about such an equation—it is, in fact, tendentious. It is difficult to hear the account of Desdemona's devouring ear without freighting her in some minimal way with the violent excesses to which the play will devolve, and of which she is the chief victim. Forcibly marking her thus is to respond to a desire to ground the passage, to produce a sense of agency in a scene of seduction without cause, with neither a seducer nor a seduced. In doing so one merely makes the figure of the cannibal the recursive image of one's own reverting force. If the tragedy is already present here at the outset, it's because one has already monstrously, self-consumingly set it in motion. And if such coercion is at work in the application of the cannibal trope to Desdemona, it is a fortiori at work in the unspoken ascription of the epithet to the self-destroying "black-amoor," a figure who in the context of the seduction narrative tends to be read either as cunning and thus rapacious fabulator or as primitive naïf, or, somehow, as both.

Such matters of interpretive force return at the close. Focusing on his account of himself as one "not easily jealous," as one who loved "too well," critics have debated how accurately Othello knows himself in his final, suicidal address (5.2.354, 353). But the question of self-recognition may be less a matter of the content of the address than its rhetorical status.

OTHELLO   .... Set you down this,
  And say besides, that in Aleppo once,
  Where a malignant and a turbaned Turk
  Beat a Venetian and traduced the state,
  I took by th' throat the circumcisèd dog,
  And smote him thus. [*He stabs himself*]
LODOVICO   O bloody period!
                              (5.2.360–65)

With his suicide, Othello seals his identification with the other insofar as the references to the "circumcised dog" and "turbaned Turk" are to Iago; he recognizes his own cultural alterity insofar as he is in fact referring to himself; and he acknowledges a certain self-difference insofar as the moment of "self-recognition" takes the form of a performative fiction.

Indeed, it's hard to avoid the sense that Othello has died in fiction—that he has somehow narrated his own end. Such an impression, recalling the cannibalizing narrative of the opening, is, again, intimately bound up with the problem of aesthetic autonomy and the interpretive ethic it implies. Othello eludes the audience to the extent that it is caught up in his fiction. And the audience is caught up in the fiction precisely to the extent that it dissolved it by supposing its transparency, by presuming an unproblematic referent in the figure of the "turbaned Turk." Such narrative captivation may be irreducible. To have kept a bead on Othello, to have more vigilantly recognized fiction as fiction and thus to have fixed indeed the moment of truth toward which the play has moved—the hero's death—simply means repeating the same self-inscribing gesture at the level of the play's own signifying structures; for to forcibly take the "bloody period" of Othello's "thus" for the teller's end is to be all the more caught out by the hero's after-death "confession" moments later.[18]

Such a return is merely one of a series of supplements marking and failing to mark the close of the drama. The play's structural similarities with comedy (the overcoming of the paternal senex at the outset, the "pastoral" change of locale to Cyprus) is picked up at the close in the correspondence between Othello's final address and a comedic epilogue: "Soft you, a word or two before you go" (5.2.347). That speech is in turn marked by a supplementary close: "Set you down this, / And say besides" (5.2.360–61). All of these amount to so many inscribing lures for the self-betraying desire to force a period to the fiction, and thus to know where one stands in mastering relation to such an end.

Recalling the inscribing seductions of his narrative of wooing, tragic recognition would thus amount to the recognition of irreducible fictionality, knowledge Othello and the audience as well had lost track of in the exacerbating demands of self-certainty.[19] But to translate the effects of the ending into a generalizable moral about fiction overlooks a significant turn toward the close. Although we've likened Othello's final address to his wooing narrative, the difference between them is significant. We move from the ear to the pen, from orality to writing, and specifically the record of state: "Set you down this," Othello says to his captors. Of course, although he speaks of his acts to protect the state, it is to evade the clutches of the law that he speaks. And yet Othello's "mar[ring]" of "all that is spoke" is precisely the condition of his becoming a matter of record (5.2.367).[20] "Myself will straight aboard, and to the state / This heavy act with heavy heart relate," Lodovico declares with the play's last lines (5.2.380–1).

There were signs enough of the state's pervasiveness before this moment. "Something sure of state / . . . / Hath puddled his clear spirit," Desdemona remarks earlier at the first signs of Othello's anger (3.4.136, 139). As the ambassadors return to deliver the letters of state commanding Othello back to Venice, Othello feigns absorption all the while eavesdropping on and cryptically responding to the account Desdemona offers the messengers of his falling out with Cassio:

OTHELLO	Are you sure of that?
DESDEMONA	My lord.
OTHELLO [*reads*]	"This fail you not to do as you will—"
LODOVICO	He did not call, he's busy in the paper.

(4.1.219–22)

And, after Othello strikes Desdemona, Lodovico remarks, "Or did the letters work upon his blood?" (4.1.272).

We take these references to the state as pretexts, distractions from the "real" domestic drama.[21] But the logic of beguiling distraction is sufficiently marked in the play to warn us against dismissing such moments. As Thomas Moisan points out, one construes the state's writs recalling Othello and installing Cassio in his place as timely punishments, even though they were obviously set down before Othello's transgressions occur.[22] That strange forseeingness of the law, as if the domestic plot and all its machinations had been inscribed in advance, is of a piece with the law's power to possess. It is not a coincidence that what we do get of the letter that hails Othello back—"This fail you not to do as you will"—figures the inescapable imperatives of symbolic law as such, a command in which resistance is equivalent to acquiescence, where the "as you will" is inseparable from the law's "fail you not." In that sense, Othello has never stopped being "in the paper," the letter working "upon his blood."

That supervention of law at the end is not a given; it depends on an opposition established from the outset, not between the ear and the eye, but between orality and writing, the fantastic traveler's tale and the record of state.[23] It would be wrong to take the distinction in any direct sense as indicating a historical transition.[24] The play is never more textual than it is in the tale of anthropophagi and cannibals, culled as it is from Mandeville, whose marvelous "discoveries" are culled in turn from other textual sources such as Pliny. What is important is the structure through which the "deception" plays itself out. With the return of the interpellating call of the state, the play reveals itself to have had the form of a seduction, but now a seduction in which one is all the more inscribed for having imagined that one occupied a space outside the law. Just as fiction—the omnivorous tale of wandering—had beguiled state and law, the illimitable letter of the law in turn beguiles fiction.

Nor does the sequence end there: what one is to "say besides"—the enveloping story of the "turbaned Turk"—succeeds upon what is to be "set down." The "bloody period" of Othello's suicide in turn mars "all that was spoke" (5.2.366–67). The significant point is not whether speech or writing is the final term, but the structure of the sequence. On the one hand, we move between discrete, oppositionally defined terms: orality and writing, fiction and law, fable and record. On the other, each turn is recursively absolute—we had never been outside the space of fiction, never outside law—and all moves in the increasingly rapidly concatenated series toward a point where the distinction between inscribing forms approaches a dissolve. Through their reversible, recursive exchanges, literature takes on in an explicit way the anonymous and inscribing force of law, manifest law the illimitability of fiction, and both constitute themselves as at once determinate and limitless forms.[25]

The play's condition as circumscribed and unbounded form is underwritten by that political/rhetorical economy. The absolutizing of the literary, its extension beyond any limit including death, means that for the literary to remain the literary it must constitute itself internally, as it were, through the dialectical, mutually inscribing, and purely formal opposition to law. Such a formal solution is bound up with the particularities of Othello's status as citizen-subject, and with the play's status as "domestic tragedy"—a generic "monstrosity" in Thomas Rhymer's view. But the structure is by the same token related to significant transformations in the literary and legal domains. With the advent of the state as, in Quentin Skinner's words, "omnipotent and impersonal power," the entire field of law takes on the supervening, self-exceeding, even phantasmatic character it assumes with modernity: law becomes Law, a purely formal, abstract, yet determining condition.[26] At the same time, that transformation brings with it as its mirror figure and opposing term a translation of the category of the literary itself, the appearance of a version of the literary absolute in the form of the reflexive, endlessly self-incorporative work.[27] Othello reveals the signifying economy out of which these determining categories—the state, the literary—constitute themselves.

Race and the Universal Citizen

There's nothing irreducible about the formal opposition between fiction and law. Indeed, the difference is fragile precisely because it is not founded, ultimately, on the apparent security of a phenomenological claim, such as that between sight and language. For that reason, the work confronts the question of its grounds, including its historical grounds, most directly in relation to that formal issue of its capacity to designate itself as literary. To take up that aspect of the text's function, we need to look not to the blazoned threats of the consuming eye or devouring ear but to a body part that recurs in the play more mutedly yet with something like the character of an obsession: "It had been better you had not kissed your three fingers so oft . . . Yet again, your fingers to your lips?" (2.1.172–73, 175); "Lechery, by this hand" (2.1.248); "When these mutualities so marshal the way, hard at hand comes the master and main exercise, th' incorporate conclusion" (2.1.251–53); "You cannot, if my heart were in your hand" (3.3.167); "Iago doth give up / The execution of his wit, hands, heart" (3.3.468–69); "Give me your hand. This hand is moist . . ." (3.4.34); "A liberal hand. The hearts of old gave hands, / But our new heraldry is hands, not hearts" (3.4.44–46); "Yours, by this hand" (4.1.168); "No, my heart is turned to stone; I strike it, and it hurts my hand" (4.1.175–76); "Give me thy hand" (4.2.208); "Whose breath indeed these hands have newly stopped" (5.2.209); "of one whose hand / Like the base Indian threw a pearl away" (5.2.355–56).

What are hands doing in *Othello*?[28] For one thing, they kill. That fact can be read as a confirmation of the brute, unmediated violence of the primitive over against the "super-subtle" world he inhabits. And yet, even at its most brutish, the violence of the hand functions in relation to questions of meaning. Desdemona is suffocated, and her voice uncannily returns. "Who hath done this deed"? Emilia asks. "Nobody, I myself" (5.2.133). That the play's misogynistic crime is explicitly bound up with such returns—reversions of guilt, reversions of language—is suggested by the auditory dynamics of the murder scene itself:

OTHELLO   Being done, there is no pause.
DESDEMONA   But while I say one prayer.
OTHELLO   It is too late.
   He smothers her
DESDEMONA   O Lord, Lord, Lord!
   Emilia at the door
EMILIA [*within*]   My lord, my lord, what ho, my lord, my lord!
OTHELLO   What noise is this? Not dead? Not yet quite dead?
                                       (5.2.90–95)

Stifled within, the voice returns from elsewhere, from outside.[29] This is a matter of dramatic contingency—Emilia happens to arrive. But it anticipates the actual returns of Desdemona's voice, and plays out at the limit a familiar economy associated with the purely negative and relational character of the signifier, one in which negation affirms, in which what's violently suppressed within recurs from without.

That redounding economy is prominent in the play. Indeed, it conditions the moment that is often considered to mark the fall, the "handkerchief scene." Othello fends off Desdemona's efforts to "bind [his forehead] hard" with her handkerchief: "Your napkin is too little" (3.3.290–91). As Othello knows, such compensation is merely the binding and effeminate sign of what it would cure. And yet it is in repudiating such a threat that one brings it about. *"[He puts the handkerchief from him. It drops]* 'Let it alone,'" Othello remarks (3.3.287). It would not be wrong to say that Othello orchestrates the disaster that befalls him. As Harry Berger has shown especially in relation to Desdemona, an entire array of motivational question unfolds from this moment of "forgetfulness."[30] But beyond the psychology of the scene, one can see in it the operations of a symbolic economy that inscribes all in its reverting effects: an unbinding that binds, a vigilance that blinds.

And yet, the hand suggests something other than that interpellating structure, something more exorbitant to judge from Iago's exercise in palm reading. Here's his commentary on Cassio's and Desdemona's dockside flirtation: "He takes her by the palm. Ay, well said—whisper. With as little a web as this will I ensnare as great a fly as Cassio. . . . [I]t had been better you had not kissed your three fingers so oft, which now again you are most apt to play the sir in. . . . [Y]et again your fingers to your lips? Would they were clyster-pipes for your sake!" (2.1.168–69, 172–73, 175–76). The hand signifies as go-between, and, as the oral and anal erotics of the passage suggest, the hand is bound up with possibilities of incorporation. And, of course, the hand points. In all these respects, the hand suggests the visible, materialized and erotically charged equivalent of language.[31] And yet, if the hand signifies, it hardly does so in a stable form, judging from the signifying cascade palm reading seems to release in and beyond the scene: "Bless'd *pudding*! Didst thou not see her *paddle* with the *palm* of his hand?" (2.1.253–54); "To Desdemona hath tonight carous'd / *Potations pottle*-deep" (2.3.53–54); "I learn'd it in England, where they are most *potent* in *potting* . . . he gives your Hollander a vomit ere the next *pottle* can be fill'd" (2.3.76–77, 84–85). "Something . . . / Hath *puddled* his spirits," Desdemona later remarks (3.4.240–43). "*Pish*," says Iago (2.1.263). "*Pish*!" mad Othello exclaims, two acts later (4.1.42 my italics throughout). There's anal sadism here, orality—consumption, expulsion—and oral violence in the repeated plosives. At the same time, we hear the sheer, empty ticking over of language, a mechanical reiteration passing from character to character, and distinct from the symmetrical recursions of symbolic negation. To pick up on this thread is to feel the play itself take on the fragmentary, desubjectified character of Othello's madness.

That virulent skittering is bound up, not with language's role as go-between, its communicative function, but with the more fundamental question of it capacity to refer. For while it is clear that the hand points, it is hard to know to what it points. "Lechery, by this hand; an index and obscene prologue to the history of lust and foul thoughts," Iago exclaims (2.1.248–49). The hand indexes Desdemona's hand and the "history of lust and foul thoughts" that coquettish hand indicates. "This hand" is also, of course, Iago's own hand, and thus a wry reference to the plot he is only now hatching.[32] And, with all the reflexiveness of the scene, it would not be wrong to imagine a reference to the author's hand as well here, the real contriver of the "history of lust and foul thought." And yet those forms of identificatory instability point toward a more radical uncertainty: how does the hand—how does language prior to its constitution of agent or object—designate itself, its own capacity to designate? The structural impossibility that vexes the gesture in Leonardo recurs: the mad reading associated with the hand derives from the necessity and impossibility of an initiatory pointing to pointing, the indexing of indexing.[33]

The uncertainties of designation are amplified at the close of the drama. "This fail you not to do"; "Set you down this"; "No way but this"; "This did I fear"; "This is thy work": the play assumes toward the end an attenuation of reference comparable to Othello's invocation of "the cause" during the murder scene.[34] That indeterminacy is a direct measure of the empowering vagueness—the "indistinct regard"—the play claims for itself as reflexive, illimitable form. At the same time, "this" marks the more radical problem of designation that comes to the fore as a consequence of that claim to recursive self-reference. At the close, the hand that fatally turns against itself converges with the hand that writes, or impossibly turns on itself to write writing: "set you down *this*," this setting down. Again, the play structures itself around a recursive vanishing point of sorts, but a radically unstable one, and one that is not assimilable to the eye or the ear, indeed to any form of phenomenal reference including the one that lets us say with any certainty that the problem is *here*, with the "bloody period" of the scripting hand.[35] At such a limit, even writing as a category, which is to say the forms of record and historicity associated with the state as well as those associated with the emerging category of literary authorship, begins to waver.

What's interesting ideologically speaking is the relation between that attenuation of reference and the luridly theatricalized scene to which the play in some privileged sense fails to refer at the close. Othello, like Desdemona, "returns" to speak: "I kissed thee ere I killed thee. No way but this: / Killing myself, to die upon a kiss" (5.2.368–69). All closes on the miscegenating kiss—no doubt it is just such an "object" that "poisons sight," as Lodovico claims at the end, and therefore must be "hid" (374–75).[36] "This" points to that riveting scene. At the same time, Othello's final lines are among the most empty in the play, hollowed out as they are by the symmetry of the purely formal chiasmus they perform; "this" can be understood to point to nothing beyond the logic of that rhetorical figure: kiss then kill, therefore kill then kiss. We recall the mad, prophetic chiasmus Othello pronounces during his epileptic dissolve: "To confess and be hanged for his labour. First to be hanged and then to confess!" (4.1.36–37). Insofar as it translates at its limit the exorbitancy of language into a form of specular return, "this"—this logic, this structure—is the condition of language's capacity for mimetic designation, as well as the index of the failure of that mimetic claim.

The point is not that the sign of miscegenation is the taint that must be violently suppressed for the play, or for the state, to sustain itself. What can be hidden and therefore can be seen, what, indeed, contagiously returns to speculation the more it is concealed from view, visible otherness is firmly enlisted within the aesthetic and ethical economy of the play. To point to the bed as the revealed crux of the drama—as the hitherto repressed "place of sexuality itself," in Edward Snow's account, or "the site of racial transgression" which, in Michael Neill's account, Snow himself "suppress[es]"—is merely to renew that redounding economy with vivifying intensity. Matters of race may have been "unutterable" to contemporary audiences, Neill remarks, "but they were there on the bed for all to see."[37] Precisely insofar as it seems to promise such deictic surety, for all it seems to threaten, the scene of transgression serves a grounding function, its apparent phenomenological certainty standing in the place of a thoroughgoing failure of ground and reference. An aesthetic ideology, and with it a distinct conception of the subject, is bound up with the illusion that "this" means *that*.

The logic, political and otherwise, of such an aesthetic solution may be brought into relief by glancing at the play's relation to its precursor on many of these issues. *Titus Andronicus*, too, is concerned with race, a category it imagines explicitly in the "archaic" terms of purities of blood and dynastic lines. "Behold the child," Marcus declaims at the close, focalizing all the tragedy's lurid miseries: "Of this was Tamora deliverèd, / The issue of an irreligious Moor, / Chief architect and plotter of these woes" (5.3.117–21). Aaron, the starkly demonized Moor, addresses his infant: "Peace, tawny slave, half me and half thy dam! / Did not thy hue bewry whose brat thou art, / Had nature lent thee but thy mother's look, / Villain, thou mightst have been an emperor" (5.1.27–30). Cannibalism, too, is here—graphically. True Senecan hero, Andronicus concludes by cooking the ravishers of his daughter and feeding the dish to their unsuspecting mother. That literalization of the self-consuming character of a "civil wound" is of a piece with the play's organic conception of the political sphere as "body politic." "Titus, I am incorporate in Rome," Tamora exclaims (1.1.459).

And the play is preoccupied with hands, hands now literally severed. After her rape, Lavinia's defilers cut out her tongue and cut off her hands in an effort to keep her from speaking or writing the names of her assailants. And Andronicus cuts off his own hand in what he is given to believe will be an exchange for the lives of his sons. Again, the hand is bound up with problems of reference. When Lavinia does designate her attackers, it is by virtue of using the stumps of her hands to find the passage in Ovid within which her plight is prefigured. The violence of the play is bound up with the violence of textuality in general— Andronicus showers his enemies with verses from Horace impaled on his arrow's tips—and with the queasy redounds of the signifier in particular: "*Stuprum*"—"rape," Lavinia writes, at the same time horribly referring back to the "stumps" with which she writes (4.1.76–78). "I'll find some cunning practice out of hand," Tamora pronounces (5.2.77). "And here's thy hand, in scorn to thee sent back," the messenger says to Andronicus, as if summarizing the workings of the linguistic recoils (3.2.236).[38]

The difference between the one play and the other can be designated: it is the distinction between pointing and pointing to pointing, which is to say the difference between a blind inscription within the redounds of the signifier, an inscription to which revenge gives thematic form, and the transformation of such recursions into aesthetic ideology. I have argued that that aesthetic turn is related to the emergence of both the state as at once abstract and determining (as the space of formal law) and the subject as "universal" (that is, determinately empty) being, as citizen-subject. At the same time, it is the aesthetic that problematizes anything like an outright developmental account, whether historical or textual. Rather than simply marking historical change, the negative, universal subjectivity *Othello* articulates emerges expressly as an effect of the il-limitability of its own figurative grounds. In that sense, the political stakes of the play need to be situated ultimately in relation to the fragility and contradiction of that figurative construction of illimitable limits.

For readers today, such a horizon is inevitably bound up with what it has meant to "throw out our eyes for brave Othello." One can read that as an allegory of the perils of an anachronistic, historically projective racialization. I would argue instead that the equivocality of the category of race, its presence as a category to come, is a function of its relation to the limits of the dialectical structures, including the historical dialectic, that inform the political and subjective domain the play announces.[39] The force entailed in the designation of race is bound up with the forced phenomenalization that sustains those symbolic economies. In that sense, race functions neither as an empirical category nor even as a discursive construction, but in a more thoroughgoing and unstable relation to the phenomenal grounds of the modern social and symbolic field *tout court*, which is to say in relation to that field's capacity to realize itself at all. To see race as one of the terms freighted thus is to discern the logic behind its virulent and paradoxical insistence within the era of the empty, "universal" subject.

CHAPTER 5

Aesthetics and Absolutism in *The Winter's Tale*

The Winter's Tale describes sovereignty in its absolutist moment, that is, in the historical interim between medieval suzerainty, the organic conception to which works such as *Gorbuduc* and *King Lear* pay retrospective ideological homage, and the rationalized state form. Which is also to say it reveals sovereignty in the context of the modern signifying universe we've seen articulated in *Othello*. That assertion will seem counterintuitive. For Jean Bodin, the great theorist of absolutism, nothing defines sovereignty more explicitly than its nonsubstitutable character; the sovereign is the indivisible figure in whose place no one can stand.[1] And yet, the very fact that such a concern appears as a signal preoccupation indicates that we have entered a political space in which the possibility of substitution has come into play, and in which sovereignty is staked on formal autonomy as a problem.

As with other late Shakespeare plays, the *Winter's Tale* is also a work in which the aesthetic achieves an explicit global function. I will make a case for the inextricability of these two concerns: the play's relation to absolutism and its relation to self-conscious aestheticization. Within an infinitized self-referential signifying domain, it will be the work qua work that underwrites any prospect of phenomenal consistency. As a formal matter, and in terms of the movement of Shakespeare's work, that translation of the aesthetic into an overriding function is evident in the shift of the vanishing point from a point of infinite self-reflection within the diegetic drama to the internal divide, temporal and otherwise, around which the drama self-consciously articulates itself as self-reflective aesthetic form, what is figured in the choral interlude mid-drama in *Winter's Tale*. Far from suggesting a retreat to mere aestheticization, the aesthetic self-consciousness of the late works is a matter of seeking out the problem of sovereignty—the sovereignty of the ruler, the sovereignty of the subject—where as a modern concern it resides.

The scope of that aesthetic turn is evident in a shift in the aesthetic's relation to law. I have traced the way law and literariness function as mutually defining counterterms in early modern drama. Even while it retains such a structure, in *Winter's Tale* aestheticization becomes the very condition for a knowable relation to law—it gives law its ratio. The sovereign becomes an aesthetic operation, in that sense. That radical, compassing stake in aesthetic autonomy gives Shakespeare's late works their distinctive ontological character: on the one hand, a super-refined aesthetic self-consciousness that anticipates the era of sensibility; on the other, the sense of being posed in relation to the possibility of a dissolution which, by-passing the Enlightenment altogether, anticipates the most extravagant self-devourments of totalitarian modernity.

Law and the Voice of the Oracle

The question of early modern sovereignty can be broadly framed around the problem of the political decision. For Carl Schmitt, early modern absolutism realizes in the figure of the sovereign the identity between legislator and creator that he takes to be the founding truth of politics.[2] Schmitt's affirmation of the metaphysical force of the sovereign decision—his claim that the decision informs law as its constitutive ground and in every instance of its application—arises, in part, as a reaction against what he takes to be the signal failures of modern liberalism, the "liberal indecisionism" of the parliamentary democracy of his own moment—Weimar Germany—and more broadly in relation to what he describes as "liberalism's onslaught against the political."[3] For Schmitt, that assault is a function of the normativism of the nineteenth century "organizational-technical" state, and is embodied particularly in the subordination of the political to the economic and the corresponding emergence of the aesthetic as the category which valorizes indecision and stands as a privileged figure for the apolitical autonomy of civic formations in general.[4]

The force and the promise of Schmitt's account of early modern political authority consist in what it suggests about the irreducibly political character of the social and juridical domains.[5] For Schmitt, the sovereign decision cannot be subsumed by the system of legal codes and norms—the grounds of the entire tradition of juristic rationalism from

Locke to Rawls—precisely because it constitutes that field and determines when it does and does not come into play. "Sovereign is he who decides on the exception," and that possibility of the exception lies at the determining core of the rule.[6] The political implications of Schmitt's decisionist argument might seem, then, to depend on whether the exceptional act need necessarily belong solely to the person of the sovereign. Decisionism, of course, does not necessarily mean monarchism, and Schmitt himself allows for a range of political embodiments, insisting only on the undivided character of the authority that decides the force of law, whatever that authority might be. And yet the more fundamental question, politically and philosophically, is whether the logic of the exception as Schmitt articulates it might imply just such a division of authority, and thus pose questions not just about who decides but about the nature of political agency as such.[7]

That issue of agency becomes apparent when we consider Schmitt's account of the sovereign act from the topological perspective. Schmitt's argument is predicated on the recognition that, as Paul Hirst puts it, "all legal orders have an outside": thus Schmitt's central claim about the exceptional character of the determining act.[8] The political act as an act is premised on the possibility of such externality—that is what assures that it is not inscribed within the dimension of norms. At the same time, the political is for Schmitt that which is without exteriority. "The political is the total, and as a result we know that any decision about whether something is unpolitical is always a political decision, irrespective of who decides."[9] The political is illimitable, a fact all the more borne out by liberalism's tendentious efforts to bracket it.

At once definitionally external and yet, because of the limitless field of its operation, incapable of assuming exteriority vis-à-vis itself—of transcending itself as an act—the political act amounts to the act that poses the problem of its own conditions.[10] Looked at "from the perspective of the norm," Schmitt writes, "the constitutive, specific element of the decision . . . is new and alien," it "emanates from nothingness."[11] The question is whether that emergence from nothing is merely an effect of the normative perspective or whether it is an irreducible element of the act as he conceives it.

Nothing is more distinctly early modern, I would argue, than that problematized understanding of the political decision. The notion of the act as what reconstitutes the grounds on which it can be known is at the heart of Machiavelli's understanding of the historicity of the political—it is what makes political society political. Moreover, it is no coincidence that at least within the domain of English theater—from *Gorbuduc* to *King Lear*—early modernity's reflections on sovereignty gravitate toward the political act in its most opaque manifestation, that is, in the act by which sovereign force undoes itself, as if in that self-annulling gesture something of the mysterious grounds of sovereignty came to view.[12]

In *Lear*, such an act is bound up with sovereignty's self-exceeding character—its illimitability—as well as with its unfathomable "something out of nothing."[13] As I noted in chapter 1, that sovereign illimitability is evident in the coincidence between the "darker purpose"—obtuse and already knowing—of the sovereign's own ritual theatricalizations and the space of the work itself, a coincidence that suggests in its very illegibility how deeply if implicitly the problem of the aesthetic is related to sovereignty's own autogenetic claims. It is worth noting the rough parallel between the "purposive purposelessness" that defines Kant's account of the aesthetic and the noninstrumental character of sovereignty, its nature as the one political form that contains its ends within itself: the aim of sovereignty, as Foucault points out, is sovereignty.[14]

What is the distinction, then, between *King Lear*, with its backward-looking feudal preoccupations, and *The Winter's Tale*, a play concerned with absolutism as a modern form? The difference between the two plays can be intuited in the differing forms their tyrants' madnesses take. With *Lear*, madness amounts to the fragmentation attending a radically totalized, organically imagined conception of the body politic, a condition in which cure is indistinguishable from disease, in which the sovereign's excision of the poisonous member reproduces the division it would resolve: "I will punish home," Lear declares, turning on his own flesh and blood and anticipating his passage into madness.

For Leontes, madness is no less reiterative and self-punitive, but derives from the recoils of delusional jealousy and mimetic desire—it is, in that sense, the madness of systems. "I am angling now, / Though you perceive me not how I give line. / Go to, go to!" Leontes says as he sends Hermione and his twinned rival Polixenes to the garden.[15] Leontes acts, in Camillo's words, "as if he had . . . been an instrument / To vice [Polixenes] to't," because he functions, as René Girard has argued, within the mimetic, circulatory structure in which the figure who bars desire simultaneously constitutes it (1.2.410–11).[16] Within such a mechanism, rivalrous difference amounts to identity, and identification merely reproduces desire's divisions within. In other words, we are in the space of limitless substitutability: "like a cipher, / Yet standing in rich place, I multiply," Polixenes says, alluding to the strange, reiterative power of the empty numerical place-holder (1.2.6–7).[17] Would I "appoint myself in this vexation?" Leontes exclaims (1.2.323): he does, apparently, and his language emphasizes the relation between his plight and the substitutive logic of the office holder.[18] In terms of political dispensations, the play belongs less to *Lear*'s world of embodiment than to *Othello*'s world of lateral equivalences and surrogacy—the world, that is, of the citizen subject.[19] Jealousy is a bourgeois ailment, and *The Winter's Tale*, a fundamentally domestic drama.[20]

What makes it a drama of absolutism, then? In one regard, nothing but the purity of the mimetic structure it invokes. As Girard remarks, *Winter's Tale* is the play in which Shakespeare realizes mimetic desire without causative alibi—no Iagos; it realizes it as a structure that emerges, again, *ex nihilo*.[21] The play's concern with sovereignty is reflected in this preoccupation with the problem of originative grounds and derivation. In its condensation of origin and outcome, the word "issue" becomes both the play's resolving term and its opaque point of obsession: "I / Play . . . a part, whose issue / Will hiss me to my grave" (1.2.185–87); "I'll not rear / Another's issue" (3.1.192–93); "gracious be [the oracle's] issue" (3.1.22); "this being . . . the issue / Of King Polixenes" (3.3.42–43); "his highness' fail of issue / May drop upon his kingdom" (5.1.27–28). "I would most gladly know the issue of it" (5.2.8); "I / . . . have preserved / Myself to see the issue" (5.3.125–28).[22]

Leontes's descent into madness is bound up with that speculative fixation on origins. "We are / Almost as like as eggs" he says to his son Mamillius (1.2.128–29). The phrase recurs: "Will you take eggs for money"? (1.2.159). Leontes is absorbed with the question of the paternity of his wife's unborn child, and seeks solace in the mirror affirmation of the child he knows to be his own. But, of course, to be alike as two eggs is to be like every other egg. To stake oneself on that ground—to fix oneself at all—is to be all the more caught within the chain of empty and limitlessly multiplying ciphers.

The often-remarked obscurity and instability of the play's language is related to the illimitability of that signifying chain. Critical discussion has focused particularly on the passage in which Leontes describes the incomprehensible *ex nihilo* of desire:

—can thy dam, may't be
Affection!—thy intention stabs the centre.
Thou dost make possible things not so held,
Communicat'st with dreams—how can this be?
With what's real thou coactive art,
And fellow'st nothing. Then 'tis very credent
Thou mayst co-join with something, and thou dost,
And that beyond commission, and I find it,
And that to the infection of my brains
And hard'ning of my brows.

(1.2.136–44)

Is Leontes describing Hermione's illicit affections or the workings of his own diseased imagination, critics and editors have wondered. That ambiguity is related to another, perhaps stranger, one; to the extent that he is describing himself, Leontes seems at once to be in the throes of his delirium and to be recognizing it as a delirium: "Thou dost make possible things not so held / . . . / With what's real thou coactive art, / And fellow'st nothing." The mixture of immersion and self-reflexive knowledge is picked up more broadly in the ways Leontes seems at some level to know he is caught up in a play, even to possess an obscure foreknowledge of its imagined end: "Go play, boy, play—thy mother plays, and I / Play too, but so disgraced a part, whose issue / Will hiss me to my grave" (1.2.185–87).[23] Such boundary crossings between identities, between insides and outsides, can be understood in terms of the spiraling relation between the infinitude of the signifying chain and the demand for grounds it exacerbates. In relation to the purely differential logic of the multiplying cipher, not only will one identity stand in the place of another, but the very impulse to situate oneself outside the structure—to differentiate—reinscribes one within it.[24]

That signifying phenomenon is not exclusive to *The Winter's Tale*, of course. But its heightened presence there, as well as its explicit framing as a problem of issue and origination, is a function of the play's historical and political moment. In the play and as a historical formation, absolutism is articulated within the horizon of a fundamentally new political / subjective configuration—the space of illimitable equivalency—and is thus oriented around autonomy as a formal problem.[25] As the end of the play will show, with absolutism, the contradiction between lineage and autonomy as the grounds of legitimacy, a contradiction that had always inhabited sovereignty, assumes an outright form.[26]

What characterizes the sovereign decision within such an order? The fact, I would argue, that it derives from elsewhere. Leontes's choice to invoke the judgment of the oracle at Delphos to determine the outcome of the public trial of Hermione might be read in terms of the proto-liberal compromises that marked absolutism as a historical phenomenon. "Let us be cleared / Of being tyrannous, since we so openly / Proceed in justice," Leontes proclaims (3.2.4–6). Even before the final decades of absolutism's historical interim, "rulers were accepted only because of what they did to weaken their rule," Ivan Nagel observes.[27] We might even see an anticipation of that characteristic Enlightenment procedure by which political authority resolved its internal contradictions and legitimized itself by suspending its force in relation to supervening grace.[28] Yet it is not grace that is drawn down in the oracle's pronouncement: it is law and judgment. In that sense, the otherness of the oracular pronouncement should be read directly in relation to the logic of sovereignty. Within the infinitized signifying domain of the political, the sovereign decision can only emerge from a radical elsewhere, from out of the blue. Whatever its thematic associations with ancient social formations, the oracle summons something new and momentous.

In a sense, of course, the oracle's word is explicitly opposed to Leontes's judgment, divine truth exposing tyrannical delusion. In fact, though, the two are explicitly aligned in their effects, which is where their meaning lies. Hermione is moved less by the content of the tyrant's false judgment than the brutality of her public exposure in the court of law, a killing visibility that lays bare the spectator as well and momentarily empties out the theatrical fiction: My past life has been as chaste, she says, "as I am now unhappy, which is more / Than history can pattern, though devised / And played to take spectators" (3.2.34–36). The oracle's consequences are no less fatal. To recall the rapidly concatenated sequence: the judgment is opened, the message read declaring that Hermione is innocent, Leontes a jealous tyrant, and that "the King shall live without an heir if that which is lost be not found" (3.2.132–33). When the King refuses the judgment, a messenger arrives to announce that Mamillius, "from mere conceit of the queen's speed," has died. Declaring "the heavens themselves / Do strike at [his] injustice," Leontes instantly forgoes his delusion (3.2.143–44).

It is, one can argue, the resistance to oracular truth that precipitates death. But the sequence feels seamless, the response fulfills the pronouncement, and we know from the previous scene in which the messengers describe their visit to Delphos that the oracle's words harbor their own violence. "But of all, the burst / And the ear-deaf'ning voice o'th' oracle, / Kin to Jove's thunder, so surprised my sense / That I was nothing" (3.1.8–11). The grounds of that annihilating power are evident in the temporal character of its enactment. The oracle's pronouncement that the King shall live without an heir is fulfilled precisely in Leontes's refusal of it. Thus, even as the reply seems to be compassed in advance by oracular law, that pronouncement is only realized—only proves law—through the response it solicits. The inscribing, desubjectivizing force of oracular truth consists in that elision of the distinction between law and response, between the inside and outside of the space of law.[29]

Insofar as it is inscriptive and without exteriority, such a conception of law is explicitly oriented around the problem of its locus. When the oracle's words "by Apollo's great divine sealed up" shall be broken open, "something rare / Even then will rush to knowledge," the messenger declares (3.1.19–21). Rush to knowledge from where? The language suggests inward as much as outward revelation. That shift to the question of law's source is specific to absolutism. When *King Lear* comes to, when he tentatively recognizes Cordelia at the close, he is attempting to know what we sense he has known and not known from the outset; knowledge is sealed within the ineluctable recesses of sovereign personhood. Leontes's instantaneous coming to is a function ultimately neither of inwardness, however occulted, nor simply of external determination; it amounts instead to the annulment of the frame within which those structuring oppositions are sustained, that is, the frame within which sovereignty itself is inscribed.

Rather than implying a necessary equivalency between judicial decision and the person of the King, the play represents law as a desubjectivizing effect. To return to Schmitt's terms, law, as figured in the oracle, is what undoes the distinction between constituting and constituted authority.[30] The aesthetic emerges in the play specifically in relation to that problematic of law. The aesthetic functions at once as law's mirroring counter-image, the autonomy of the one reflecting the autonomy of the other, and as the necessary term for the constitution of any sort of ratio or rapport between sovereign agency and a law without source.

Devouring Art

The play's self-conscious turn in its second half to the category of the aesthetic is most evident, of course, in the famous statue scene at the close. Hermione's artful return, however, merely crystallizes the larger structure through which the play itself passes into the register of the aesthetic by returning upon itself across the sixteen-year caesura at its center. That aesthetic translation is an aspect of the late "romances" generally, and is bound up with their tragicomic form. It is clunky but not wrong to read Shakespeare's late plays in terms of the passage from comedy to tragedy to a sublation of death through the reflexive return by which death is internalized as the condition of the work's status as self-reflective, self-consciously aesthetic form.[31] That apparent formal solution bears directly on the problem of sovereign autonomy in a relational universe; as I will show, the thematic particulars of Leontes's reformation play themselves out within the ultimately fragile logic of the play's own aesthetic turn.[32]

That Shakespeare is conscious of the stakes of the structure is evident in the calculated tonal instabilities of the hinge scene where the play passes from tragedy to comic/romance mode. "Thou metst with things dying, I with things newborn," the Old Shepherd declares to the pastoral clown during the scene in which he discovers the abandoned infant amidst the carnage on land and at sea—devouring bears, drowning sailors (3.3.109–10). The forced character of the turn is represented specifically as a problem of narrativizing in the Clown's comically veering attempts to accommodate the grisly and disparate elements of the scene: "I would you did but see how [the sea] chafes, how it rages, how it takes up the shore; but that's not to the point. O, the most piteous cry of the poor souls! . . . And then for the land-service, to see how the bear tore out his shoulder-bone . . . But to make an end of the ship, to see how the sea flapdragoned it; but first, how the poor souls roared . . ." (3.3.85–96). "To make an end of the ship": the complicity between the telling and the destruction it describes suggests how thoroughly violence is affiliated here with narrative mastery, all oriented around the problem of death's inassimilability.[33]

The caesura that opens the possibility of aesthetic autonomy and self-inclusiveness also brings to the fore these prospects of narrative instability, and it does so insofar as that division is shown to have a foundational rather than just a mediating relation to the work. The "wide gap" to which the chorus makes reference, and to which Leontes will return in the final lines of the play—"Lead us from hence, where we may leisurely / Each one demand and answer to his part / Performed in this wide gap of time since first / We were dissevered" (5.3.152–55)—reappears in the context of Autolycus's considerably less elevated aesthetic:

> He hath songs for man or woman of all sizes—no milliner can so fit his customers with gloves. He has the prettiest love songs for maids, so without bawdry, which is strange, with such delicate burden of dildos and fadings, "jump her and thump her"; and where some stretch-mouthed rascal would, as it were, mean mischief, and break a foul gap into the matter, he makes the maid to answer, "Whoop, do me no harm, good man"—puts him off, slights him with "Whoop, do me no harm, good man."
>
> (4.4.193–202)

To "break a foul gap into the matter" is, according to Stephen Orgel's note, to "interpolate something indecent into the song." But, in the context of "dildos" and "fadings," the "foul gap" carries its own sexual and misogynistic connotations. Indeed, the sexual and the interpolative are inextricable in the passage. As Orgel notes, although "dildos and fadings" appear as empty nonce words in contemporary ballads, it is precisely the speaker's severing and isolating them from their generally bawdy context that gives them their prurient cast. Such inadvertent interpretive complicity is of a piece with the broader transferential logic of the scene. The way in which the "stetch[ed] mouth" of the interpolating rascal mimes the "foul gap" he would open in the matter of the song picks up on the larger uncertainty about whether the interpreter is a figure within a dialogic ballad—Orgel's reading—or an intrusive audience member whose responses are inscribed in advance by the ditty. And that ambiguity about the interpreter within figures, in turn, the ambiguities of the playgoer's own inescapably complicit, prurient, and anticipated relation to the passage. Such transferential effects arise because the interpolated, and interpellating, gap—foul or otherwise—is not within the matter of the play or song; it is that matter, the constitutive division the would-be mastering auditor can only reiterate.[34] Listening to his ballad, all, male and female alike, are gelded—"all their other senses stuck in ears—you might have pinched a placket, it was senseless; 'twas nothing to geld a codpiece of a purse" (4.4.605–7)—and what they are lost to or inscribed by is "the nothing of it" (4.4.609). Such is the logic of a groundless, prosthetic aesthetic that manages for that very reason to fit every customer, especially the most resistant customer, like a milliner's glove.

That Autolycus should embody such an aesthetic makes sense, given his cheerful embrace of the possibilities of self-annulment.[35] In the scene in which Autolycus snares the Clown by posing as the abject victim of highwaymen, picking the rustic's pocket as he comes to his assistance— "You ha' done me a charitable office"—and then announces he has been victimized by an "ape-bear[ing]" rogue named Autolycus, the self-making man converts the tyrant's reflexive, self-rivening masochism into a casually self-annihilating power (4.3.76, 93). The gratuity of his gestures— there is no need to name himself, no need to announce his ruses as he performs them—signals the aesthetic character of the pleasure; he stands for a self-theatricalization more clarified than Leontes's. But that explicit passage into the register of the aesthetic allows something like the powers of sovereign self-encompassment Leontes fulfilled only in the form of madness. Indeed, in his gratuitousness, Autolycus achieves something like the *ex nihilo* of sovereignty, for his aim is less the profits of his undertakings than the pleasures of speculation's potentially illimitable returns: "if I make not this cheat bring out another, and the shearers prove sheep, let me be unrolled and my name put in the book of virtue!" (4.3.118–20).

The ease with which Autolycus empoweringly abrogates himself can be read in terms of class distinctions between the court, with its taut investment in lineal selfhood, and the more free-form, demotic culture of country and market, an ideological ranginess made possible by the capaciousness of the romance genre.[36] Yet, it is important to recognize what nevertheless holds together Autolycus's seemingly unbound world. Through Autolycus, the aesthetic is affiliated with economy: it is a matter of customers and commodities. And through economy, substitutability is translated into a systematic, thus thematizable, logic of exchange, including the exchange of identities. "Yet for the outside of thy poverty we must make an exchange; therefore discase thee instantly," Camillo says, preparing Autolycus to change forms with Florizel (4.4.627–28). "What an exchange had this been, without boot! What a boot is here with this exchange!" Autolycus exclaims, emphasizing the perfect symmetries of economy's limitless surplus value (4.4.670–72). Rather than being ontological and originative—what has already eroded identity from the outset—exchange amounts to a socioeconomic theme defined over and against "flesh and blood," even as what comically reverses lineal derivation. The Clown describes the literally "preposterous" sequence through which he and his shepherd father are abruptly elevated at the discovery of the lost child: "but I was a gentleman born before my father, for the King's son took me by the hand and called me brother, and then the two Kings called my father brother" (5.2.142, 134–37).[37]

The fact that Autolycus ultimately devotes his roguery to the needs of the prince he had once served, as well as the fact that he drops out of the drama before the finale, can be read in terms of the play's need to recover its aristocratic bearings and the totalizing aesthetic particular to court and sovereign. At the same time, though, in its final turns, and precisely insofar as it does return to the problem of totalization, the play engages the aesthetic beyond its stabilizing affiliation with economy, and beyond the relatively manageable perils of self-fashioning. That more compassing and problematic conception of the aesthetic draws it into relation to sovereignty in part by drawing it into relation with what amounts to art's counterterm in the divided structure of the play: law, and particularly oracular law.

The Winter's Tale has a double resolution, and the stakes of the final scene of Hermione's return are only really apparent in relation to the immediately preceding discovery scene in which Perdita, the lost daughter, is recovered. The odd theatrical withholding of that moment of recognition—the fact that it is conveyed through a series of reports—should be seen as a consciously failed attempt to buffer the audience from a scene whose clinching resolutions merely reiterate the violence of the oracular pronouncement they would miraculously fulfill and allay: "They seemed almost with staring at one another to tear the cases of their eyes," one of the reporting gentlemen says of the long-awaited reencounter (5.2.11–13). Recognition threatens to repeat the rending possessiveness that necessitated it, a violence animated now by an exacerbated desire to forcibly manage loss. Paulina "had one eye declined for the loss of her husband, another elevated that the oracle was fulfilled. She lifted the princess from the earth, and so locks her in embracing as if she would pin her to her heart, that she might no more be in danger of losing" (5.2.73–77).

The scene's affective contradictions are bound up now with larger aesthetic and epistemological demands in which narrative force is equated with juridical truth. "That which you hear you'll swear you see, there is such unity in the proofs," one of the tellers declares (5.2.31–32). Constituted through what it excludes, such a version of unity reproduces the divisions it would efface. The reports proliferate, each reiterating the violence of what it seeks to mediate: "I make a broken delivery of the business"; "I never heard of such another encounter, which lames report to follow it, and undoes description to do it" (5.2.9–10, 55–57). Such violence is explicitly associated with aestheticization's queasily forced chiastic symmetries: "till from one sign of dolour to another she did, with an 'Alas!,' I would fain say bleed tears; for I am sure my heart wept blood" (5.2.85–87).

Hermione's return, the marvel that transpires this time right before our eyes, is an explicit corrective to the fatal overproximity of the prior recognition scene. "Good my lord, forbear," Paulina declares when Leontes moves too soon to embrace the figure (5.3.80). The vicariousness that had been a perverse effect of jealousy's possessive drive—"go to, go to"—now becomes a function of willing deference. "I am content to look on," Leontes remarks. "So long could I / Stand by, a looker-on" Perdita says (5.3.92, 84–85). Even Hermione, the object of every gaze, amounts to a looker-on, merely offering back when she finally does speak her spectators' question in inverted form: "Tell me, mine own, / Where hast *thou* been preserved"? (5.3.123–24; my italics). The aesthetic here is not simply the willing adoption of a distance toward a determined object; it is a function of the larger movement of return through which the "wide gap" of death and loss is retained as the forming condition of subject and object alike, and thus as the vacant ground of all rapport. In the gradualness of the statue's coming to life, object and spectator are transferentially suspended in the condition of living dead, a state in which the blind masochism of tyrannical jealousy is now transformed into desire's knowingly engaged condition:

PAULINA   No longer shall you gaze on't, lest your fancy
  May think anon it moves.
LEONTES   Let be, let be.
  Would I were dead, but that methinks already—
  . . . .
  Would you not deem it breathed? . . . .
  . . . .
  No settled senses of the world can match
  The pleasure of that madness.
                        (5.3.60–73)

That aesthetic condition—a dream state—is also the scene of coming to. In the play's doubling back over itself to recover and fail to recover what it lost, the play brings the spectator to know what it had and had not known in its mimetic absorption: that living Hermione was already, of course, art. What follows the momentary breathing space of such suspended knowledge—the subsequent "culmination"—suggests reversion and intimations of fatality:

POLIXENES   She embraces him.
CAMILLO   She hangs about his neck.
(5.3.111–12)

The return from death, the canceling passage from the rigors of ancient law to faith—we are clearly, as Roy Battenhouse and Julia Lupton have argued, within the ambit of a Christianizing Pauline transformation.[38] I would argue, however, that the theological reading of the close is inscribed within an aesthetic turn that is at once narrower historically and formally supervenient. The specificity of that aesthetic operation is evident in the nature of its relation to law, a relation that is something more complex than one of supercession. Like law, art is illimitable. Whatever Paulina's directorial role at the close, the mystery of Hermione's return, which figures the mystery of representational origins in general, extends beyond Paulina and beyond the explanatory horizon of the drama; with Hermione's return, the play's representational logic exceeds its narrative logic. And, like law, art inscribes—subject and object alike are constituted and sustained within the ratio and distance the aesthetic maintains.[39]

Indeed, what becomes critical at the close is the mutual articulation between law and the aesthetic. "If this be magic, let it be an art / As lawful as eating," Leontes exclaims (5.3.110–11). Even as art seeks the grounding of law, the aesthetic functions to naturalize and to normativize law. From being the desubjectivizing and inscriptive force of sheer negation—the oracle's law—law, articulated within art's sublimating return, becomes the comprehensible division or ratio that gives the subject its bearing as a relational being. At once opposed and reflected in one another like the halves of the play, the infinitudes of art and law are stabilized by way of the chiasmus of their mutual relation. And yet, that reflective, chiasmic structure—the structure of the play itself—is itself an aesthetic operation.

The contradictory nature of that solution, where the aesthetic dictates the structure within which it is constituted, poses the question of just how stable such a resolution is. It is hard not to hear something troubling in the likening of art to eating. Autolycus utters his tunes "as he had eaten ballads," the Clown declared (4.4.187). Dion, the oracle's messenger, had spoken of dangers should the King remain without issue that will descend on the kingdom and "devour / Incertain lookers-on" (5.1.28–29). Is the prospect of aesthetic violence allayed at the close? Dion described the "sacrifices" attending the oracle's ceremonies, and we may have reason to wonder at the close if such sacrificial violence belongs only to the domain of truth. What do we make of the unremarked disappearance of Mamillius at the close? All members of the family return except the boy.

Particularly given the unstable narcissism of Leontes's relation to the child at the opening, one can read the son's death as the offering that ensures the exogamous logic of the genealogical resolution, the breach that all the more secures patrilinealism, in this instance through the daughter. But to understand the unacknowledged character of the child's disappearance we need to understand it in terms of the aesthetic function itself, the aesthetic now conceived in its radically inclusive character. The title of the play derives from the story Mamillius whispers to his mother—as critics have noted, the play itself gradually converges with that tale of the supernatural.[40] We should take seriously the formal question posed by that inclusion of the title within the drama. Can the aesthetic work incorporate everything, including its ground and origin? Yes, except of course for a small remainder, the trace of the hand that recursively inscribes itself. Egg and, as Polixines says of his own son, "parasite," Mamillius is posited at once as source and as the sacrificial remainder that constitutes the possibility of the work as totality. The dissolution of agency implied by the figure of art as eating—art as what simultaneously is devoured and devours—derives from the instability of that conception of the radically self-incorporative work.

Of course, to take the child as a figure for the aesthetic is tendentious—a forced reading. That is the point. The problem of the aesthetic is the problem of interpretive force, as the scene of Mamillius's tale-telling suggests. Having put him aside Hermione calls the child back—"Come, sir, now / I am for you again. Pray sit you by us, / And tell's a tale" (2.1.21–23). "I will tell it softly, / Yon crickets shall not hear it," Mamillius says, alluding to the chattering ladies in waiting. Hermione: "Come on, then, and give't me in mine ear." Stanley Cavell observes the sexual resonances of Hermione's line, and argues that Leontes enraged entrance at this moment to revoke the child occurs "as if it were brought on by" the scene of the child in his mother's lap, filling his pregnant mother's ear.[41] In other words, it amounts to a fantasy of origins within the play.

However, it is the audience, not Leontes, that hears the phrase, and the question of the erotics of the passage—the question of what is really there—cannot be distinguished from the question of the interpretive pressure we bring to bear on it. If there are intimations of force in Hermione's words, they are hard to separate from whatever animates our own desire to put ourselves in the place of that scene of absolute origination, to know what the child whispers back into the maternal ear. Her words are our words: "giv't me in mine ear." That exclusive impulse holds the microscopic seeds of the violence against mother or child that will flower in the drama. And yet, it is just that need to assert possessive force in the name of our own autonomy and self-completion that confirms the fact that the words are not our own, and that the sexuality of the scene is a function of our jealous and reiterated exclusion from its unknowable intimacy. In other words, the line has the function of a lure. Consuming and consumed, the audience of "incertain lookers-on" interpretively constitutes the scene—it is indeed an ur-scene—but as one within which its desires are from the outset already alienated and inscribed.[42]

To return to Carl Schmitt's own fantasies of origination and autonomy and to sum up. Rather than being decisionism's foundational scene, the representation of early modern sovereignty brings to the fore the ungrounded, dispossessive character of the political act. With absolutism, that problem of grounds becomes an explicitly aesthetic matter. The aesthetic appears, not as an effect of the prince's creative hand—Burckhardt's state as work of art—but as a function within which sovereign agency and positive law are sustained; in giving itself over to the aesthetic sovereignty establishes its ratio, that is, its law.[43] And yet, that political aesthetic disposition opens a risk more profound than modern sovereignty's definitionally suspended power. Foreclosing the gap or ratio altogether, the radically incorporative, or self-incorporating, work threatens to abolish the very space of the subject, a loss of loss figured in the unmarked disappearance of the child from a scene already centered on the acknowledgment of death's structuring function.[44]

That version of desubjectivizing extends beyond the force of law as it is enacted in the play. For it amounts to the undoing of the opposition between law and art around which the play is structured. Law understood as a formal category based on negation and prohibition—as an interpellating mechanism—dissolves, as does the aesthetic understood as a self-referential and phenomenologically coherent operation. With that, the play intimates the two political futures its account of the aesthetic harbors. The aesthetic implies a subjectivity sustained by a law or ratio that has no space because it ceaselessly opens space in the divisions of its becoming. In that sense, the aesthetic implies the possibility of a radically open, sheerly relational political subject without recourse to totalization. At the same time, the infinitely refined aesthetic operation through which sovereign and subject articulate themselves around a knowing acknowledgement of their limits—the play as a document of proto-Enlightenment liberalism—reveals its proximity to its totalitarian inverse: an incorporative and self-devouring annulment of the "other scene" that opened the space of the social in the first place. With that, law becomes disastrously equivalent to its corporeal embodiments.[45]

CHAPTER 6

The Beating Mind: *The Tempest* in History

However, the decisive spatial perspective was that of England, i.e., the view from the *sea*, of the balance of territorially defined continental European states represented as sovereign persons.

—Carl Schmitt, *The Nomos of the Earth*[1]

Full fathom five thy father lies
. . . .
Those are pearls that were his eyes

—The Tempest[2]

S overeign authority, autonomy, and aesthetic formation most obviously converge in the island kingdom of *The Tempest*. If that kingdom is a fragile one—the domain of an exiled ruler, and a closed space nevertheless reverberate with voices from who knows where—that is because it engages autonomy precisely as a problem. A correlative to the play's self-consciously unitary form, the heightened sense of boundedness implied by the island world of the drama is sign enough that, whatever its concerns with genealogy and descent, the play conceives sovereignty within the newly formalized and relational space of the *jus publicum Europaeum*. Within that space, autonomy is always autonomy *vis-à-vis* the field of others. The transformative character of that conception of the *jus gentium*—what Schmitt describes as a new *nomos* of the earth—can be teased out from Pascal's well-known lament, *un méridien decide de la vérité*. Therefore, Pascal continues, *le droit a ses époques*—the law has its own epochs.[3] Where the boundary is not determined by a prevenient truth—where inscription decides truth—we enter the sphere of contingency and historicity.

The Tempest explores that real problem of sovereign autonomy in the time of history by way of the fantasy of political and artistic autogenesis—a self-contained world made from within itself. The problem of grounds implied by such a trope of self-creation is consonant with the thought of colonial or imperial conquest, where the fantasy of an absolutely incorporative power always threatens to annul the mark of difference that defines it. Even if the play is inflected by the more modest and ironic conceptions of global expansion—the "empire nowhere" of Jeffrey Knapp's description—by which England distinguished its ventures from Spain's, the speculative fantasy of radical encompassment nevertheless underwrites *The Tempest*'s engagement with the problem of aesthetic and political autonomy.[4] Indeed, the play's scrupulous ambiguity about whether it should be mapped according to Atlantic or Mediterranean coordinates, New or Old Worlds, is a measure of the radical character of Shakespeare's reflections on a form of self-creation and compassment that cannot be said to draw itself from a determinate prior ground, even the imagined *tabula rasa* of the New Found Lands.

The shift from the *respublica Christiana* to a global *jus gentium* meant a shift in symbolic ordering evident at the level of the state form. That emerging form involved at once a localization of what had been the universal community of Christendom and an abstraction of such a territorial conception into juridically fluid versions of *civitas* applicable beyond the physical limits of the city. Secured neither from above nor from below, obligation derives, in Francisco Suárez's phrase, "as if by the mediation of the place."[5] The "as if" of that mediated space corresponds with the remarkably fluid margin between natural and civil law by which a new citizen subject is articulated in the political and legal thinking of the period.[6] And as purely mediated, the problem of the *civitas* becomes the problem of its boundaries.

Such a transformed ordering, what Schmitt describes as a new *nomos*, is evident symptomatically, as it were, in the very fabric of the political thought of the era. Schmitt may be correct in his argument that Francisco de Vitoria's *Relectiones* is the work of an older scholastic tradition.[7] Yet it is not hard to detect the undercurrents of a rhetorical sea change in Vitoria's analysis of the case for Spain's imperial claim in the Americas. Vitoria's argument is governed from beginning to end by a double imperative. On the one hand, there is an acknowledgement of contingency, including differences of faiths: "Those who are not Christians cannot accept the judgment of the pope, since the pope cannot condemn or punish them by any right other than that he is the vicar of Christ." On the other, there is an often astonishingly fluid reference to historical and political equivalency. The Amerindians cannot be dispossessed for their failure of faith just as "the Sarcens who live amongst Christians have never been despoiled of their goods or otherwise oppressed on this pretext." The fact of discovery "of itself provides no support for possession of these lands, any more than if they had discovered us."[8] That conjunction of contingency and equivalence is the sympton of a fully relational conception of the political domain. Taken to its limit, such a structure inevitably risks the dissolution of its determining terms in the potential infiniteness of its own extension. Difference in such an illimitable context becomes at once impossible and pervasive: the necessarily unachievable defining limit of the system of equivalencies as such and therefore that which comes to inhabit every equivalence as its most intimate kernel.

For Schmitt, that paradoxical inside/outside of the new *nomos* has a name: England. England's transition to maritime empire marks for Schmitt an epochal transition away from the territorial organization of continental power. At the same time, it is the "*view* from the sea" that is all-important for Schmitt because the space of the *jus publicum Europaeum* qua relational domain only becomes a space at all by virtue of the extrinsic perspective from which it can be conceived, whether we take that as the "free space" of the barbarian lands or of the island kingdom.[9] Although Schmitt construes that perspective in empirical terms, insofar as it is what opens the possibility of autonomous space as such, the "view from the sea" amounts to the alien condition of sovereign identity itself for the age—something like the intimate and inhuman gaze returning from *The Tempest*'s depths. That is the gaze of autonomous personhood, whether we are describing the being of the sovereign, the authoring magus, or the all-mastering theatergoer.

Legible in relation to a new geopolitical order, *The Tempest* also indexes a subjectivity coordinate with the time of absolutism.[10] With their preoccupation with aestheticization and the romance form, with court masques and aristocratic rule, Shakespeare's late plays have been read as a backward-looking reaction to the modern, citified concerns of Jonsonian comedy with their more outright focus on contingencies of economy and material culture. And yet, one can equally argue that the late plays radicalize the question of political subjectivity. For Jonson, the individual is *homo economicus*, that is, the purely negatively defined being of the bourgeois era for whom liberty means freedom *from* the other, even if in Jonson's intractably social world that impulse for social separation always redounds against the isolate.[11] For Shakespeare, and particularly in *The Tempest*, subjectivity is a matter of autonomy understood in terms of the question of self-grounding and self-authorization. That difference between individualism and autonomy is a historical one, a matter of engaging the subject prior to its full consolidation as a specifically bourgeois form. But it is also a matter of picking up the problem of the subject at a more fundamental political and ontological point, a recognition that subjectivity is something other than an economic category insofar as it founds itself at the point where the possibility of relationality as such is constituted.

In *The Tempest*, that conception of autonomy is among other things an ethical matter, and one that brings us back to the question of Shakespeare's relation to revenge. Forgiveness in the play is what releases from the cycle of revenge, which means the redounding logic of condign punishment, but also the reciprocal structure of indebtedness generally, including the this-for-that of the demand for contrition and forgiveness as answering forms. Imperialism's fantasized annulment of difference in an illimitable *answering for* rather than an *answering to* the other provokes a counter-image of liberty as a more radical unbinding of the answer's very form, I will argue.[12] Forgiveness means freedom insofar as it passes beyond the closed, reciprocal structures within which the self's imagined completion is bound. That beyond—the posited promise of a relation to nonrelation—is the condition of autonomy as the play conceives it.

Understood in these terms, although cast as a matter of an aristocratic ruler's release, the freedom the play articulates intimates the version of political right that comes to view in the historical interval between normative, quasi-theological or Aristotelian conceptions of civic virtue—what is associated sometimes with Florentine Republicanism, for instance—and Locke's essentializing description of individual private rights that will underwrite doctrines of self-interest. Describing the emergence of the category of right, Annabel Brett remarks that "the term . . . involves of itself a reference to what we might term a 'zone of non-coincidence' between individuals and the positive legal order of the state." That zone refers to a constituting though always unspecifiable difference from either church or state, but it also opens, Brett argues, the possibility of a political or civic subjectivity articulating around the fact of its own civic historicity—that is, the fact of its temporal self-difference.[13]

That "zone of non-coincidence"—equivalent to the ungrounded interval beyond the reciprocity of answering forgiveness or revenge in Shakespeare—is also, as we've seen, the space of the aesthetic. Aestheticization grants—or would grant—that elliptical noncoincidence and contingency phenomenal form, and thus make such a historical subject knowable to itself, if only as the effect of an artificial and inhuman gaze. The most self-consciously artsy of Shakespeare plays—the most fantasy-like—*The Tempest* is also the play that engages the problem of history most profoundly, I will argue: The *problem* of history, inasmuch as the play as aesthetic form posits such a noncoincident subject as the irresolvable juncture between empirical or phenomenal history and the historicity that exceeds and opens such a causal accounting.

The Tempest is the right place to take up head-on the relation between aesthetics and history, for that relation is at the heart of one of the play's central riddles. The most "aestheticizing" of Shakespeare's plays, the most preoccupied with its own formal autonomy, *The Tempest* is also the play most concerned with the "brave new world" of exogamous contact. Rather than addressing that apparent contradiction, critical reception of the play has tended simply to play it out over time, with the tide more or less shifting from a preoccupation with, say, the neo-Platonic roots of Shakespeare's spiritualizing art to reading the play as the *mis-en-scène* of colonial encounters. The play suggests what is at stake in the failure of those traditions to engage each other, what that nonencounter protects against. I will say in advance that the intuitive solution to the play's riddle—the argument that the work's aspiration to aesthetic self-sufficiency buffers or ameliorates the alien encounter—is wrong. The relation between the aesthetic and historical causation is at once more complex and more direct.

The Tempest's concern with aestheticization is evident enough in its formal reflexivity, as well as its thematic concern with the magician as artful conjurer. But the relation between materiality and aesthetics is explicitly there in the preoccupation with sublimation both in the precise alchemical sense of the term—the metaphors drawn from that arcane transformative process run through the play—and more generally in the work's apparent etherealizing aims: the translation—or declared failure to translate—gross matter into spirit. Such a movement into spirit is consistent with the play's dialectical place in Shakespeare's oeuvre. It is not wrong to read *The Tempest* in terms of a Hegelian passage from comedy through tragedy to another form in which death is sublated—at once negated and inwardly retained—and thus redeemed. The reflexive, internalizing dimension of such a dialectical movement is consistent with the play's general preoccupation with memory and inwardness. The social/historical dimensions of the structure might then be apparent in the recursive movement of the play's opening, where we discover that the initiating storm scene, with its thrilling class inversions—with death looming, the mariner/laborers freely command the courtiers—turns out to have been the work of the aristocratic humanist sorcerer all along; one might be tempted to see in that Shakespeare's revisionary account of the redeeming passage from artisanal stage into the illimitable space of authorial letters.

The aesthetic logic of the play is more complex, however, and what it implies of sovereign power is not of such a clinching sort. We can intuit that in the play's most striking formal trait. No Shakespeare drama is more tightly controlled, one of just two to observe the classical unities. And yet, no Shakespeare play is so dispersed, with its ambient voices, its projective relation between characters (Prospero imputes the usurping crimes of the father to the prospective son), its expansive web of specular correspondences in which, for instance, the "forward" and "backward" voices of a monster can figure the self-divisions of the master, and where characters eerily anticipate themselves—the hollow, bellowing voices Antonio concocts to cover his intended crime foretell the form his actual guilt will later take (2.2.86–87, 2.1.311–13).[14]

In fact, those qualities of the play—its totalizing character, its dispersal—are of a piece. The autonomous character of the project is apparent in the play's attempted incorporation of its own limits precisely as constitutive limits: the storm scene, through which the play retroactively attempts to inscribe its own precipitating cause, the epilogue through which the fiction as fiction—Prospero stays in role—would include its reception and end. The play's knowingness about the contradiction of such a self-constituting gesture—the fact that it depends on a remainder simultaneously included and excluded—is evident from the curious formal status of the tempest itself, a founding, eponymous event that nonetheless remains ostentatiously marginal in relation to the play. Precisely because the play would establish itself as self-generative fiction, the division that constitutes that domain as such inhabits every element within it, producing the play's endlessly dissolvative, endlessly recuperative effects. The play secures itself, to the extent that it secures itself at all, not at the level of its mimetic or empirical particulars, but as an aesthetic field within which all tends toward a generalized and fluid allegoresis.

One can understand that formal trait in local literary terms—the dispersed character of the play, and of the romances in general, have been read as Shakespeare's response to the individuating tendencies of Jonsonian realism.[15] But the aesthetic logic of the drama can also be understood more ambitiously in relation to the political/representational logic of the era. The mechanism through which the work would compass its own limits as limits and thus become, as it were, internal and external to itself is the aesthetic operation that seeks to redeem the untranscendable immanence of the social field generally: thus the epochal, and specifically aesthetic, character of the sovereignty the play articulates.

The Tempest's preoccupation with autogenesis or self-constitution is most evident in the fantasy of patriarchal creation, and thus too in its demonization of the mother. It is not the only play to engage in that abjecting gesture. But the differences are telling. In *King Lear*, where sovereignty remains a thematic concern, the maternal is radically foreclosed and luridly returns, precisely in relation to the sovereign's madness: "O, how this mother swells up toward my heart! / *Hysterica passio*."[16] Founding demonization in *The Tempest* is virtually evoked as such—the witch, Sycorax, is represented as Prospero's mirror, the one's history directly and ironically mappable onto the other, the one conquest of the island repeating the other, one off-spring and heir for another. The maternal figure assumes the form of that included exclusion through which sovereign and play alike seek to constitute themselves as autonomous forms. When Prospero describes the crabbed woman "grown into a hoop," the strange image at once figures the woman as sheer negation—the familiar "naught" of the feminine—and as the very image of Prospero's own dream of self-completion (1.2.258). The two meanings are consubstantial insofar as the hooped woman figures the negation and exclusion on which that possibility of auto-completion is founded.

In other words, the maternal is of a piece with the play's larger efforts to figure within itself its own inscribing grounds, positing that ground as a naturalized and thus legible continuum ranging from the gross matter upon which "any print of goodness wilt not take" to the "printless foot" of the ethereal spirits (1.2.351, 5.1.34). Along with the preoccupation with dynastic continuity, the play's extravagant investment in chastity should be understood in terms of the problem of grounds in general; the play stakes itself on Miranda's status as *tabula rasa*, a pure, groundless ground secured in the determinate interval between matter and spirit.[17] But it is also precisely around that question of inscription—the play's capacity to mark its own power to inscribe, to *take*—that one feels its greatest perturbations. "I pray thee mark me" . . . "Dost thou attend me?" . . . "pray thee mark me" . . . "Mark his condition," Prospero declaims (1.2.67, 78, 88, 117). "Do you mark me?" Gonzalo declares (2.1.169). Such moments have a psychological dimension; Prospero betrays his anxiety, perhaps even his own reluctance, at the point where he is to hand on his daughter. But the fact that the concern is reiterated across characters suggests its bearing on the way in which the radically incorporative and totalizing work, the absolute work, necessarily encounters the question of its own power to take. We reencounter the problems of inscriptive reference we saw, for instance, toward the end of *Othello*, but now as the condition of the work qua work and as thematic preoccupation.

The problem of inscription appears most vividly in the scenes where the play's creationist themes come to bear directly on the formation of subjectivities, including the moment that has received the most critical attention—Prospero's curiously overwrought response at the point where, recalling Caliban's plot, he dissolves the wedding masque. "Never till this day / Saw I him touched with anger so distempered," his daughter remarks (4.1.144–45). "I am vexed," Prospero says, "my old brain is troubled. / Be not disturbed with my infirmity . . . . A turn or two I'll walk / To still my beating mind" (4.1.158–63). Stephen Orgel is right to suggest that Prospero's reaction exceeds what can be explained by the recalled machinations of the hapless monster and his drunken coconspirators. What disturbs the magician, Orgel observes, is more the fact of his own self-forgetfulness—such a realization brings thoughts of mortality.[18]

That moment of forgetfulness is the point where auto-creation threatens to become sheer repetition. Having restaged the entire history of his betrayal to rewrite its close, Prospero risks repeating the fall itself, the moment of his being lost to his books. He risks closing the hoop, as it were. Such forgetfulness can be psychologized; Prospero's uncharacteristic absorption in his own theater is a stay against the paternal loss the wedding masque will inevitably bring with it for him. But there is something originary and irreducible in the moment. To have given oneself over thus is already to enact the mortal loss one fends against, a self-loss that by definition can only be known after the fact, at the point of coming-to. We recall Caliban's earlier, equally ravishing account of his own indeterminate coming to, his dream of a bereaved waking, and of waking to dream again. For the authorial master, as for the acculturated slave, consciousness is the consciousness of a recursive loss, neither absorption nor transcendence but the belated knowledge that one had already been inscribed.

"A turn or two I'll walk to still my beating mind." Prospero's phrase does in fact bring beginnings to mind, as well as ends: the opening tempest, or at least Miranda's response to that precipitating event. After the clamor of the shipboard scene, we shift to Prospero and his daughter on the island, and hear Miranda's cry: "O, I have suffered / With those that I saw suffer: a brave vessel—/ Who had, no doubt, some noble creature in her—/ Dashed all to pieces!" (1.2.5–8) Of course, what she has viewed is not a real event; her magician father has staged the storm, as she herself seems to know. Part of the ethical force of the scene derives from the audience's awareness of the discrepancy between its response to that stagy opening scene of drowning and Miranda's pure, absorptive sympathy. The distinction is not a matter of the status of the event—it is theater for us, it is art for her—but of the condition of the subjectivity that apprehends it. Miranda responds with absolute identification because, as yet unformed, she is, in a sense, everywhere. "Be collected," Prospero says, and, setting aside his robes, he proceeds to give her the means to be collected, the inclusive and to this point unspoken narrative of her life from her birth to the present moment (1.2.13).

It is Miranda herself, however, who completes the circuit of that narrative, drawing its thread back to the event Prospero set out to explain: "And now I pray you, sir, / For still 'tis beating in my mind, your reason / For raising this sea-storm" (1.2.175–77). What beats in Miranda's mind is, of course, the tempest. But the status of that cause and end is hard to know. It is no longer the immediate impress of the event—the storm has past. Nor, however, is the beating mind a function of the recollective, narrativized self. Belonging neither to the mark of outward spectacle nor of inward narrative, distraction here suggests subjective causation—subjectivity's opening—precisely as what exceeds symbolic or cultural interpellation, a causeless cause.

A reverberation of the storm that went before, the beating mind is also the sound of something still to come. "Now my charms are all o'erthrown," Prospero announces as he turns outward to the audience at the close:

And what strength I have's mine own,
. . . . . Now 'tis true
I must be here confined by you,
Or sent to Naples. Let me not,

> . . . . . dwell
> In this bare island by your spell
> But release me from my bands
> With the help of your good hands.
> Gentle breath of yours my sails
> Must fill, or else my project fails,
> Which was to please . . . .
> . . . . my ending is despair
> Unless I be relieved by prayer,
> Which pierces so that it assaults
> Mercy itself, and frees all faults.
> As you from crimes would pardoned be,
> Let your indulgence set me free.
>
> (5.1. 319–38)

The tonal oddities of the epilogue, the suggestions of force—of assaults and piercings—the freighted language of crime and punishment, is bound up with the unstable agonism of those moments where the Shakespearean spellbinder within—Puck, Prospero—address himself without, directly to the all-mastering audience. The audience might clap gently, graciously freeing the magician. Then again, given the perils of captivation figured throughout the drama but especially at the end in the circle of the spellbound adversaries—image of our own absorbed relation to the stage—an audience would have more tendentious reasons to wish Prospero on his way, to clap with a spell-breaking vengeance, thus marking the play's limits, and its own knowing place beyond them.

But to claim one's power thus, to speed his ship on its way with something more violent than a gentle breath, is, of course, to repeat the tempest with which the play began, and thus to be back where one started, all the more bound-up. To release oneself from that double-bind would be to applaud knowingly, precisely with the consciousness that one's response is already inscribed, and thus to hear it—one's own clapping—as something, again, at once inward and alien: to come to with the lingering, familiar and strange, sound of a beating in the mind. That state anticipates the *savoir faire*—the knowing that one does not know—of aesthetic subjectivity. But the effect equally recalls the traditional status of the sovereign as *major et minor se ipso*, above and below himself, beyond and within the law.[19] Crucially, it is now the logic of the aesthetic that sustains that sovereign condition.

Groundless, reflexive, knowing: such an irresolute resolution embodies the play's version of aesthetic subjectivity in ideal form. And yet the beating mind remains disquieting. "Thou most lying slave, / Whom stripes may move, not kindness," Prospero says to Caliban (1.2.344–45). But if force lingers in the beating of the mind, it is unsettling precisely because it is intransitive and causeless—one thinks of the phantasmatic scene at the center of Freud's essay, "A Child is Being Beaten."[20] We might also hear Lacan's account of the drives where he recalls the butterfly that inspires in Freud's Wolfman "the phobic terror of recognizing that the beating of little wings is not so very far from the beating of causation, of the primal stripe marking his being for the first time with the grid of desire."[21] What pulses in the drives is the workings of a negation indistinguishable from the foundations of being: " 'Ban, 'Ban, Ca-Caliban," the monster reverberates (2.2.179).

The relation between that inhuman iteration and aestheticization can be recognized in the play's "recognition" scene, a scene of self-recognition, ultimately, articulated around revenge and forgiveness. Prospero has gathered his "spell-stopped" adversaries into the conjuring circle he has drawn—figure for all those porous circles that figure the stage and our own relation to it. As many have noted, Prospero's words of forgiveness are unheard by the figures to whom they are addressed: the island visitors remain charm-bound and lost to themselves. It would be wrong, however, to see that fact as questioning the force of Prospero's gesture.[22] Given the circumstances, given the magician's power and orchestration of the moment, what answer could the adversary give that would not be a forced one? More to the point, the very demand for such a moment of recognition—conventional tragedy's promised end—remains bound within the closed circuit of the answering pardon, the this-for-that of an economic exchange, and thus to an act that is neither free nor ethical. If forgiveness frees it does so by passing beyond that circuit. In that regard, Prospero's apostrophizing address, an address to the other that is simultaneously a self-address, opens that circuit precisely insofar as it enacts the missed encounter, even the missed self-encounter, as the play's ethical ground—it is Ariel, the inhuman spirit, that prompts the turn to forgiveness, we should remember.

Indeed, the scene only fully makes sense when it is imagined from the vantage point of the other. Prospero does not break the charm; he lets his adversaries come to. And for a moment they hold back:

> Not one of them
> That yet looks on me, or would know me. Ariel,
> Fetch me the hat and rapier in my cell.
> I will discase me, and myself present
> As I was sometime Milan.
>
> (5.1.82–86)

By displaying himself as he was of old—as Milan—Prospero makes himself a figure of memory for them, something inward. And in actively choosing to recognize that figure, they would release themselves from their tormenting bonds and return to themselves: "Not one of them . . . would know me." By turning within, they return without. Recognition would be, by such an account, a story of the restorative power of conscience based on an embrace of the other.

And yet, Prospero is something more than a figure of memory here. He is a figure that returns from the depths; for them, he drowned long ago. King Alonzo had described earlier his experience of the spell-binding words that left them guilt-bound, "all knit up / In their distractions," and in a "strange stare" (3.3.89–90, 95):

> O, it is monstrous, monstrous!
> Methought the billows spoke and told me of it,
> The winds did sing it to me; and the thunder,
> That deep and dreadful organ-pipe, pronounced
> The name of Prosper: it did bass my trespass.
> Therefore my son i' th' ooze is bedded; and
> I'll seek him deeper than e'er plummet sounded,
> And with him there lie mudded.
>
> (3.3.95–102)

This is an account of inwardness and the awakened debt of conscience. It is monstrous, however, because it is something more. Prospero, who prompts conscience, is himself a monstrous being, a name—nothing but the name—emerging from the sound of the beating waves, and yet a name that leaves you in "a strange stare." He is, in that sense, something at once inward and alien, like the pearl-eyed creature of Ariel's song, phenomenal and nonphenomenal. There is no certainty that what draws one to him is the "free" choice of ameliorating conscience, or the inhuman hold of another causation, a rending distraction associated with the reiterative inscription of the signifier, where the distinction between the embrace and the repudiation of the other dissolves into a difference that ceaselessly conjures what it excludes. "*If thou beest Prospero,*" Alonzo says at the close, and his only assurance is the sound of a beating: "Whe'er thou beest he or no, / Or some enchanted trifle to abuse me, / As late I have been, I not know. Thy pulse / Beats as of flesh and blood" (5.1.134, 111–14; my italics). "As of": the pulse of the play is the beating of the language—the play's own language—within which the very question of whether it is or is not human opens. Recognition, and thus release, is a matter of retaining the "as of" of aestheticization, which means holding onto the impossibility of knowing whether one's choice is a choice.

That conception of freedom clarifies the distinction between Shakespeare's aesthetic subject and that of the Enlightenment, or at least of a received version of the Enlightenment. The beating mind bears the mark of fatality insofar as it undoes because it passes beyond the distinction between the blind, inscribing recoils of revenge and the reflexive, inward turn of conscience and reflective consciousness, the outward law of the one becoming ultimately indistinguishable from the spirit of the other.[23] Consciousness itself redounds like something poisonously extrinsic—"Do not infest your mind with beating on / the strangeness of this business," Prospero says to his spellbound adversaries in their coming to (5.1.246–47). Because it takes the ground with it in its self-including completion, pure aesthetic internalization—sublimation—turns out to be indistinguishable from the incorporative atavism of the drives. "A grace it had, devouring," Prospero says of the apparitional banquet Ariel conjures for the conscience-stricken courtiers (3.3.84). We devour it, it devours us, and what is devoured is nothing, death: "What, must our mouths be cold?" the storm-tossed mariner says (1.1.52). And that consumption is reflexive consciousness: "they devour their reason," Prospero says of his wide-eyed audience within the play (5.1.155). The line suggests the prophylactic aspect of the distinction a latter era will forge between aesthetic judgment and pure reason.

Understood in these terms, aestheticization conditions the world of the play from its heights to its depths. On the one hand, the arbitrary nature of the difference between law and inward spirit means the inevitably forced character of the political-theological translation the play would articulate; it is the *violence* of prayer the play enlists at the close. On the other, aestheticization defines the most immanent of the play's creatural embodiments. The riddle of Caliban's anagrammatical name is bound up with the reverting consumption the play intimates at its close. The cannibal who eats his own kind is for Shakespeare always a figure for a self-devouring, as if the fascinating, illegible "primitive" in fact offered back nothing but the consuming figure of our own aesthetic consumption, a truth that returns upon us exactly in proportion to the super-subtle interpretive force through which we claim the power to know him for the cannibal he is.[24]

Such a reversionary understanding of the creatural at once bears out and complicates recent accounts of the politics of "bare life." "'Ban, 'Ban, Ca-Caliban": it would not be wrong to hear in Caliban's self-referring chant what Giorgio Agamben describes as the logic of the "sovereign ban," that auto-exclusion through which the sovereign would establish itself as "self-constituting self-relation."[25] At the same time, insofar as the monster figures itself as nothing but the abyssal reduplication of that structure, he also implies a critique of the translation of bare life into the object or referent of sovereign force, the hypostasization which forms the unspoken ligature between the dialectal and the bio-political dimensions of Agamben's undertaking.[26]

I've been arguing that political aestheticization, that historical process by which sovereignty is recouped through a mechanism that might seem to be ameliorative—a sublimation of power—in fact brings to view something dire at the ontological core of the political, something more troubling than the death of kings. But *The Tempest*'s engagement with the aesthetic as I have traced it also bears on the riddle with which I began. It is precisely because *The Tempest* is the most aestheticizing of Shakespeare's plays that it is the play most preoccupied with radically extrinsic causes, with history as sheer contingency.

The beating mind suggests causation as the returning trace of a missed encounter, in Lacan's formulation, an encounter "forever missed"—it is that status as missed encounter that gives material causation its traumatic, inassimilable character. The beating mind marks the point where the play encounters its own best-known cause in just such a form. In 1610, William Strachey, the secretary and one of the stockholders of the Virginia Company's colony in Jamestown, wrote a letter describing the storm that left their ship wrecked on the Island of Bermuda, suspending the expedition intended to reimpose government on the dissolving colony. Anticipating the play's opening moments, Strachey describes the scene in which the tempest, striking all with "amazement" and "distraction," seems to unhinge all human government. The sea "beat [the governor] from his hold . . . [and] struck him from the place where he sate, and grovelled him, and all us about him on our faces, beating together with our breathes all thoughts from our bosoms else than that we were now sinking."[27]

The mingling of the beating of the storm and "our breaths" recalls the opening of *The Tempest*—"you do assist the storm," the Boatswain tells the bellowing courtiers—and the epilogue, where we are made conscious of our own breaths; one can imagine the description of the encounter with watery death as something like the imaginative kernel of the play—the revolutionary kernel, even, given its relation to the undoing of sovereign governance. However, to recognize that relation to the limits of sovereignty, it is important to hold off on the overhasty referential claim. The force of the account, and its status as source, is less a function of the dramatic fact of death's approach than of the rhetorical slippage that marks that approach. "Beating together with our breaths all thoughts from our bosoms." Does the storm knock from the mariners both their breaths and all thoughts save of death? Or does breath join with storm to beat away all thoughts except of death? Mingled indistinguishably with the storm as it is at the play's close, breath figures at once as effect and cause, an ellipsis equivalent to the impossible act of thinking one's own death. The disaster that turns the entire colonial enterprise into a missed encounter—Bermuda, not Jamestown—is the disaster of the irreducibly missed encounter, a reaction that is also its cause.

That beating amounts to Shakespeare's brush with historical cause insofar as we imagine him hearing in it the echo of an enterprise that is still to come and already past. In that sense, it resonates with Walter Benjamin's account of the revolutionary, elliptical instance that breaks the narrative continuums of historicist history.[28] What Strachey's and Shakespeare's (and for that matter Benjamin's) storms evoke of the limits of the political imaginary in the undoing of human governance and state should be understood in relation to that opening of historical causation. It would be a mistake to imagine such vexations as a function of the aesthetic's encounter with history in any simple sense, as if history breached art from some space beyond. This is a textual encounter, of course. More to the point, precisely in its totalizing movement, the aesthetic solicits and provokes history as the trace of an inassimilable cause, an infraction that occurs neither exactly from within nor from without. Aestheticization makes that missed encounter knowable even as it blindly reiterates it in its own self-devouring movement.

Such an account of the relation between aesthetics and history brings us back to cultural materialism, and the claims for the aesthetic work as embedded in culture, and thus, a fortiori, as embedded in history. Such a model, which casts the work as an apartment in the mansion of culture, fails to allow for what aesthetic ideology might suggest about the limits and thus the conditions for the possibility of culture and narrative history as consolidating forms. In bringing those limits to account, the aesthetic reorients cultural analysis broadly, but also in its particulars, suggesting, for example, that the imperial project in the time of globalism may stake itself ultimately less on the empirical instance of the over-mastering confrontation than on the forcible conversion of the missed encounter into a scene of first encounters, a translation of the intractable beating of causation into a manageable drama of disciplinary force. To lose sight of that forced translation is to lose sight of the relation between empire and the most intimately familiar and ongoing forms of aesthetic consciousness.

CHAPTER 7

Hobbes and the Hydrophobes: The Fate of the Aesthetic in the Time of the State

I have been describing a genealogy of the aesthetic understood as a response to the politicization of space in the early modern era, a solution to the problem of grounds that also radicalizes that problem. I now want to cross the historical divide of war and regicide to pick up the fate of political aesthetics in relation to a new dispensation. Hobbes's *Leviathan* explicitly turns away from conscience to the passions and interests—above all, self-interest—and to the formal, contractual state as governing terms.[1] The institution of the political as neutral, scientific, even geometrical system might seem to suggest an outright abandonment of the rapport between politics and art. In fact, for Hobbes that new political space involves a conception of art that seems, on first blush, more thoroughgoing than the accounts of art as "second nature" encountered in Leonardo and the Renaissance. Here is *Leviathan*'s well-known opening:

> Nature (the art whereby God hath made and governs the world) is by the *art* of man, as in many other things, so in this also imitated, that it can make an artificial animal. For seeing art is but a motion of the limbs, the beginning whereof is in some principle part within, why may we not say that all *automata* (engines that move themselves by springs, and wheels as doth a watch) have an artificial life? . . . *Art* goes yet further, imitating that rational and most excellent work of nature, *man*. For by art is created that great LEVIATHAN called a COMMONWEALTH, or STATE . . . which is but an artificial man, though of greater stature and strength than the natural, for whose protection and defence it was intended.[2]

Indeed, the Hobbesian moment might be considered a high-water mark for political aesthetics. As Victoria Kahn argues, mid-seventeenth-century contractual theory, and Hobbes in particular, represents a significant historical interval between an understanding of the body politic as a given natural order centered on the virtues—an Aristotelian conception—and a later order in which legitimacy becomes equivalent to legality and where the political and aesthetic domains are securely cordoned from one another, an interval during which the political sphere was for the first time explicitly understood as a fictive domain available to creative invention.[3]

Yet from the vantage point of the "prehistory" of political aesthetics that I have been tracing here what is striking is not the invention of a political art but the transformation of political aesthetics from its generative and creationist form—the "foetalism," as Simon Palfrey puts it, of a play like *The Tempest*—to the thorough instrumentalization of art implied by Hobbes's automaton of state and his contractual fiction.[4] Hobbes is the right place to look for an understanding of what informs such an aesthetic transformation. For as Kahn persuasively argues, the ground against which Hobbes stakes his theoretical system is already art, not the raw matter of "nature"—a fictive construction—but the corrosive dangers of mimetic contagion and emulative desire associated, among other things, with romance fiction. The solution to that mimetic risk is mimesis, Kahn argues, and specifically the metalinguistic awareness that lets us comprehend the fact of our fictiveness.[5]

And yet, given that mimetic contagion is precisely what undoes the capacity to assume such exteriority to its effects—that is what makes it a contagion—the challenging question becomes how that metadiscursive turn is possible at all.[6] The prospect of such a turn depends, I will argue, on Hobbes's relation to the prior and more untoward aesthetic logic I have been tracing, a noninstrumental aesthetic the formal state can neither accommodate nor do without. Much depends on that aesthetic negotiation: contract, the ability to comprehend the political sphere as a manipulable fiction, as well as the distinctive version of transcendence that defines the modern state form.[7]

Reckoning on Death

Engaging the relation between the aesthetic and the political in Hobbes means beginning with the irreducible term of Hobbes's political construction: death, or, rather, the fear of death. Self-preservation is foundational for Hobbes. "A Law of Nature . . . is a precept or general rule, found out by reason, by which a man is forbidden to do that which is destructive of his life or taketh away the means of preserving the same" (79). Indeed, while Hobbes goes on to list an array of "Other Laws of Nature," including abiding by contracts, the law against self-destruction remains in a certain sense the only natural law, for as he points out in certain circumstances in the state of nature—a war of all against all— abiding by natural laws can lead to self-destruction and in that sense must be abrogated.

The relation between the fear of death and the founding of the state can be understood specifically as a response to the deontologized and agonistic character of early modern political space, a relational space without secure transcendental reference, as I have suggested. Death is the pivot in the dialectical operation through which the ceaseless division and finitude of that limitless space is projected outward as the ahistorical and, indeed, purely imaginary domain of raw, aboriginal "nature"—the place of the battle of all against all—in order that it can then internally underwrite the transformation that founds the state on a universalizable and consolidating fear of such a condition.[8] In other words, death is both exteriorized as threat and absorbed as the grounds of the state, a process that accounts for its double status in Hobbes's analysis: fear of death is the source of our woes—the cause of the anticipatory, self-protective violence that endlessly brings on the destruction it would ward against—and the solution, the source of the contractual sovereign's power to sustain peace. "The passion to be reckoned upon is fear" (88).

And yet, if death must be forcefully enlisted as the state's anchoring term it is precisely because it is always at risk of being no limit at all. As Kahn argues, the state of nature is defined, not so much by brute passions, as by a susceptibility to mimetic desire associated particularly for Hobbes with the deleterious effects of reading—a "vain-glory" "nourished by the histories or fictions of gallant persons" (32).[9] The emulative impulse, derived from the radical equivalency of men, poses the greatest danger precisely because it carries men past death's limit, a situation that arises when reflexive self-regard converts the act into the display of the act. Men will "tak[e] pleasure in contemplating their own power in the acts of conquest" leading them to pursue glory "farther than their security requires": once they do, others must follow (75). "All signes of hatred, and contempt provoke most of all to brawling and fighting, insomuch as most men would rather lose their lives . . . then suffer reproach," Hobbes remarks in *De Cive*.[10] Bound up with Hobbes's conception of the radical equivalency of man, emulation is particularly associated with the imitative recoils of revenge, a "glorying to no end" amounting to the negative, *tu quoque* equivalent of the *quid pro quo* of contract. Here, too, self-destruction is a function of a passage into the register of signs: "because all signs of hatred or contempt provoke to fight, insomuch as most men choose rather to hazard their life than not to be revenged" (96).

Aligned at moments with a subset of the political body—young men, readers of romances—emulation in fact brings us to the essence of what constitutes man as a political being for Hobbes, and why the human condition amounts to something less and something more than Aristotle's *zoon politikon*. Whereas for the peaceable bees "the common good differeth not from the private; and being by nature inclined to their private, they procure thereby the common benefit," man, "whose joy consisteth in comparing himself with other men, can relish nothing but what is eminent" (108). Man is distinct from the creatural, not because of his egoism, but because of his dangerous and ineradicable sociality.

Man is consigned to be a reader of men, and limitlessly so, insofar as man's condition as linguistic being is absolute. Truth is, for Hobbes, "the right ordering of names" (19).[11] Insofar as man is mimetic, a supervening authority, though underwritten by the fear of death, is also required because death is not enough.[12] Hobbes writes of a contagion of suicides afflicting the "young maidens" of an ancient Greek city. The plague was stopped only when the magistrates determined to "strip such as so hanged themselves, and let them hang out naked. This, the story says, cured that madness" (43). Just a story, but a story about the limitless force of imitative stories.

The fictive and real, absolute and posited character of the fear of death in Hobbes is hardly subterranean. It enables his political construction and is directly bound up with its founding term: the law against self-destruction. That law passes unaltered between natural and civil domains, and articulates the relation between them. In the state of nature, man is conditioned by two fundamental axioms: the "Right of Nature," that is, "the liberty each man hath to use his own power, as he will himself, for the preservation of his own nature, that is to say, of his own life," and the "Law of Nature," which is "the precept or general rule . . . by which a man is forbidden to do that which is destructive of his life" (79).

The proximity of the content of the two descriptions highlights the crucial aspect of the formulation: the very fact of the inclusion of a version of law as prohibitory injunction—law as formal constraint—within the field of nature. Natural Law is, of course, not Hobbes's invention, but the category has a significant structural function in his schema. The logic of the inclusion of the conventional within nature—a kind of proto-norm—becomes apparent with the passage into the civil domain, where the constitutive force of the covenant that founds the state—the fact that it "is more than consent, or concord; it is a real unity of them all, in one and the same person"—is borne out by the status of the law against self-destruction now as a true and irrefutable fiction (109). The conventionality of the law of nature symmetrically mirrors and reinforces the real truth of a purely social law: "If he that attempteth to depose his sovereign be killed, or punished by him for such attempt, he is author of his own punishment, as being, by the institution, author of all his sovereign shall do" (111). One cannot complain of injury from the sovereign, for "to do injury to oneself is impossible" (112). To claim a right to depose the sovereign is as unthinkable as to say "the Roman people might depose the Roman people" (112).

Hobbes will at other moments hold onto the distinction between the natural and legal forms of that law of self preservation, but in a strikingly minimalist form: "The consent of a subject to sovereign power is contained in these words *I authorize, or take upon me, all his actions*, in which there is no restriction at all of his own former natural liberty; for by allowing him to kill me, I am not bound to kill myself when he commands me. It is one thing to say *kill me, or my fellow, if you please*, another to say *I will kill myself, or my fellow*" (142). The preoccupation with whether the condemned are obliged to participate in their own deaths derives from the scholastic political literature and particularly the work of Domingo de Soto. What is distinctive to Hobbes is the casting of the issue as a matter of contract, an orientation which on the one hand places emphasis on intentional aims and on the other highlights the purely rhetorical character of the distinction between subject and sovereign.[13] The juxtaposition between the natural and the legal, between what belongs to the subject and what to the sovereign, is "contained in these words" in a form in which all comes down to a mere shift in the structure of enunciation ordered around death's insecure stake.

Before dismissing Hobbes's contractual fiction as mere authoritarian fantasy, it is important to recognize what is at stake in that imagined event. For Hobbes, the domain of nature amounts, ultimately, to a retroactive fiction, civility's posited ground.[14] Natural law is, as it turns out, no law at all except as an effect of sovereign power (181). There is no sin, no good or evil, nothing intrinsic, before the law (77).[15] Virtue and merit are, for Hobbes, "valued for eminence, and consisteth in comparison" (38). "The *value* or Worth of a man is, as of all other things, his price . . . and therefore is not absolute, but a thing dependent on the need and judgment of another" (51). Thought as such is a purely differential operation, a matter of similitude and difference through and through (38). In other words, meaning and value are entirely interpretive effects. "Because words (and consequently the attributes of God) have their signification by agreement and constitution of men, those attributes are to be significative of honour that men intend should so be" (242). Meaning—the meaning of nature, the meaning of God—is contractual; it is in that sense an aftereffect of the institution of the state.

To note this is to note the self-constituting character of Hobbes's founding contract. The profoundly reduced status of political subjectivity, the fact that for Hobbes the state of nature is a condition in which there is as yet "no propriety," no "*meum* and *tuum*," no just or unjust, no "*good, evil, lawful* and *unlawful*," allows the institution of the sovereign state its constitutive force (114). And yet, such radical constructivism inevitably opens the question of its own grounds. Of course, Hobbes develops those grounds at length: his entire theory of the contractual basis of the Commonwealth. But the circularity of that account remains remarkably close to the surface. "The nature of justice consisteth in keeping of valid covenants; but the validity of covenants begins not but with the constitution of a civil power sufficient to compel men to keep them; and then it is also that propriety begins," which is to say the notion of "*own*," of "*meum* and *tuum*." And with "*meum* and *tuum*" begins the conceptual possibility of contract in the first place (89). Insofar as it represents fear of death at once as what prompts law and what law posits, the law against self-destruction crystallizes that circularity as the opaque ground of law as such.

The self-constituting character of Hobbesian political authorization is intimated in the "as if" that initiates it. "This is more than consent or concord; it is a real unity of them all" made "as if every man should say to every man *I authorize and give up my right of governing myself to this man* . . ." (109). The fictitious status of the moment is a practical matter: given the multiplicity of citizens, no such scene of transference would actually be possible. But it is also a function of the self-authoring character of authorization itself. A necessarily retroactive instance, that authorization can only be imaginary. And yet, Hobbes does not just allude to the content of the contract—he iterates the authorizing address as an address, in italics, and later states that "sovereign power is contained in these words *I authorize, or take upon me, all his actions.*" A mere fiction, the words of authorization are also an absolute fiction. For given the vicarious nature of man as mimetic being—given his character as ineradicably signifying creation—the instance of constitution will necessarily assume the form of just such a transferential address, one in which the distinction between enunciation and enunciator is nugatory because it has yet to appear. It is in this sense that we should understand the equation Hobbes draws between political constitution and the *ex nihilo* of divine creation, "that *fiat*, or the *let us make man*, pronounced by God in the creation" (4).

Hobbes's story of origins is of course inveterately statist. But to read that scene of founding contract simply as an imposition against the prepolitical person's independence is to misunderstand the scope and nature of the project. For Hobbes is concerned, not with the management of already given individuals, possessive or otherwise, but with how subjectivity is precipitated from the limitless equivalencies of economically conceived social and signifying worlds. One should balk at the totalizing and seamless character of the contractual foundation he posits, but not at his reading that scene in terms of the interpellative dimension of law. The relation between law and the autonomous subject is there *ab origine* in Hobbes's negative conception of the golden rule, a formulation that defines the relation between autonomy and sociality in Hobbes: "*Do not that to another, which thou wouldst not have done to thyself*" (99). Insofar as the subject is a precipitate of a purely relational signifying structure, it will be conditioned from the outset by the negational character of law. The characteristic of Hobbes's social thought that has understandably most troubled his critics then and now—his equation of liberty and constraint—is also the measure of how closely he approaches the inherent contradictions of an emerging conception of a *society* of *individuals*.[16]

That engagement with the founding dimensions of law indicates the radical character of Hobbesian social thought vis-à-vis a later liberal tradition, particularly Locke, which attempts to resolve the problem of foundations through, on the one hand, an essentializing of the subject and its liberties, and, on the other, a corresponding reduction of sociality and law to a purely mediating and formal function—the state as vehicle for competing rights.[17] The cotemporal grounds of law and subjectivity in Hobbes also suggest the misplaced nature of the debate as to whether Hobbes belongs on the side of liberalism or absolutism; insofar as it involves the law of the negatively constituted individual, absolutism is historically inseparable from modern individualism.

Sovereign Monsters: From Biopower to Political Aesthetics

The aporetic force of Hobbes's conception of political origination is condensed in the very oddity of the notion of a law against self-destruction. What does it mean that one would need such a law as law, as distinct from a right to life? To posit the law against self-destruction as law— that is, as prohibition—is to posit the possibility of its transgression from the origin. In a political philosophy marked by the proximity of cure and punishment, in which the terror of death resolves the terror of death, that thanatotic prospect is never far off. Hobbes imagines such a drive luridly under the heading of rebellion, and in relation, again, to the dangers of reading, in this case "books of policy and histories of the ancient Greeks and Romans" advocating tyrannicide (214):

> In sum, I cannot imagine how anything can be more prejudicial to a monarchy than the allowing of such books to be publicly read without present applying such correctives of discreet masters as are fit to take away their venom, which venom I will not doubt to compare to the biting of a mad dog, which is a disease the physicians call *hydrophobia*, or *fear of water*. For as he that is so bitten has a continual torment of thirst, and yet abhorreth water, and is in such an estate as if the poison endeavoured to convert him into a dog, so when a monarchy is once bitten to the quick by those democratical writers that continually snarl at that estate, it wanteth nothing more than a strong monarch, which nevertheless out of a certain *tyrannophobia* (or fear of being strongly governed), when they have him, they abhor. (215)

Rebellion against the monarch amounts to hydrophobia insofar as it means a turning against the wellsprings of life. But the horror of the condition consists in its circular and self-perpetuating character—Hobbes will also liken the contagion of emulative rebellion to "hot bloods that, having gotten the itch, tear themselves with their own nails, till they can endure the smart no longer" (214). And that circularity of the relation between desire and transgression exposes the possibility that the "thirst" for sovereignty's waters never was separable from the disease it must cure. The relation between the coursing venom of such an effect and reading is apparent in the instability of the metaphor itself: the self-swallowing way in which the disease that makes us like dogs turns us into dogs, and the way monarchy itself turns out to be the envenomed creature, what is afflicted with an insatiable, self-poisoning desire for monarchy.

Hydrophobia is a calamity—the ruination, not just of the monarch, but of the entire structure of exchange that undergirds the Hobbesian system. And yet, the hydrophobes may also tell us something about the grounds of modern power insofar as the passage suggests the logic of the autoimmune disorder which contemporary theory associates with the expansive character of a distinctly modern sovereign force. For Roberto Esposito, the immunological paradigm is bound up specifically with the emergence of biopower, that self-generative operation through which power constitutes itself, not by way of the regulative finality of law, but through an ever-increasing capillary insinuation into the functions of life. Hobbes, for Esposito, realizes modernity's significant break from classical political thought insofar as with him the *conservatio vitae* enters fully into the political sphere, becoming "by far its most privileged dimension."[18]

Hobbes reveals the immunitary logic that informs that conservative operation, insofar as in the state of nature self-preservative impulses cannot be separated from countervailing acquisitive and destructive forces. "If life is abandoned to its internal powers, to its natural dynamics, human life is destined to self-destruct because it carries within itself something that ineluctably places it in contradiction with itself."[19] For Esposito, the passage from nature to artifice in Hobbes amounts to a protective doubling over of this primordial immunological operation: "In order to save itself, life needs to step out from itself and constitute a transcendental point from which it receives orders and shelter." Modern sovereign is that *metaimmunitary* redoubling of life.[20]

The question, however, is whether those two phases or dimensions—a prior vitalistic operation and the sheltering movement of sovereignty—actually are distinguishable in Hobbes. Esposito sees Hobbes's natural state, not as a posited effect inextricable from the contradictory foundations of sovereignty, but as a field of fully individuated desires and even communal impulses which will be abolished with the institution of the cocooning autonomy of sovereignty. In that sense, the passage into the political sphere is a sacrificial operation, a matter of life "giv[ing] up something that is integral to itself," that "acquisitive desire . . . that places itself in the path of a deadly reprisal."[21]

The critical point is the way in which this division of fields—a vital field of "primordial intensity" on the one hand, the field of sovereign law on the other—bears on Esposito's own thought. Esposito is careful to avoid essentializing *bios*. Biopolitical life is less a substantive category or ontological ground than a "moving margin" conditioned from the outset by its own antinomies.[22] And yet, Esposito's antinomian orientation—his positing of biopower as an operation "antecedent to . . . the subject of law"—raises a question as to what that vital antinomy entails.[23] Modern power arises not as an external imposition but as "the *intrinsically* antinomic mode by which life preserves itself through power" (my italics).[24] Intrinsic to what, however? Life's constituting division consists, for Esposito, in the movement through which life negationally "separates itself from itself," the "fold" or "interval" through which life "is separated from itself."[25] But if that antinomy is constitutive, can we speak of it as an operation of life, as what life itself does to itself? What is that constituting interval or divide prior to if inseparable from life but *nomos*, law in its heteronomic inextricability from life?[26] In that regard, what Hobbes's exorbitant law against self-destruction "inaugurates" is not an immunological function of life, or even a thanatotic impulse, but a matter of "thinking life otherwise." In other words, it is an autoimmune operation that precedes (because it determines) the opposition between *bios* and *zoe*, between life and positive, civil law, and that cannot in any pure sense be separated from the workings of sovereignty.[27]

For Hobbes, the critical term is neither life nor the body and its needs, nor the subject even—a fungible category for him—but economy: the *quid pro quo* of contract, but more generally the system of equivalencies that informs his political thought from beginning to end and out of which, in his account, subject and sovereign are constructed. Hobbes's thought is staked on its own systematicity, and particularly the mathematical and geometrical logic that, for him, underpins the possibility of a coherent political philosophy—the modernity of Hobbes lies in the neutral, compassingly inscriptive character of that artificial system. And that possibility of economy as an autonomous and purely formal operation is directly bound up with art, art conceived in distinctly post Cartesian terms as a self-functioning mechanism. Consider the opening paragraph of *Leviathan* in its entirety, where state, man, and the human body are evoked, not vitalistically, but as animate artifice:

> Nature (the art whereby God hath made and governs the world) is by the *art* of man, as in many other things, so in this also imitated, that it can make an artificial animal. For seeing life is but a motion of limbs, the beginning whereof is in some principle part within, why may we not say that all *automata* (engines that move themselves by springs and wheels as doth a watch) have an artificial life? For what is the *heart*, but a *spring*; and the *nerves*, but so many *strings*; and the *joints*, but so many *wheels*, giving motion to the whole body, such as was intended by the artificer? *Art* goes yet further, imitating that rational and most excellent work of nature, *man*. For by art is created that great LEVIATHAN called a COMMONWEALTH, or STATE (in Latin CIVITAS), which is but an artificial man, though of greater stature and strength than the natural, for whose protection and defence it was intended; and in which the *sovereignty* is an artificial soul, as giving life and motion to the whole body. (3)

Art, according to such an account, remains a mimetic and secondary operation—a matter of imitating nature, or imitating the artificer who created nature. And yet, the automaton of art presses close to a "going yet further" of its imitative ground insofar as it approaches a description of man's capacity to artifice himself, an abyssal prospect related to the paragraph's concluding comparison—a likening that amounts to something more than a mere analogy—between the founding contract and the opaque "*fiat*, or the *let us make man*, pronounced by God in the creation" (4).[28]

That Hobbes is cognizant of the ambiguities of the simultaneously immanent and transcendent sphere he elaborates becomes evident when we place the opening description in the context of the introduction as a whole. The book's brief preamble stakes the claims of the treatise entirely on the operations of comparison or emulation, and ultimately on readers' ability to compare themselves to or read themselves in the relational system that allows them to perform such a comparison—a judgment on the possibility of judgment.[29]

The introduction consists of four paragraphs: the opening description of the artificial man of the state, a listing of the sections of the book, and then two paragraphs turning their attention to the artificer himself: man, that is, the reader.

> There is a saying much usurped of late, that *wisdom* is acquired, not by reading of books, but of *men*. Consequently whereunto, those persons that for the most part can give no other proof of being wise take great delight to show what they think they have shown in men, by uncharitable censures of one another behind their backs. But there is another saying not of late understood, by which they might learn truly to read one another, if they would take the pains; and that is, *nosce teipsum, read thyself,* which was not meant, as it is now used, to countenance either the barbarous state of men in power . . . or to encourage men of a lower degree to a saucy behavior towards their betters, but to teach us that for the similitude of the thoughts and passions of one man to the thoughts and passions of another, whosoever looketh into himself and consider what he doth, when he does *think, opine, reason, hope, fear*, &c, and upon what grounds, he shall thereby read and know, what are the thoughts and passions of all other men. (4)

The dangers of sheer, emulative differentiation—the limitless aggression of the backbiters—can be checked only by first turning the gaze within, by reading oneself. As Kahn points out, Hobbes's turn here to introspection and with it, an acknowledgment of similitude, should be read in relation to the ascendancy of the abstract, universal subjectivity of the bourgeois era. Insofar as the turn from the outward gaze of the backbiters to the inward gaze of self-knowledge also entails a turn from the object as such, introspection ensures a focus on the universal cause of passions rather than their infinite varied object-forms, as Hobbes will go on in the paragraph to suggest.[30]

And yet such a solution feels problematic at best. Kahn speaks of the distinction between the "simple perception of likeness" that enables one to " 'know [in] oneself' the " 'thoughts and passions' of others" and the "bad mimetic desire" of romance, but it is difficult to know how such similitude is distinguishable from the mimetic dangers of emulation (150). Mimetic desire is a contagion precisely because it dissolves the distinction between similitude and differentiation—in asserting ourselves against others we become equivalent to them. The mere fact of an inward-turning does not resolve the matter. In the course of the paragraph, Hobbes goes on to note that how one reads depends on whether "he that reads is himself a good or bad man," and, if the project as a whole stakes itself against anything, it is against the false claims of those who would claim to discover truth within. Indeed, those who claim conscience, that is, inwardness, as a ground have merely forgotten that conscience itself is nothing but a metaphor of an original sociality—the supposed authority of conscience evolved, Hobbes claims, from the fact of being "conscious," that is, having a shared knowledge with another (34).

The fact that introspection amounts to a provisional solution—a turn—becomes apparent with the final permutation in his account of epistemological grounds; the last paragraph begins:

> But let one man read another by his actions never so perfectly it serves him only with his acquaintance, which are but few. He that is to govern a whole nation must read in himself, not this or that particular man, but mankind, which though it be hard to do, harder than to learn any language or science, yet when I shall have set down my own reading orderly and perspicuously, the pains left another will be only to consider if he also find not the same in himself. For this kind of doctrine admitteth no other demonstration. (4–5)

We move, then, from reading men—the outward gaze of emulation—to reading oneself, to reading all men within oneself, that is, to conceiving the subject (Hobbes, the reader) as Commonwealth, the being that contains the multitude within himself. In other words, what one reads within is not another but relationality as such. And yet despite whatever dialectical resolution might be implied by that incorporative turn in which the object converges with the text itself, and perhaps precisely because of the overreaching suggested by its vast encompassment, the passage returns us to the bare workings of emulative rivalry, now played out at the level of the reader's relation to Hobbes. Having called on all to "take the pains" to learn to read themselves, Hobbes now says, though the task be "harder than to learn any language or science," you need take no pains at all, for I have taken them for you; if you are able to discover the same within yourself, it is because I have led the way. This is Hobbesian wit and hauteur, but the stakes are notable. All that follows—the entire "doctrine" of a neutral, scientific ground of man's political existence—will have "no other demonstration" than the act of comparison it provokes in the reader.

To make sense of the performative turn of the introduction, the fact that it stakes itself ultimately on the emulative, self-definitional act of our own reading, we need to view that opening address in relation to the image with which it was yoked, the famous frontispiece whose design Hobbes oversaw (Figure 7-1).[31] For the looming sovereign who re-

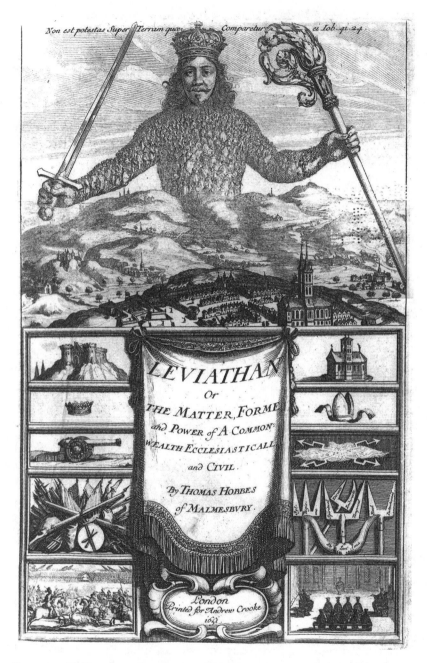

Figure 7-1. Hobbes, *Leviathan*. Frontispiece (1651).

turns our gaze and whose body is made up of the multitude of the citizenry visually figures the multitudinous self-reflection Hobbes enjoins at the conclusion of the introduction. Those who knew that the frontispiece image was in fact—or purportedly—Hobbes's self-portrait would have been all the more aware of the visual play on *nosce teipsum*. Given that, the image's superscription becomes striking. "*Non est potestas Super Terram quae Compareteur ei*"—"There is no power on earth which can be compared to him."

How does the image that solicits comparison establish the sovereign's incomparability, and thus the securing limit of the mimetic function? That possibility, which is also the condition for something like an immanent transcendence, depends on the way the viewer is doubly figured in the image: eye to eye as its mirroring spectator beyond the frame, and within the image in the form of the spectators making up the sovereign body and gazing obliquely up at the face. In other words, the frontispiece figures not just the concluding turn of the introduction but a condensation of the entire dialectical sequence. We see the Leviathan at once outwardly, as the object of our gaze, and inwardly, as self-reflective form. As inward alien form, the image has something of the character of the metaphor that for Hobbes reveals the actual sources of interiority— conscience as "a thousand witnesses" (33).

The consequence of that splitting of the gaze is felt in the force of the sovereign's eye. The passage from Job from which the inscription is drawn continues: "Leviathan . . . is made so as not to be afraid. He seeth everything below him, and is a king of all the children of pride." "Shall not one be cast down even at the sight of him? . . . Who can discover the face of his garment? . . . Who can open the doors of his face? . . . His eyes are like the eyelids of the morning" (41:34, 41:9, 41:13, 14, 18).[32] To understand the Leviathan's ability to cast down the viewer's level gaze with eyes that nevertheless remain as "close-sealed"—as blind—as the scales of his body, we simply need to grant the artificial man the originative force Hobbes claims for him (41:15). What one sees in the eye of the sovereign is the locus of one's own seeing in the alien form of blind spectacle—as artifice. In other words, it represents the grounds of subject and sovereign as a divisive effect prior to subject or object—"read thyself." What is significant is the dynamic of that effect. For it is precisely the subject's desire to know—that is, to master—the phantasmatic figure by objectifying it that renews its subjecting force, that gives the Leviathan its power to inscribe all within its gaze.[33]

To understand Hobbesian sovereignty in such terms—not, ultimately, as a contractual construction, not as a concept at all, but as a reduplicative effect whose power to overawe derives from its very groundlessness—is to see how thoroughly the phantasmatic figure is of a piece with the fabric of Hobbes's universe.[34] For Hobbes, the world itself is a phantasm. "Sense in all cases, is nothing else but original fancy" created, not from the world's impingement on perception, but from the "resistance, or counter-pressure, or endeavour of the heart, to deliver itself" of those pressures, pressures no different in kind or redounding effect than the spectator's resistant objectification of the sovereign figure (7, 6). The illusion of outwardness is produced by that extrusive movement; memory—the illusion of inwardness—by the fading of those ghost traces. In other words, the Hobbesian universe is a political universe through and through, one conjured by the reiterated included exclusion of the sovereign ban.[35]

The figure of the Leviathan, that is, the figure of the state, derives its hold specifically from what there is of the purely artificial man beyond any instrumental conception of art. What derives solely from man yet exceeds every subjectivity, the sovereign as gaze realizes the immanent transcendence of a new state form, even as it consolidates man as a primordially collective being. The self-exceeding character of the act which had in Machiavelli been the ongoing source of political creativity is reconfigured in Hobbes as the fixed and fixative limit of a systematic and homogenous economic space within which the "free" and "autonomous" agency of contracting subjects can be imagined.[36]

The blindingly visual character of that threshold is directly related to the sovereign's monstrosity. Hobbes alludes to the exorbitance of what he has contrived, and Leibniz will make the point explicit: the sovereign is monstrous insofar as it is a leviathan—a sea monster—but also monstrous in the root sense of the word, as the effect of an exorbitant showing. If in the ideology of an earlier age, sovereignty is a visible phenomenon—a matter of what is seen, or what hides itself from sight in the *arcana imperii*—with the everywhere and nowhere of the modern state, sovereign force becomes the function of an extravagant and horizonless showing in advance of seeing, what exceeds, even as it opens, an economy of speculation, that is, economy per se. "As monstruum, the Latin root of 'monster,' indicates," Paul Kottman writes, "the Leviathan 'gives itself to be seen' in such a way that it comprises the visual horizon itself."[37] The incomparable Leviathan is neither a creature of the land nor is it subterranean, neither seen nor unseen—it derives from elsewhere: that enigmatic elsewhere is alone what distinguishes the sovereign from the phantasms of the primitives who "mak[e] [the] creatures of their own fancies their gods" (62).[38] In the engraving, the figure is situated in an indeterminate space beyond the walls of the city, beyond the land—the sea can be glimpsed at the left of the image—but at the same time emergent from those rolling, undifferentiated hills which are themselves like billowing waves. The Leviathan evokes the "view from the sea"—Schmitt's phrase—but as the view from within.

Leviathans fetch from the depths, and their capacity to overawe derives, ultimately, not from finality—the fact of certain death—but from groundlessness. I have already noted the relation between water and a terrifying loss of purchase in the reiterative contagion of the hydrophobia brought on by the reading of "democratical writers." Hobbes cites another, quizzical instance of mimetic contagion linking a specifically literary delirium with aquatic monsters, the case of the people of Abdera who fell ill at a production of "the tragedy of *Andromeda*" about the terrors of the sea monster of myth: they "did nothing but pronounce iambics, with the names of *Perseus* and *Andromeda*; which, together with the fever, was cured by the coming on of winter" (43).

But the depths return in a similitude more directly linked to Hobbes's theoretical stakes. When Hobbes conceives his minimalist version of political liberty, he thinks of a sinking ship. "Fear and liberty are consistent, as when a man throweth his goods into the sea for *fear* the ship should sink, he doth it nevertheless very willingly, and may refuse to do it if he will" (136). The conceit represents a conception of liberty in the face of mortality—the condition of Hobbes's political subjectivity. It also suggests the exchange that founds the economy of his system on death's fixed limit: my goods for my life; if I give up nothing else, certainly I'll give up this for that. And yet, understood thus, the original version of the metaphor becomes all the more striking. In *De Cive*, Hobbes described liberty in terms of the man who is free, if he is willing, to throw *himself* from a sinking ship.[39] The example, which figures in its most extreme form Hobbes's understanding of the compatibility of fear and consent, is based on his understanding of the identity between passion and deliberation, and thus the voluerism of all passions.[40]

The real primal scene of the Hobbesian structure consists less in either metaphoric usage than in the (tropic) movement between them.

We can imagine the modification of the original metaphor as a matter of Hobbes amending the excesses of his claims with a more conventional understanding of self-preservation. If so, self-protection merely opens the more extravagant subtext implied by the convergence of the systemic and the affective dimensions of the figure. Insofar as man is himself a definitionally economic and mimetic being, he necessarily begins with his own free casting away, a breach of the law of self-preservation as the grounds of self-preservation and self-interest. As what constitutes sovereign and subject alike, the authorizing fiat will entail, not a *quid pro quo* within an already constituted system of exchange, but an initiatory positing or blind carrying-over that institutes the possibility of exchange and contract. In other words, it is a metaphor for the metaphoric transport, the necessary, originative, and nonphenomenal "as if" of political foundations, even as it suggests why metaphor is what Hobbes must proscribe for the structure to retain a calculable form.[41]

Understood as that founding "as if," political aesthetics bypasses the instrumentality of the state as artificial man, or even the chains of mimetic captivation against which the contractual state explicitly sets itself. Whatever its uncanny and agentless character, the gaze of the sovereign remains a phenomenal effect—a matter of showing. Yet, as aesthetic instance, sovereign force also harbors the enabling trace of what does not resolve into phenomenal form.

Such a nonphenomenal residue can be deduced from *Leviathan's* textual logic in its broadest terms. The call to readers to find themselves in the Leviathan—commonwealth and treatise—and to find the Leviathan already within themselves corresponds with the introduction's own status as what is within and beyond *Leviathan*, an integral part of the text but also what governs the terms of its reading from beyond it. That divided, self-incorporative logic opens the distinction between text and reader, and establishes sovereign, subject, and text as internal and external to one another, as what is to be constructed and what is already there.[42] And yet, articulating its authoring operation in its sparest terms, the text also suggests the risk of Hobbes's foundational conception of "self-reading": a dissolution of the distinction between text and reader, in which text and self are shown to depend, not on the temporal movement of a performative or inscriptive effect, but on an "as if" posited in no time and by no one. In that sense, the burden of Hobbes's account of political grounds—the burden of the founding "as if"—becomes the forced translation that sustains and disrupts its logic: the equation between *nosce teipsum*, "know thyself"—a mimetic and phenomenal operation—and "read thyself," Hobbes's translation of the phrase.

The engraving as well is legible in terms of the formal logic of self-incorporation, in this instance explicitly in the relation between its visual and textual registers. A critical part of the text, the frontispiece also oversees the text and the reader's entry into it. Following the recursive logic of self-incorporative sovereignty, the divided, correspondent relation between image and text is duplicated within the title page, where the borderless figure of the artificial man stands over the framed title matter, which in turn contains its own series of framed visual icons of civil and ecclesiastical power. The limit of those securely delimited, correspondent relations between the visual and textual is manifest in the writing inscribed within the image that makes known the sovereign's incomparability: the citation from Job. The cursive script, neither quite text nor image, suggests the nonphenomenal cut or incision out of which text and vision alike emerge. The sovereign's sword, tilted inward and backward, drawing us to the script, cuts or superimposes itself against that founding inscription even as it reiterates its incision.

The logic of the severed, reiterated cut conditions sovereignty from the marks on a page to the *nomos* of the *jus publicum europaeum*.[43] For Schmitt, the relation between *Leviathan* and *nomos* is a matter of historical irony. The text which more than any other articulated the grounds for the European nation state was produced in a country whose maritime and mercantile status was already passing beyond those territorial terms.[44] And yet, as I suggested in chapter 6, the state form was always dictated by the view from elsewhere, and the pure mechanism of the commonwealth as Hobbes articulates it will always be something of an aquatic monster insofar as the *nomic* division that institutes the boundary logic of the state remains inassimilable to it. In that regard, the historic irony runs deeper. The limitless self-division Hobbes stakes his commonwealth against, he builds into the Leviathan as its sovereign core.

Strange Stares

Aesthetics and sea monsters recall *The Tempest*, of course. When Trinculo discovers Caliban, he sees him as a "strange fish," in fact, a cloven thing: a man, a fish, and an artifice: "Were I in England now . . . and had but this fish painted, not a holiday fool there but would give a piece of silver. There would this monster make a man" (2.2.27–30).[45] But Caliban is not the play's most alien creature. Sovereignty's phenomenal/non-phenomenal mark recalls Prospero's name returning from the deep, a signifier with the power to put its listeners in a "strange stare." "O, it is monstrous, monstrous!" The sound of that name, which "did bass" King Alonzo's "trespass" is enough to prompt him to seek his son, whom he presumes has drowned, "deeper than e'er plummet sounded, / And with him there lie mudded" (3.3.95–102). Alonzo's response is dictated by the substitutive logic of guilt, a matter of putting himself in the place of the son who fills the place of the long-gone Prospero. But his line anticipates Prospero's own pronouncement at the close that he will "drown his book" "deeper than did ever plummet sound," as if the depths were associated with a signifying dimension that passes beyond characterological matters, the dimension from which the book derives and to which it returns (5.1.56–57).

Indeed, the waters are associated with a form of abandonment not so easily aligned with the stings of conscience. Ariel describes the sinking ship:

> Not a soul
> But felt a fever of the mad, and played
> Some tricks of desperation. All but mariners
> Plunged in the foaming brine and quit the vessel,
> Then all afire with me, the King's son, Ferdinand,
> With hair up-staring,—then like reeds, not hair—
> Was the first man that leapt, cried "Hell is empty,
> And all the devils are here."
>
> (1.2.208–15)

Why leap from a sinking ship? Ferdinand in particular embodies the mad fever of that exchange of certain death for certain death, perhaps because he will become the embodiment of mourning for the dead father, the primordial guilt that authorizes authority. That guilt is primordial, the passage suggests, because it comes before the death of the father—a mad legitimation. Such an act transpires outside the authorizing operations of time—after "all" had plunged "then" Ferdinand leapt, and yet he "was the first man that leapt"—and beyond the structuring terms of subjectivity: the passage elides the distinction between outward and inward (is it the ship or the boy that is "all afire"?); between human and inhuman (reed for hair); between sight and spectacle in the "up-staring" hair. The last phrase suggests the unstable source of a possessive terror that is nothing but the response it solicits.[46]

And the play famously evokes what draws one beneath the sea, a monster and an artificial man:

> Full fathom five thy father lies,
> Of his bones are coral made;
> Those are pearls that were his eyes;
> Nothing of him that doth fade,
> But doth suffer a sea-change
> Into something rich and strange.
> Sea-nymphs hourly ring his knell.
>   (1.2.397–403)

For Ferdinand, the inhumanness is curative. Left by the storm "sigh[ing]" "in an odd angle of the island," sitting with "his arms in this sad knot," Ferdinand is turned in on himself, bound up in the mourning guilt that attends the death of the father; Prospero knows calling him a usurper will hit its mark (1.2.223–24). Ariel's song unties that knot, letting him imaginatively move where he does and does not want to go—beneath the waves—even as it unbinds inwardness in the alien artifice of the scene it evokes. Whereas Miranda is gathered together ("be collected"), Ferdinand is dispersed, "Burthen dispersedly" the song's text says. Where those trajectories cross, the two join: such is the calculus of Prospero's social and psychic engineering.

And yet, the ditty is what holds us, not what we seek—"I have followed it, / Or it hath drawn me rather"—because it does not belong to a logic of compensatory exchange—outward for inward, dispersed for bound (1.2.394–95). Its alienness is already also within; its empty gaze holds because it figures one's own as it derives from elsewhere. The figure's inscribing effect remains a feature of personhood at all only by virtue of the aesthetic function that maintains the illusory relation between the recursive working of the gazing figure and the sheer material sounds of the song; that is also what assures that the drowned father is in any way distinguishable from the book that tells the tale.

Shakespeare's maritime suicides and sea creatures let us specify the status of the aesthetic in Hobbes. The aesthetic is what must be foreclosed to establish the encompassing fiction of the modern state—what the neutral state as the space of reason stakes itself against. And the aesthetic is what returns with a force directly proportionate to that exclusion, not dispersedly as in Shakespeare, as the medium within which subjectivities are sustained, but as the refused lining and support of sovereign force. Both in its partitioning and in its crystallizing effect, such a foreclosure anticipates the emergence of the aesthetic as a discrete and vexed category: no Kant without Hobbes. The shift in the placement of the aesthetic corresponds with a change in the disposition toward death, from death as what must be sustained as the condition of any rapport to what is conjured solely through the thin fiction of its banishment, as a legislated fear of death. Rather than a progressive inclusion of death within the expanded political field as biopower describes it, death is what is always at once far off and too close at hand in the modern state.[47]

Particularly given the redounding logic of the aesthetic, it makes sense to compare the dispensations I have described in terms of their symmetrical contradictions. On the one hand, the humanist play, by virtue of the aestheticization that should secure sovereignty, encounters at the deepest reaches of conscience an inhuman dimension that in some sense already anticipates the automaton of state: it is not hard to get from the dispersed and agentless voice of Prospero's island to the impersonal apparatus of state, a phantasm in its own right.[48] On the other hand, it is as if the pure, neutral mechanism of the state encounters at its political aesthetic foundation the binding force of just what Hobbes has pointedly excluded from his calculus, something like the reiterated death of the king and the compulsive hold of reverting conscience, a conscience exacerbated by the force of its foreclosure from the formalized world Hobbes constructs and the independent beings that inhabit it.[49] Prospero and the Artificial Man, both inside and outside the limits of their texts and worlds, might be read in that sense as the inverted images of one another, each revealing in the other what the other cannot by definition see in himself.

It is as if the works corresponded, and that "as if" must be retained; the persistence of the aesthetic both keeps this from being a legitimate history and problematizes historicization insofar as it conditions its possibility. The movement from Shakespeare to Hobbes can be read genealogically, as moments in a history of the aesthetic. At the same time, because it coincides with the politically freighted separation of the domains of reason and aesthetics we inhabit, Hobbes's recursive and ungrounded "as if" also articulates an unstable horizon structure. In relation to such a historical/ahistorical limit, the Shakespearean aesthetic amounts to a phantom formation—a forerunner and a residue—whose devouring exorbitance can never be purely separated out from a perturbation within our own post-Kantian division of the faculties that troubles the narratives by which we would determine its causes. The critical posture that supposes the absolute character of that horizon—assumes that it marks a clarified before and after of the aesthetic—remains within the terms of such a division even as it shores against the dimension of the early modern that disorders that universe.

Temporal perturbation does not in itself mean subversion. That point is evident enough in *The Tempest*, where theatrical momentousness dissolves into an elliptical forward and backward hearkening of correspondent voices all in the service of an encompassing aesthetic ideology. *The Leviathan* is no less untimely: historically speaking, all its Euclidian certainties are constructed around a revenant, as Hobbes knew. Rather than taking us outside the ambit of sovereign power, sovereignty draws its effects from just such recursive, causeless causes.

Does that mean there is no beyond to sovereignty? Only if sovereignty and the aesthetic are presumed to be equivalents, the aesthetic another name for sovereignty and vice versa. But they are not. Whatever disjunctures it implies, the recursive causeless cause of sovereignty is governed by a logic of temporalization. In that sense, sovereignty remains narratable. The aesthetic enables that minimal phenomenalization, a condition evident at the point where sight and inscription intersect: the superscript drawn across the frontispiece, the punctuating sound of a beating that leaves one in a "strange stare": those are the reference points of sovereignty. At the same time, precisely because it amounts to a sheerly posited instance, the aesthetic also exceeds phenomenalization, engaging a dimension that remains unavailable to temporalizing. Even as it conditions sovereignty, something of the incisive event of the aesthetic remains open to versions of freedom and community not governed in advance by the speculative thought of the autonomous commonwealth—a commonality, rather than sovereignty, without compare.

Notes

INTRODUCTION

1. The temporality of sexuality in the psychoanalytic context has been engaged most exactingly by Jean Laplanche. See especially "The Time of the Other" in *Essays on Otherness*, ed. John Fletcher (London: Routledge, 1999) and, with Jean-Bertrand Pontalis, "Fantasy and the Origins of Sexuality" in *International Journal of Psychoanalysis* 49 (1968): 4–12.

1. EARLY MODERN POLITICAL AESTHETICS

1. On the opposition between "embeddedness" and the "free-standing" artwork, see Stephen Greenblatt, *Shakespearean Negotiations: The Circulation of Social Energy in Renaissance England* (Berkeley: University of California Press, 1988), 95, 127. For summaries of the view, see Hugh Grady, *Shakespeare and Impure Aesthetics* (Cambridge: Cambridge University Press, 2009), 36–37; Louis Montrose, "The Poetics and Politics of Culture," in *The New Historicism*, ed. H. Aram Veeser (New York: Routledge, 1989), 15, 24; and H. Aram Veeser, introduction to *The New Historicism*, xiii.

2. See Thomas M. Greene, *The Light in Troy: Imitation and Discovery in Renaissance Poetry* (New Haven, CT: Yale University Press, 1982), 3.

3. Anthony Kemp, *The Estrangement of the Past: A Study in the Origins of Modern Historical Consciousness* (Oxford: Oxford University Press, 1990), 106.

4. Greene, *Light in Troy*, 8.

5. On "supercessive history," see Kemp, *Estrangement of the Past*, 108–10. Greene develops the idea of "historical solitude" in *Light in Troy*, 4–27.

6. Lisa Frienkel, *Reading Shakespeare's Will: The Theology of Figure from Augustine to the Sonnets* (New York: Columbia University Press, 2002), 73–80, 88–90.

7. Montrose, "Poetics and Politics of Culture," 20.

8. Ibid., 23.

9. Douglas Bruster, *Shakespeare and the Question of Culture: Early Modern Literature and the Cultural Turn* (Houndsmills, UK: Palgrave, 2003), 191–205. Subsequent references to Bruster will be cited in the text.

10. On the limit-positing structure of empiricism, see Jacques Derrida, *The Politics of Friendship*, trans. George Collins (London: Verso, 2006), 90, and *Rogues: Two Essays on Reason* (Stanford, CA: Stanford University Press, 2005), 128, 140.

11. See Julia Reinhard Lupton, *Afterlives of the Saints: Hagiography, Typology, and Renaissance Literature* (Stanford, CA: Stanford University Press, 1996), 8. For a subtle account of the relation between aesthetics and the historical operation of acculturation, see Marc Redfield, *The Politics of Aesthetics: Nationalism, Gender, Romanticism* (Stanford, CA: Stanford University Press, 2003), 12–16.

12. The relation between cultural analysis and aesthetics may come most strongly to view in a footnote at the end of Bruster's book. Having acknowledged that the work of cultural study will always be a composite matter, "the sum of various and multiple studies of that culture," he adds a note: "This totality, of course, will not be seamless but full of contradiction and conflict. Like the early modern culture such studies seek to revive and describe, the aggregate 'fantasy' of culture among these critical works generates contestations and may even operate dialectically in terms of them" (268). Whether it's a matter of "solo" pleasure, or the collective process through which a critical field posits a frame which at the same time governs it, the "fantasy" of culture seems hard to separate from the logic of aesthetic desire.

13. Michael McKeon, "Politics of Discourses and the Rise of the Aesthetic in Seventeenth Century England," in *Politics of Discourse: The Literature and History of Seventeenth Century England*, ed. Kevin Sharpe and Steven Zwicker (Berkeley: University of California Press, 1987), 49, and *The Origins of the English Novel, 1600–1740* (Baltimore, MD: Johns Hopkins University Press, 1987), 119–20.

14. McKeon, "Rise of the Aesthetic," 44.

15. Jürgen Habermas, *The Philosophical Discourse of Modernity*, trans. Fredrick Lawrence (Cambridge, MA: MIT Press, 1987), 10. On the aesthetic and autonomy, see Andrzej Warminski, "Introduction: Allegories of Reference," in Paul de Man, *Aesthetic Ideology*, ed. Warminski (Minneapolis: University of Minnesota Press, 1996), 21.

16. On the relation between the self-exceeding character of the aesthetic and its historicality, see Heidegger, "The Origin of the Work of

Art," in *Poetry, Language, Thought*, trans. Albert Hofstadter (London: Harper and Row, 1977), 72–78.

17. On the aesthetic and individualism, see Terry Eagleton, *The Ideology of the Aesthetic* (Oxford: Wiley-Blackwell, 1991), 9–15.

18. For a particularly rich account of the "untimely," metaleptic character of English material culture in early modernity, see Jonathan Gil Harris, *Untimely Matter in the Time of Shakespeare* (Philadelphia: University of Pennsylvania Press, 2009).

19. Ernst Cassirer, *The Individual and the Cosmos in Renaissance Philosophy* (London: Dover, 2011), 159, 91–92.

20. Paul A. Kottman, *A Politics of the Scene* (Stanford, CA: Stanford University Press, 2007), 200.

21. Robert Williams, *Art, Theory, and Culture in Sixteenth Century Italy: From Techne to Metatechne* (Cambridge: Cambridge University Press, 2011), 23, and *Art Theory: An Historical Introduction* (Oxford: Blackwell, 2004), 77.

22. Williams, *Art, Theory, and Culture*, 6. On Renaissance art and the dream of "cultural totality," see Clark Hulse, *The Rule of Art: Literature and Painting in the Renaissance* (Chicago: Chicago University Press, 1990), 19. Hugh Grady suggests the way Renaissance Platonism can be seen to anticipate Kantian aesthetics. "Aesthetics in the Renaissance" in *Cambridge Shakespeare Encyclopedia*, forthcoming in *The Cambridge Guide to the Worlds of Shakespeare*, ed. Bruce Smith (Cambridge: Cambridge University Press, 2015). I thank Professor Grady for sharing a manuscript copy of the entry.

23. Robert Matz, *Defending Literature in Early Modern England* (Cambridge: Cambridge University Press, 2000), 22, 52–53, 58–85.

24. See Jonathan Goldberg, *Writing Matter: From the Hands of the English Renaissance* (Stanford, CA: Stanford University Press, 1990), 45, and Matz, *Defending Literature*, 30–37.

25. "Tudor Aesthetics" in *The Cambridge Companion to English Literature, 1500–1600*, ed. Arthur F. Kinney (Cambridge: Cambridge University Press, 2000), 32.

26. *As You Like It*, *The Norton Shakespeare*, 2nd ed., ed. Greenblatt, Cohen, Howard, and Maus (New York and London: Norton, 2008). Subsequent references to Shakespeare's works will be to this edition and cited in the text.

27. The association of the circle of the stage with the conjurer's circle and of applause with the clap through which the magus brought the demonic event to a close was, since Marlowe, conventional.

28. Or, as Frienkel describes in *Shakespeare's Will* (203) the Shakespearean turn, the possibility of "a lie that lies like truth."

29. "But the poet . . . never affirmith; the poet never maketh any circles about your imagination, to conjure you to believe for true what he writes." *Sidney's "The Defence of Poesy" and Selected Renaissance Literary Criticism*, ed. Gavin Alexander (London: Penguin, 2004), 34.

30. Such an account of literature as reiterative inscription obviously complicates claims for literary "framing" as a form of social distantiation. See, for example, Hugh Grady, *Shakespeare and Impure Aesthetics* (Cambridge: Cambridge University Press, 2009), 29, and Victoria Kahn, "Political Theology and Liberal Culture: Strauss, Schmitt, Spinoza, and Arendt" in *Political Theology and Early Modernity*, ed. Graham Hammill and Julia Lupton (Chicago: University of Chicago Press, 2012), 41. On the aesthetic and the aporetic operation of framing, see Jacques Derrida, *The Truth in Painting*, trans. Geoffrey Bennington and Ian McLeod (Chicago: University of Chicago Press, 1987), 17–147, and Marc Redfield, *The Politics of Aesthetics: Nationalism, Gender, Romanticism* (Stanford, CA: Stanford University Press, 2003), 10.

31. On the undecidable character of Hymen's "if," see Malcolm Evans, *Signifying Nothing: Truth's True Contents in Shakespeare's Text* (Athens: University of Georgia Press, 1986), 152–58, and Robert H. Bell, *Shakespeare's Great Stage of Fools* (New York: Palgrave Macmillan, 2011), 72.

32. Jacques Lacan, *Ecrits: A Selection*, trans. Alan Sheridan (London: tavistock, 1977), 193. Lacan refers to Fechner's "eine andere Schauplatz."

33. On the *ex nihilo* character of Renaissance artistic production, see Lupton, *Afterlives of the Saints*, 67–69. On *ex nihilo* creation in relation to the constitution of the world without presupposition of anterior substance, see Jean-Luc Nancy, *The Creation of the World, or Globalization*, trans. François Raffoul and David Pettigrew (Albany: SUNY Press, 2007), 51–54.

34. Such a reading is borne out by the ornate, periodic and quite controlled rhetoric of Lear's speech in response to Cordelia's refusal of his demand for the display of love—"For, by the sacred radiance of the sun, / The mysteries of Hecate and the night, / By all the operation of the orbs"—and by the obscure, vastly overdetermined self-knowledge implied by his likening himself to the "barbarous Scythian" "that makes his generation/Messes" (1.1.109, 116–17; Norton conflated edition). That cannibalistic erosion of distinctions between self and other relates to the incestuous themes of the play, as well as to the vertiginous loss of boundary between the sovereign act and the space of the play itself. See Christopher Pye, *The Vanishing: Shakespeare, the Subject, and Early Modern Culture* (Durham, NC: Duke University Press, 2000), 95–96.

35. de Man, *Aesthetic Ideology*, 61–69. See also Warminski's introduction to the collection, 14. On inscription and the limit of the self-

referential, self-negational claims of the literary, see de Man, "Hypogram and Inscription," in *The Resistance to Theory* (Minneapolis: University of Minnesota Press, 1986), 39, 42–43.

36. See Redfield, *Politics of Aesthetics*, 24.

37. The difference can be understood in terms of Jean-Luc Nancy's account of the most radical dimensions of Kant's understanding of aesthetic judgment as world creation: "What is actually missing in the reflective judgment is not the concept of reality (universal) but the very existence of that reality as given" (*The Creation of the World*, 25).

38. John Parker similarly takes the play as emblematic in relation to the general equivalency between early modern English theater and commodification. *The Aesthetics of Antichrist: from Christian Drama to Christopher Marlowe* (Ithaca, NY: Cornell University Press, 2007), 242. For a particularly acute account of the relation between capitalization and the emergence of self-conscious literariness in the English Renaissance context, see Matz, *Defending Literature*, 6–16. For a broad equation of aesthetic autonomy and economic rationalism, see Arnold Hauser, *The Social History of Art*, vol. 2, *Renaissance, Mannerism, Baroque* (London: Routledge, 1999), 12; for the difference between aesthetic value and exchange value, see Michael McKeon, "The Origins of Aesthetic Value," *Telos*, no. 57 (September 1983): 80.

39. *The Tragical History of Doctor Faustus A-Text*, in *Doctor Faustus and Other Plays*, ed. David Bevington and Eric Rasmussen (Oxford: Oxford University Press, 1995). All references will be to this edition and cited parenthetically in the text.

40. *Faustus Myth: Religion and the Rise of Representation* (Gordansville, VA: Palgrave, 2007), 38, 21.

41. Ibid., 68.

42. Ibid., 68–71.

43. According to a Greek tradition, Helen herself was an "*eidolon*," a mere image (ibid., 71).

44. For the argument, see Catherine Belsey, *The Subject of Tragedy: Identity and Difference in Renaissance Drama* (London: Methuen, 1985), 42–46.

45. On the aesthetic as that which explicitly passes beyond the system of economic exchange, see Jacques Lacan, *The Seminar of Jacques Lacan, Book VII, The Ethics of Psychoanalysis 1959–1960,* trans. Dennis Porter (New York: Norton, 1992), 216–48.

46. My account of the play bears comparison with two supple readings that see in the work a reflection of deracinating commodification even while suggesting a subversive dimension of the aesthetic. For Richard Halpern, the literary in the play is ultimately related to a

"resistant power of negation" that promises a "blocked or denied sensuality" beyond economic commodification. "Marlowe's Theater of Night: *Doctor Faustus* and Capital," *ELH* 71, no. 8 (Summer 2004): 489. I'm placing the aesthetic at a prior point, in relation to the conditions for sensuous phenomenalization. Graham Hammill connects the play to the advent of a form of literariness and literary subjectivity associated with the infinite extension of commodification and exchange. *Sexuality and Form: Caravaggio, Marlowe, and Bacon* (Chicago: University of Chicago Press, 2002), 124–27. I align the play with the aesthetic as the beyond of economy as a speculative operation. In that sense, it differs as well from the argument that the aesthetic as autonomous sphere arises as an occlusion of the truth of material economic conditions. See the particularly shrewd accounts by Richard Wilson, *Shakespeare in French Theory: The King of Shadows* (London: Routledge, 2007), 138–39, and Richard Burt, *Licensed by Authority: Ben Jonson and the Discourses of Censorship* (Ithaca, NY: Cornell University Press, 1993), 84, 95–96.

Vis-à-vis commodification, my argument coincides with Adorno's, for whom the aesthetic bears on the antagonistic, nonidentical dimension of society not recuperated by the reified, "administered" world of capitalism, including its exchange structures. The difference arises around how that relation to social antagonism is conceived. For Adorno, for whom the aesthetic entails a kind of riven monadism, the relation between work and world is always veiled—aesthetic autonomy is "windowless." And yet, the work corresponds by virtue of what he refers to as its "internal mimesis," that is, the "proportion" between the "ratio" of the work's own irreconcilable divisions and the divisions of the world. Through that ratio, one experiences in the work the "primal shudders" of a prereified world. Theodor W. Adorno, *Aesthetic Theory*, ed. and trans. Robert Hullot-Kentor (Minneapolis: University of Minnesota, 1997), 7–13, 20–21. Such an account leaves open the question of the relation between the aesthetic and that internally mimetic function itself, the fact that the process by which division whether in the work or in the world assumes the form of a ratio, and thus become cognizable, is already an unstable aesthetic operation. Adorno's structure of correspondent division bears, I think, on the larger tension in his account between his sense of the aesthetic as definitionally illimitable—that one must reject art for the sake of art—and his analytical reliance on the aesthetic/"extra-aesthetic" distinction (53).

47. Greenblatt, *Shakespearean Negotiations*, 19–20.

48. Carlo Galli, *Political Spaces and Global War*, ed. Adam Sitze, trans. Elizabeth Fay (Minneapolis: University of Minnesota Press, 2010), 17–19.

49. Claude Lefort, "The Permanence of the Theological-Political," in *Democracy and Political Theory*, trans. David Macey (Minneapolis: University of Minnesota Press, 1988), 225.

50. Ibid., 232. On political "disincorporation" more broadly, see Claude Lefort, *The Political Forms of Modern Society: Bureaucracy, Democracy, Totalitarianism*, trans. David Thompson (Cambridge, MA: MIT Press, 1986), 303–6.

51. Claude Lefort, *Machiavelli in the Making,* trans. Michael Smith (Evanston, IL: Northwestern University Press, 2012), 140, 297–98. On power becoming "an immanent dimension of history" for early modern political thought, see Graham Hammill, *The Mosaic Constitution: Political Theology and Imagination from Marlowe to Milton* (Chicago: University of Chicago Press, 2012), 123–24.

52. Lefort, "Permanence of the Theological-Political," 223.

53. See Jacques Derrida, "What is Relevant Translation?," trans. Lawrence Venuti, *Critical Inquiry* 27, no. 2 (Winter 2001): 194–97, and Jacques Lezra, "The Instance of the Sovereign: The Primal Scenes of Political Theology," in *Political Theology and Early Modernity*, 204. Such a minimalistic account of the political-theological limit might be read in relation to a tension within critical engagements with that domain. Understanding political theology as *translatio* corresponds, for instance, with Graham Hammill's and Julia Lupton's description of the political theological as an "impasse" or "aporia" in political and religious dispensations. It resists the persistent conversion of that limit into a substantified category, the way, for instance, in Eric Santner's analysis of the returning residue of archaic sovereignty within modern political formations that remainder becomes a "fleshly substance," the "spectral yet visceral" remainder of nonsymbolizable carnal being (47, 81). If the " 'flesh' " of sovereignty needs to remain in scare quotes, where Santner is careful to place it, that's because such a limit cannot be understood in cognizable terms, including as the "real stuff" of fantasy (81). It nevertheless persists as the horizon of symbolization because it's located at the contradictory limits of tropic phenomenalization, in other words, the point where, I would argue, political theology becomes inextricable from political aesthetics. See Hammill and Lupton, introduction to *Political Theology and Early Modernity* (Chicago: University of Chicago Press, 2012), 5, and Eric L. Santner, *The Royal Remains: The People's Two Bodies and the Endgames of Sovereignty* (Chicago: University of Chicago Press, 2011).

54. In this, I echo Graham Hammill's call for modes of analysis that "reconceive the social and its relation to history through the aesthetic" (*Sexuality and Form*, 2, 85). On the inhuman dimension of the aesthetic,

see Heidegger, "The Origin of the Work of Art," 67–72; on aesthetic and techne, see Derrida, *The Truth in Painting*, 20–22.

55. Lefort, *Machiavelli*, 216. On "becoming original by imitation," see also Leonard Barkan, *Unearthing the Past: Archaeology and Aesthetics in the Making of Renaissance Culture* (New Haven, CT: Yale University Press, 1999), 287–88. Heidegger provides the classic articulation of the constitutive dimension of the artwork, its relation to the possibility of conceiving the createdness of the world immanently. See "The Origin of the Work of Art," 60–66, and J. M. Bernstein, *The Fate of Art: Aesthetic Alienation from Kant to Derrida and Adorno* (University Park: Penn State Press, 1992), 123.

56. Claude Lefort, "The Death of Immortality?" in *Democracy and Political Theory*, trans. David Macey (Minneapolis: University of Minnesota Press, 1988), 270–71.

57. Ibid., 273. The work, in that sense, amounts to an event without "existence" or being, as what is always past or still to come—an event as such; rather than being a paradox, the association between aesthetics and event is of a piece with the aesthetic's inassimilability to the universalizing structures of cognition. As Adorno writes in *Aesthetic Theory* (176), "Artworks are such only *in actu* because their tension does not terminate in pure identity." On the historicity and dialectic of the image, see Samuel Weber's analysis of Benjamin in *Benjamin's -abilities* (Cambridge, MA: Harvard University Press, 2008), 34. As event, the work exposes its relation to history in a form congruent with Machiavelli's radical conception of *virtù*, not as a destined act, nor as a merely contingent act, but as the act that opens the very distinction between necessity and chance, and thus opens the temporality within which it is at the same time inscribed. See Miguel E. Vatter, *Between Form and Event: Machiavelli's Theory of Political Freedom* (Dordrecht: Kluwer, 2000), 8, and Antonio Negri, *Insurgencies: Constituent Power and the Modern State*, trans. Maurizia Boscagli (Minneapolis: University of Minnesota Press, 2009), 39–41. For a superb account of this ambiguity as inherent in the notion of contingency understood as what is at once aleatory and dependent, see Jacques Lezra, *Wild Materialism: The Ethic of Terror and the Modern Republic* (New York: Fordham University Press, 2010), 168–70. On the event-character of aestheticization, see Marc Redfield, "Derrida, Europe, Today," in *Late Derrida*, ed. Ian Balfour, *South Atlantic Quarterly* 106, no. 2 (Spring 2007): 379, 384, and Nancy, *Creation of the World*, 54. On the aesthetic as an *ek-stasis*, a being outside time, that also opens historical consciousness, see Giorgio Agamben, *The Man Without Content*, trans. Georgia Albert (Stanford, CA: Stanford University Press, 1999), 99–100.

58. Ernst Kantorowicz, *The King's Two Bodies: A Study in Medieval Political Theology* (Princeton, NJ: Princeton University Press, 1997), 191, 445, and Lefort, "Death of Immorality," 271.

59. On absolutism as the model for emerging conceptions of individual liberty, see Richard Helgerson, *Adulterous Alliances: Home, State, and History in Early Modern European Drama and Painting* (Chicago: University of Chicago Press, 2003), 10.

60. On legislative power as the newfound dimension of sovereignty in Bodin, see Perry Anderson, *Lineages of the Absolute State* (London: Verso, 1974), 50.

61. On Bodin and the absolutist sovereign state as self-originating, see Negri, *Insurgencies*, 98. See also Franco Moretti, *Signs Taken for Wonders* (London: Verso, 1988), 45.

62. On divisible sovereignty as consubstantial with its explication, and thus radically historical, see Lezra, *Wild Materialism*, 85–7.

63. See Claude Lefort, *Machiavelli in the Making,* trans. Michael Smith (Evanston, IL: Northwestern University Press, 2012), 121. Subsequently cited in the text.

64. Carl Schmitt, *Political Theology: Four Chapters on the Concept of Sovereignty*, trans. George Schwab (Chicago: University of Chicago Press, 2006), 1, 12–14.

65. Giorgio Agamben, *Homo Sacer: Sovereign Power and Bare Life*, trans. Daniel Heller-Roazen (Stanford, CA: Stanford University Press, 1998), 7–11. Subsequently cited in the text.

66. Samuel Weber, *Benjamin's -abilities*, 198.

67. Bruno Gulli, "The Ontology and Politics of Exception," in *Giorgio Agamben: Sovereignty and Life*, ed. Matthew Calcarco and Steven DeCaroli (Stanford, CA: Stanford University Press, 2007), 235. On sovereignty as what subtracts itself from itself, see Giorgio Agamben, *The Kingdom and the Glory: For a Theological Genealogy of Economy and Government*, ed. Chiesa and Mandarini (Stanford, CA: Stanford University Press, 2011), 99, and Derrida, *The Beast and the Sovereign*, vol. 1, trans. Geoffrey Bennington (Chicago: University of Chicago Press, 2009), 49.

68. On the exception exempting itself, see Nancy, *Creation*, 109. For a superb account of the self-referential character of the *Grundnorm*, see Julia Reinhard Lupton, "Invitation to a Totem Meal: Hans Kelsen, Carl Schmitt, and Political Theology," in *The Return of Theory in Early Modern Studies*, ed. Cefalu and Reynolds (Houndsmills, Basingtone, Hampshire: Palgrave, 2011), 128.

69. For a critique of the ontologizing strain in Agamben, see Adam Thurschwell, "Cutting the Branches for Akiba: Agamben's Critique of

Derrida," in *Politics, Metaphysics, and Death: Essays on Giorgio Agamben's Homo Sacer*, ed. Andrew Norris (Durham, NC: Duke University Press, 2005), 191n8.

70. This is a characteristic turn for Agamben. Note in his more recent analysis of political theology and governmentality in *Kingdom and the Glory* the way the indeterminable "threshold of economy and immanence" that generates the political becomes what is "captur[ed] *by* the mechanism" of the political (251; my italics).

71. Sovereignty is that "infinite institution that nevertheless includes within it the imperious necessity of the finite moment of its institution." Nancy, *Creation*, 100. For an important account of the indeterminable temporal/historical status of the sovereign focused on the problem of how one reads his indivisibility, see Jacques Lezra, *Wild Materialism*, 66–72.

This may be the right moment to indicate the commonalities and points of difference between the current project and Jacques Rancière's analysis of political aesthetics. For Rancière, the transformative potential of the aesthetic work is a function of its continuity with the entire field of the sensible, its capacity to effect a distribution—or redistribution—of that field. The aesthetic and the political are indissociable for Rancière insofar as both operate not normatively but according to the logic of the universal singular, the irreducible exception that disrupts and constitutes the aesthetic and the political fields alike. *The Politics of Aesthetics: The Distribution of the Sensible*, trans. Gabriel Rockhill (New York: Continuum, 2004), 17, 23, 52, 63–64. The potential for a reordering of the sensory dimension derives from the aesthetic's suspension of ideological aim, of causality as such—Kantian purposeless purposiveness unreclaimed for any universal form; with that comes the potential for a disruption of the "way in which bodies fit their functions and destinies." *The Emancipated Spectator*, trans. Gregory Elliott (London: Verso, 2011), 63–64, 72.

My point of difference concerns Rancière's central claim that the aesthetic should be conceived precisely as a "distribution of the sensible," a phrase that implies a domain of the sensible in advance of its aestheticization. Rancière's argument for the suspension of ideological purposiveness is vitiated by the predicative assumptions underlying a "distribution *of* the sensible." Following de Man, I have argued that the historicity of the aesthetic can only be understood in terms of the mechanism of phenomenalization as such, the process through which the sensible is made sensible. To put this another way, the problem of the aesthetic is the fact that the sensible cannot be separated from its distribution, that is, its framing; it is that fact that makes the aesthetic an unstable operation, and its politics an effect of that instability.

2. LEONARDO'S HAND: MIMESIS, SEXUALITY, AND THE POLIS

1. Roger J. Crum and John T. Paoletti, eds. *Renaissance Florence: A Social History* (Cambridge: Cambridge University Press, 2006), 13.

2. See, for instance, Rebecca Zorach's introduction to *Renaissance Theory*, which concludes with the assertion that autonomy is a "modern fetish." *Renaissance Theory*, ed. James Elkins and Robert Williams (New York: Routledge, 2008), 27. For accounts that do, nevertheless, emphasize an incipient privileging of autonomy in Florentine arts and letters, see Catherine Soussloff, *The Absolute Artist: The Historiography of a Concept* (Minneapolis: University of Minnesota Press, 1997), 44–57; Anthony Blunt, *Artistic Theory in Italy, 1450–1600* (Oxford: Oxford University Press, 1963); and Alfonso Procaccini, "Alberti and the 'Framing' of Perspective," *The Journal of Aesthetics and Art Criticism* 40, no. 1 (Autumn 1981): 35–37. On autochthony in the German Renaissance context, especially in relation to Dürer's project of self-portraiture, see Joseph Leo Koerner, *The Moment of Self-Portraiture in German Renaissance Art* (Chicago: University of Chicago Press, 1993), 80–126. On the valorization of artistic authorship with the later emergence of connoisseurship, see Karen-edis Barzman, *The Florentine Academy and the Early Modern State: The Discipline of "Disegno"* (Cambridge: Cambridge University Press, 2000), 179.

3. In the field of art history, Arnold Hauser most notably forwards such claims in relation to the Renaissance emergence of the category of artistic genius; see *The Social History of Art*, vol. 2, *Renaissance, Mannerism, Baroque* (London: Routledge, 1999), 65–66. More broadly, New Historicism's "rediscovery" of history staked itself explicitly against what it took to be a totalizing, hermetic, and historically inaccurate aestheticization, a point it bears out at the level of claims and in the detouring, fragmentary form of its anecdotal method (a form that nevertheless has its own aesthetic).

4. See Sylvia Ferino Pagden, "From Cult Images to the Cult of Images: The Case of Raphael's Altarpieces," in *The Altarpiece in the Renaissance*, ed. Peter Humphrey and Martin Kemp (Cambridge: Cambridge University Press, 1991), and Stephen J. Cambell, "Vasari's Renaissance and Its Renaissance Alternatives," in *Renaissance Theory*, 61–63.

5. Robert Williams, "Italian Renaissance Art and the Systematicity of Representation," *Rinascimento* 43 (2004): 327.

6. Alexander Nagel, "Leonardo and Sfumato," *Res: Anthropology and Aesthetics* 24 (Autumn 1993): 20.

7. Stephen Cambell explicitly argues in "Vasari's Renaissance" (63) that the systematicity of art gives the lie to conceptions of the autonomous work.

8. Williams, "Systematicity," 320.

9. Ibid., 323.

10. Claire Farago, "The Concept of the Renaissance Today: What is at Stake," in *Renaissance Theory*, 78. Alexander Nagel and Christopher S. Wood understand the substitutive relation of images and the originative, authorial impulse to be competing functions during the era, though ultimately suggest that the work as anachronic form may be the space in which that opposition is suspended. *Anachronic Renaissance* (New York: Zone Books, 2010), 16–17, 18. Located in the interval between medieval figural syncretism and a fully developed authorial ideology, the Renaissance work engages origins at the *ex nihilo* limits of the substitutive operation itself, I argue.

11. On the problematic severing from natural grounds implied by the systematicity of art, see Williams, "Systematicity," 321. The absolute character of this aesthetic caesura and the problems of reference it entails distinguish the argument I offer here from Julia Lupton's superb analysis of the *ex nihilo* theological grounds of Renaissance secular literature; see *Afterlives of the Saints: Hagiography, Typology, and Renaissance Literature* (Stanford, CA: Stanford University Press, 1996), 69–70. With a focus on the era of the icon, Georges Didi-Huberman argues that the incarnation amounts to a rent in classical *imitatio*, as well as an opening in flesh and world, that will be suppressed by the speculative logic of humanist, and especially Vasarian, dialectical history. *Confronting Images: Questioning the End of a Certain History of Art*, trans. John Goodman (University Park: Penn State Press, 2009), 186, 217. I will argue that the incarnation is the topos in which the Renaissance image engages its novel historicity most radically, in relation to the breach that opens mimesis.

12. On the relation between incarnationalist thought and the rise of naturalism in the visual arts, see David Summers, *The Judgment of Sense: Renaissance Naturalism and the Rise of Aesthetics* (Cambridge: Cambridge University Press, 1987), 311–13, and Gerhart B. Ladner, *Ad Imaginem Dei: The Image of Man in Medieval Art* (Latrobe, PA: Archabbey Press, 1965).

13. Walter Benjamin, "The Work of Art in the Age of Mechanical Reproduction," in *Illuminations: Essays and Reflections*, ed. Hannah Arendt (New York: Schocken Press, 1969), 222–26. I owe the latter formulation to Graham Hammill.

14. The decisive break between the Byzantine and Renaissance image arises from that distinction between solicited response and constitutive representational effect; however self-consciously it is oriented around the determining character of the viewer's response, the Byzantine "image" conceives itself on a continuum with the things of the world.

For an argument for the continuity between the traditions, see Claire Farago, "Aesthetics before Art: Leonardo through the Looking Glass," in *Compelling Visuality: The Work of Art In and Out of History*, ed. Claire Farago and Robert Zwijnenberg (Minneapolis: University of Minnesota Press, 2003), 45–47, 66–67.

15. See, for example, Stephen Greenblatt, *Shakespearean Negotiations: The Circulation of Social Energy in Renaissance England* (Berkeley: University of California Press, 1988), 95, 127.

16. On society's fiction of self-immanence—the illusion that it can assume objectifiable and self-founding form—see Claude Lefort, *Democracy and Political Theory*, trans. David Macey (Minneapolis: University of Minnesota Press, 1988), 232–33.

17. On the Renaissance artwork's ability to put into question cultural materialist accounts of art's historical status, see Nagel and Wood, *Anachronic Renaissance*, 17–18.

18. Sigmund Freud, *Leonardo da Vinci: A Study in Psychosexuality*, trans. A. A. Brill (New York: Moffat, 1947); André Green, *Révélations de l'inachèvement: A propos du cartoon de Londres de Léonard de Vinci* (Paris: Flammarion, 1992).

19. See Bradley Collins, *Leonardo, Psychoanalysis, and Art History* (Chicago: Northwestern University Press, 1997), 56.

20. For a compelling discussion of the relation between Leonardo's hand and his musical theory, see Lea Dovev, "The Musical Hand in Leonardo da Vinci's Anatomical Drawings," *Reinsprung 11: Zeitschrift für Bildkritik* (2012): 20–33.

21. Collins notes that the maternal figures in Leonardo's St. Anne images "must struggle to accept with a smile a beloved son's suffering and death" (*Leonardo*, 171). That contemporaries read the dynamic of these scenes of Virgin and Christ child as prefigurations of the Passion is evident from Pietro da Novellara's analysis of the Louvre version of the *Virgin and Child with St. Anne* and Leonardo's "Yarnwinder" Madonna. *Leonardo dopo Milano: La Madonna dei fusi*, ed. A. Vezossi (Florence, 1982), 27–28, 60–61n44.

22. As I will show, *designo* ranges in the thought of the era from elevated Platonic form to the contentless, autonomous movement of the hand; both senses—the totalizing and the sheerly inscriptive—are in play here.

23. Understood in these self-compassing terms, Leonardo's image anticipates the elevation of *designo* during the sixteenth century to a constructed form that subsumes, not just all inward and outward reality, but also the act that conceives it—consider Frederico Zuccaro's claim "that his very ability to explain what *disegno* is comes to him from

disegno itself" in Robert Williams, *Art, Theory, and Culture,* 20. On the problematic of the hand's self-representation in relation to portraiture, see Koerner, *Moment of Self-Portraiture,* 140.

24. On the recursive, self-sustaining character of the Renaissance work, see Nagel and Wood, *Anachronic Renaissance,* 17.

25. Pietro Marani, *Leonardo da Vinci: The Complete Paintings* (New York, 2000), 261.

26. On *invenzione* as discovery and the lack of tension between imitation, the laws of nature, and artistic originality, see Martin Kemp, "From 'Mimesis' to 'Fantasia': The Quattrocento Vocabulary of Creation, Inspiration, and Genius in the Visual Arts," *Viator: Medieval and Renaissance Studies* 8 (1977): 348–52. On the Renaissance work occupying a "unique median status between originality and imitation," see Leonard Barkan, *Unearthing the Past: Archaeology and Aesthetics in the Making of Renaissance Culture* (New Haven, CT: Yale University Press, 1999), 302.

27. Barkan notes the connection between the groundlessness of the exhumed fragment and the process through which art came to be conceived as art in the era. *Unearthing,* xxxii. On Aby Warburg's account of the retroactively posited character of classicism, see Lupton, *Afterlives of the Saints,* 22.

28. See John Shearman, *Only Connect: Art and the Spectator in the Italian Renaissance* (Princeton, NJ: Princeton University Press, 1992), 1058.

29. Martin Kemp, *Leonardo da Vinci: The Marvelous Works of Nature and Man* (Cambridge, MA: Harvard University Press, 1981), 341–42.

30. For an evocative analysis of the lost and found character of the image within the structuring trajectories of art history, see Michael Ann Holly, "Mourning and Method," in *Compelling Visuality,* 157–59. The Baptist's role as "pointer"—what Luther will term "the Indicator of Christ"—is evident in images such as the Isenheim Altarpiece. With the Reformation, and the privileging of word and faith, that deictic function will become strongly aligned with John's purely signifying role as the one who points beyond himself. See Joseph Koerner, *The Reformation of the Image* (Chicago: University of Chicago Press, 2004), 191–200. On *sfumato* as a means to create an effect of "autonomous creation," see Alexander Nagel, "Leonardo and *Sfumato,*" *RES* 24 (Autumn 1993): 18. On the transubstantial character of the image, see Gabriele Paleotti, *Discorso intorno alle imagini sacre e profane* (1582) in *Trattati d'arte del cinquecento,* ed. P. Barocchi (Bari: G. Laterza, 1960), 3:134. On Renaissance naturalism and incarnationalism, see Summers, *Judgment of Sense,* 311–13, and G. B. Ladner, *Ad Imaginem Dei.*

31. On the image's relation to narcissistic satisfaction, see Collins, *Leonardo,* 16. On painting as the art of Narcissus, see Leon Battista Alberti, *On Painting,* trans. John R. Spencer (New Haven, CT: Yale University Press, 1966), 68.

32. On the Baptist's role as mediator between law and grace, see Hans Belting, *Likeness and Presence: A History of the Image before the Era of Art,* trans. Edmund Jephcott (Chicago: University of Chicago Press, 1994), 468.

33. Zwijnenberg, *The Writings and Drawings of Leonardo da Vinci: Order and Chaos in Early Modern Thought,* trans. Caroline van Eck (Cambridge: Cambridge University Press, 1999), 79.

34. Ibid., 36. See also Cicero, *De natura deorum,* ed. A. S. Pease (Cambridge, MA: Harvard University Press, 1979), 2:147–53. On Cicero on the hand, see Summers, *The Judgment of Sense,* 243.

35. Leonardo da Vinci, *The Literary Works of Leonardo da Vinci,* 2 vols., ed. Carlo Pedretti (Berkeley: University of California Press, 1977), 1:259.

36. Giorgio Agamben, *The Man without Content,* trans. Georgia Albert (Stanford, CA: Stanford University Press, 1999), 60–61; Zwijnenberg, *The Writings and Drawings,* 29–30. On the increasing reputation of *techne,* see Summers, *Judgment of Sense,* 263–64, and Paolo Rossi, *Philosophy, Technology, and the Arts in the Early Modern Era,* trans. Salvator Attanasio (New York: Harper and Row, 1970), 29–30.

37. On Renaissance mimesis as the correspondence between *poesis,* the act of making, and *aisthesis,* the experiencing of the work, see Jacques Rancière, *The Emancipated Spectator,* trans. Gregory Elliott (London and New York: Verso, 2011), 60–61.

38. On the mathematical principle as the *a priori* ground of empirical reality and mind, see Ernst Cassirer, *The Individual and the Cosmos in Renaissance Philosophy* (New York: Dover, 2000), 164–65. On *ars productio,* see Kemp, "From Mimesis to Fantasia," 381, and Zwijnenberg, *The Writings and Drawings,* 33.

39. See Alberti, *On Painting,* 26, 78.

40. See Shearman, *Only Connect,* 192, 239.

41. Hubert Damisch, *The Origin of Perspective,* trans. John Goodman (Cambridge MA: MIT Press, 1994), 49; Graham Hammill, *Sexuality and Form: Caravaggio, Marlowe, and Bacon* (Chicago: University of Chicago Press, 2002), 36. On the relation between perspective construction and the autonomous, self-referential work, see Procaccini, "Alberti and the 'Framing' of Perspective," 35–37.

42. On the *Madonna of the Rocks,* see Kemp, *Marvelous Works,* 281. On the drawing project, see Zwijnenberg, *Writings and Drawings,* 173.

43. On the detached and thus transcendent dimension of the pointing hand in *The Last Supper*, see Leo Steinberg, *Leonardo's Incessant Last Supper* (New York: Zone Books, 2001), 68, 71. Koerner in *Moment of Self-Portraiture* (176) speaks of a similar impulse on Dürer's part to grant a "sacramental aura" to the artist's indicating hand.

44. On the *per se facta* icon, see Belting, *Likeness and Presence*, 314. Koerner, in *Moment of Self-Portraiture* (80–98), connects the image not made with human hands—the *acheiropoetoi*—with Dürer's totalizing conception of self-portraiture.

45. On the continuity between the medieval devotional work and world, see James Trilling, "The Image Not Made by Hands and the Byzantine Way of Seeing," in *The Holy Face and the Paradox of Representation*, ed. Herbert Kessler and Gerhard Wolf (Rome: Nuova Alfa, 1998), 118–26. See also Agamben, *Man without Content*, 34.

46. Belting, *Likeness*, 427–30; Koerner, *Moment of Self-Portraiture*, 81.

47. On the conception of supersessive history, see Claude Lefort, *The Political Forms of Modern Society*, ed. John B. Thompson (Cambridge, MA: MIT Press, 1986), 222, and Anthony Kemp, *The Estrangement of the Past: A Study in the Origins of Modern Historical Consciousness* (Oxford: Oxford University Press, 1990), 120.

48. Richard Trexler, *Public Life in Renaissance Florence* (Ithaca, NY: Cornell University Press, 1980), 267.

49. See Roger Crum and David Wilkins, "In the Defense of Florentine Republicanism: Saint Anne and Florentine Art, 1343–1575," in *Interpreting Cultural Symbols: St. Anne in Late Medieval Society*, ed. Kathleen Ashley and Pamela Sheingorn (Athens, GA: University of Georgia Press, 1990), 149–50.

50. Giorgio Vasari, *The Lives of the Artists*, trans. Julia Conaway Bondanella and Peter Bondanella (Oxford: Oxford University Press, 1991), 293. Translation modified. See Vasari, *Vite de' più eccellenti pittori, scultore e architetti* (Milan: Società Tipografica de Classic Italiani, 1809), 7:58–59.

51. C. Ripa, *Iconologia; overo descrittione di diverse imagini cavate dall'antichita, e di propria inventione*, ed. E. Mandowsky (Rome, 1603, repr. Hildesheim, 1970), 305.

52. *Painting and Experience in Fifteenth Century Italy* (Oxford: Oxford University Press, 1988), 1.

53. Trexler, *Public Life*, 21, 112, 89, 119.

54. Ibid., 92.

55. Ibid., 98.

56. In a wide-ranging study, Rebecca Zorach associates the prevalent structuring motif of the triangle in Italian Renaissance art with the

relational interval of viewership, and thus associates it with a mode of analysis that reorients the subject-object focus of art historical analysis toward a mode cognizant of the inherently social and relational character of the art of the period. *The Passionate Triangle* (Chicago: University of Chicago Press, 2011), 18–23, 129, 146–48.

57. Trexler, *Public Life*, 99.

58. Aldo Mazzacane, "Law and Jurists in the Formation of the Modern State in Italy," in *The Origins of State in Italy 1300–1600*, ed. Julius Kirshner (Chicago: University of Chicago Press, 1995), 67.

59. Giorgio Chittolini, "The 'Private,' the 'Public,' the State," in *Origins of the State*, 36, 37.

60. Ibid., 34.

61. Piero Schiera, "Legitimacy, Discipline, and Institutions: Three Necessary Conditions for the Birth of the Modern State," in *Origins of the State*, 27, 26. The language of "grafting" reappears in accounts of the emergence of the autonomous state; see Manlio Bellomo, "Poteri dei gruppi e gruppi al potere del medioevo agli inizi dell'età moderna," in *Potero, poteri emerggenti e loro vicissitudini nell'esperienza giuridica italiana*, ed. G. Piva (Padua, 1986), 90. Cited in Chittolini, " 'Private,' " 53.

62. Chittolini, " 'Private,' " 52.

63. Schieri, "Legitimacy," 25.

64. For both sides of this condition, see Louis Althusser, *Machiavelli and Us*, trans. Gregory Elliott (London: Verso, 1999), 57, 73, 80.

65. Victoria Kahn, *Machiavellian Rhetoric* (Princeton, NJ: Princeton University Press, 1994), 53, 27.

66. The rhetorical character of Machiavelli's thought follows from that contingent, deontologized conception of the act. For Machiavelli, the affiliation between rhetoric and the political extends beyond an instrumental notion of language's powers to achieve ends. For, as Kahn points out in *Machiavellian Rhetoric* (39, 25), the very notion that ends justify the means is itself a rhetorical conceit, a belief of the populace and therefore available to (rhetorical) manipulation. Neither normative nor technical/instrumental, functioning without reference to a ground beyond its own effects, political rhetoric becomes fully performative, and representation inseparable from force. On *virtù* constituting the structure of its own legitimacy, see J. G. A. Pocock, *The Machiavellian Moment: Florentine Political Thought and the Atlantic Republican Tradition* (Princeton, NJ: Princeton University Press, 2003), 194.

67. Leonardo da Vinci, *The Notebooks of Leonardo da Vinci*, 2 vols., trans. E. MacCurdy (London: Reprint Society, 1954), 1:116.

68. On the Renaissance trope of art as idealizing supplement to nature, see Harry Berger, Jr., "Second World Prosthetics: Supplying

Deficiencies of Nature in Renaissance Italy," in *Early Modern Visual Culture*, ed. Peter Erickson and Clark Hulse (Philadelphia: University of Pennsylvania Press, 2000).

69. Although I'm considering an earlier historical moment and addressing the problem at the level of representation, my account of the relation between aesthetics and polis is not inconsistent with Barzman's Foucauldian analysis of the disciplinary, subject-forming function of *disegno vis-à-vis* the state. See Barzman, *The Florentine Academy and the Early Modern State*, 8–10, 189.

70. On the sketch, see Carlo Pedretti, "The Angel in the Flesh," *Achademia Leonardi Vinci: Journal of Leonardo Studies* 4 (1991): 34–51, and Daniel Arasse, *Leonardo da Vinci: the Rhythm of the World*, trans. Rosetta Translations (New York: Konecy and Konecky, 1998), 469–70.

71. On the aesthetic domain, see Leonard Barkan, *Transuming Passion: Ganymede and the Erotics of Humanism* (Stanford, CA: Stanford University Press, 1991); on the civic domain, Trexler, *Public Life*, 278.

72. *The Childhood of Art: An Interpretation of Freud's Aesthetic*, trans. W. Woodhull (New York: Columbia University Press, 1988), 78–80.

73. Green, *Révélations*, 58.

74. Jean-Luc Nancy contrasts what he terms the sacredness of the aesthetic image—its fundamental separation—with the forms of sacrificial logic underwriting religion's claims to a bond with such a beyond. *The Ground of the Image* (New York: Fordham University Press, 2005), 1–3. On the "obscene enjoyment at the heart of law" and its relation to the limit point of the dialectic of symbolic and imaginary that underpins social meaning, see Julia Reinhard Lupton, *Afterlives of the Saints: Hagiography, Typology, and Renaissance Literature* (Stanford, CA: Stanford University Press, 1996), 48–51, and Slavoj Žižek, "Neighbors and Other Monsters," in *The Neighbor: Three Inquiries in Political Theology*, ed. Žižek, Eric L. Santner, and Kenneth Reinhard (Chicago: University of Chicago Press, 2006), 150–59. On the relation between the aesthetic and the death drive, see Jacques Lacan, *Ethics*, 248–50, 295–97.

75. On this visual structure, see Christopher Pye, *The Vanishing: Shakespeare, the Subject, and Early Modern Culture* (Durham, NC: Duke University Press, 2000), 68–86. The symbolic dimensions of the perspectival structure is a vast topic—see especially Erwin Panofsky, *Perspective as Symbolic Form*, trans. Christopher Wood (New York: Zone Books, 1996) and Damisch, *Origin of Perspective*. My focus here is limited to the intersection of language and sight in the construction of the Annunciation image. Contrast my emphasis on chiasmic articulation with Daniel Arasse's reading of such images, which emphasizes the way in which the lateral, verbal/enunciatory structure parallels the perspectival insofar as

both block an absorptive relation to the scene of the unrepresentable sacred event. "Annonciation/énonciation," *VS, Quaderni di studi semiotici* 37 (January–April 1984): 6–17.

76. Louis Marin analyzes these reiterative forms in Leonardo's work in terms of the oscillating movement between near and far view through which the pictorial work at once broaches and accommodates its descriptive and mimetic limits. *On Representation*, trans. Catherine Porter (Stanford, CA: Stanford University Press, 2001), 267–68.

77. Jean-Luc Nancy speaks of the double movement through which the image at once separates itself from a ground thus constituting that ground as ground—as insensible substrate conjured in its withdrawal—and cuts itself out of that ground, thus constituting itself as image. "The Image—the Distinct" in *Ground of the Image*, 7, 13.

78. Stephen J. Milner, "The Florentine *Piazza Della Signoria* as Practical Place," in *Renaissance Florence*, 90, 94. The Piazza was also a self-consciously aesthetic space. Cosimo di Medici undertook a concerted project of multiplying the sculptural figures, often systematically decontextualizing them from their original placements, all in the name of claiming for the state a new status as pure aesthetic form. See Marvin Trachtenberg, *Dominion of the Eye: Urbanism, Art, and Power in Early Modern Florence* (Cambridge: Cambridge University Press, 1997), 276–77.

79. Shearman, *Only Connect*, 47–48, 55–57.

80. The epitaph in its entirety reads in Latin:

Me veram pictor divinus mente receipt,
Admota est operi deinde perita manus.
Dumque opere in facto defigit lumina pictor,
Intentus nimium, palluit et moritur.
Viva igitur sum mors, non mortua mortis imago,
Si fungor quo mors fungitur officio.

Giorgio Vasari, *Lives of the Most Eminent Painters, Sculptors and Architects*, ed. E. H. and E. W. Blashfield and Hopkins (London: Bell, 1897), 2:314. On the significance of the motif of the speaking epigraph for Renaissance visual artists, see Nagel and Wood, *Anachronic Renaissance*, 125–26.

81. Latini, *La rettorica*, ed. Francesco Maggini (Florence: Le Monnier, 1968), 13.

82. Vasari, *Ragionamenti sopra le invenzioni da lui dipente*, ed. Carlo Ragghianti (Milan: 1949), 16–17. Cited in John Najemy, "Florentine Politics and Urban Spaces," in *Renaissance Florence: A Social History*, 52–53.

83. On that conception of the internal and alien entity—what he terms the "extimate" form—see Jacques Lacan, *The Seminar of Jacques Lacan, Book VII: The Ethics of Psychoanalysis 1959–1960*, trans. Dennis Porter (New York: Norton, 1992), 139.

84. Martin Heidegger, *Introduction to Metaphysics*, trans. Gregory Fried and Richard Polt (New Haven, CT: Yale University Press, 2000), 152.

85. On the self-consuming character of the Florentine Republic, see Pocock, *Machiavellian Moment*, 217. On its precocity, see Lupton, *Afterlives*, 35. That relation between aesthetics and the thanatotic aspect of the state may be evident in Leonardo's most explicitly political image, the (lost) mural of *The Battle of Anghiari* created for the council hall of the Florentine Republic. The mural's tautly spiraled, self-compassing form makes martial agonism indistinguishable from self-mutilating violence—note the mirroring swordsmen and the illusion that the standard bearer is run through by his own staff.

3. SHAKESPEARE DISTRACTED: POLITICAL AESTHETICS FROM *SPANISH TRAGEDY* TO *HAMLET*

1. Stephen Greenblatt, "Psychoanalysis and Renaissance Culture," in *Literary Theory/Renaissance Texts*, ed. Patricia Parker and David Quint (Baltimore, MD, and London: Johns Hopkins University Press, 1986), 223.

2. Ibid., 218.

3. Ibid., 217.

4. See Adam Sitze, introduction to Carlo Galli, *Political Spaces and Global War*, ed. Sitze, trans. Elizabeth Fay (Minneapolis: University of Minnesota Press, 2010), xxxiii–xxxiv, and Antonio Negri, *Insurgencies: Constituent Power and the Modern State*, trans. Maurizia Boscagli (Minneapolis: University of Minnesota Press, 2009), 15, 49. On politics as founded upon the constitutive impossibility of society, see Ernesto Laclau, "The Time Is Out of Joint," in *Emancipations* (London: Verso, 2007).

5. On the infinitizing of political space in Machiavelli and Harrington, see Negri, *Insurgencies*, 109. On the hermeneutic dilemmas of nontranscendental truth claims in early modern drama, see Katharine Eisaman Maus, *Inwardness and Theater in the English Renaissance* (Chicago: University of Chicago Press, 1995), 47.

6. Walter Benjamin, *Origin of the German Tragic Drama*, trans. John Osborne (London: Verso, 1998), 66–71. See also Samuel Weber, *Benjamin's -abilities* (Cambridge, MA: Harvard University Press, 2008), 187–90. "Cut off from any transcendent consolidation," Weber states,

"the strict immanence of the modern world takes the form of perpetual disintegration" (286).

7. Claude Lefort, *The Political Forms of Modern Society: Bureaucracy, Democracy, Totalitarianism*, ed. John Thompson (Cambridge: MIT Press, 1986), 201, 222.

8. Lukas Erne, *Beyond the Spanish Tragedy: A Study of the Works of Thomas Kyd* (Manchester: Manchester University Press, 2001), 278.

9. For a subtle account of the distinctly mimetic preoccupations of the Renaissance revenge genre, see John Kerrigan, *Revenge Tragedy: Aeschylus to Armageddon* (New York: Oxford University Press, 1998), 20–22. Gregory M. Colón Semenza sees the metatheatrical element in the play as a tool of self-consciousness in response to post-Reformation epistemological uncertainty. "*The Spanish Tragedy* and Metatheatre" in *The Cambridge Companion to English Renaissance Tragedy*, ed. Emma Smith and Garrett A. Sullivan (Cambridge: Cambridge University Press, 2010), 153.

10. *The Revenger's Tragedy*, in *Four Revenge Tragedies*, ed. Katharine Eisaman Maus (Oxford: Oxford University Press, 1995), 5.1.3–6. On the recursive, self-annulling dimension of revenge, see Michael Neill, "English Revenge Tragedy," in *A Companion to Tragedy*, ed. Rebecca Bushnell (Oxford: Blackwell, 2005), 335–37.

11. For a Girardian reading of early modern drama in terms of the shift from ritualized culture to the centerless operations of modern exchange systems, see Richard van Oort, "Shakespeare and the Idea of the Modern," *New Literary History* 37, no. 2 (Spring 2006): 328–30.

12. See René Girard, *Violence and the Sacred*, trans. Patrick Gregory (Baltimore, MD: Johns Hopkins University Press, 1977), 39–67.

13. *The Spanish Tragedy* in *Four Revenge Tragedies*, 3.11.15–25. Subsequent references to the play will be to this edition and will be cited in the text.

14. As Scott McMillin points out, those implements of suicide are the implements Lorenzo used to commit the crime. "The Figure of Silence in *The Spanish Tragedy*," *ELH* 39, no. 1 (1972): 42.

15. *The Concept of the Political: Expanded Edition*, trans. George Schwab (Chicago: University of Chicago Press, 2007), 25–37. On the class division in the play, see Maus, *Inwardness and Theater*, 57–63.

16. On the relation between Hieronimo's madness and class fragmentation, see Maus, *Inwardness and the Theater*, 60. Garrett A. Sullivan Jr. associates that decentering fragmentation with the constitution of tragic subjectivity in the drama. "Tragic Subjectivities" in *Cambridge Companion to English Renaissance Tragedy*, 75–76.

17. On divided sovereignty, see Jacques Lezra, *Wild Materialism: The Ethic of Terror and the Modern Republic* (New York: Fordham University Press, 2010), 63–86.

18. See Christopher Pye, *The Vanishing: Shakespeare, the Subject, and Early Modern Culture* (Durham, NC: Duke University Press, 2000), 122–23.

19. See Jacques Lacan's analysis of *Antigone* in *The Seminar of Jacques Lacan: Book VII: The Ethics of Psychoanalysis 1959–1960*, trans. Dennis Porter (New York: Norton, 1992), 270–90.

20. "If destiny thy miseries do ease," Hieronimo declares, "happy shalt thy be; / If destiny deny thee life . . . / Yet shalt thou be assured of a tomb. / If neither, yet this thy comfort be: / Heaven covereth him that have no burial" (3.13.14–19).

21. That indeterminate belonging at once to this scene and a scene elsewhere—what makes the revenger the privileged figure for the notion of an unconscious subject—crystallizes in an ambiguity about what it means to give leave and to take leave, to invite and to disappear. Hieronimo's mad exits and entrances are prompted by an exchange with a foreigner: First Portingale: "By your leave, sir." / Hieronimo: "Good leave have you; nay, I pray you go, / For I'll leave you, if you can leave me so" (3.11.1–3).

22. On the debate over the determining force of the choral figures, and on the play's relation to an emerging drama of intention, see Lukas Erne, *Beyond the "Spanish Tragedy": A Study of the Works of Thomas Kyd* (Manchester, UK: Manchester University Press, 2001), 104–7.

23. See Carl Schmitt, *Hamlet or Hecuba: The Intrusion of the Time into the Play*, trans. David Pan and Jennifer Rust (New York: Telos, 2009), 35, 45; Douglas Bruster, *Shakespeare and the Question of Culture: Early Modern Literature and the Cultural Turn* (Houndsmills, UK: Palgrave, 2003), 81, 93; Anthony Dawson and Paul Yachnin, *The Culture of Playgoing in Shakespeare's England: A Collaborative Debate* (Cambridge: Cambridge University Press, 2001); Walter Cohen, *Drama of a Nation* (Ithaca, NY: Cornell University Press, 1985).

24. See Weber, *Benjamin's -abilities*, 269.

25. On primary substitution, see Jacques Derrida, *Adieu to Emmanuel Levinas*, trans. Pascale-Anne Brault and Michael Naas (Stanford, CA: Stanford University Press, 1999), 115, and Thomas Keenan, *Fables of Responsibility: Aberrations and Predicaments in Ethics and Politics* (Stanford, CA: Stanford University Press, 1997), 21.

26. Carla Mazzio subtly aligns the scene with Hieronimo's confrontation with what Horatio figuratively embodies: *oratio*, language as such. *The Inarticulate Renaissance: Language Trouble in an Age of Eloquence* (Philadelphia: University of Pennsylvania Press, 2009), 108. McMillin in "The Figure of Silence" (36, 48) views the confrontation as figuring a silence and fatality beyond language and time.

27. On the play's consciousness of itself as an autonomous, "self-contained artistic system," see Barry Adams, "The Audiences of *The Spanish Tragedy*," *JEGP* 68 (1969): 234.

28. Mazzio, *Inarticulate Renaissance*, 110–12.

29. Neill refers to "the senseless butchery of the innocent Castile"; see "English Revenge Tragedy," 332.

30. Jean-Luc Nancy, *The Creation of the World or Globalization*, trans. François Raffoul and David Pettigrew (Albany: SUNY Press, 2007), 98.

31. Linda Woodridge, *English Revenge Drama: Money, Resistance, Equality* (Cambridge: Cambridge University Press, 2010), 60–96. On revenge as a specifically economic version of justice, see Jacques Derrida, *Specters of Marx: The State of the Debt, the Work of Mourning, and the New International*, trans. Peggy Kamuf (New York and London: Routledge, 1994), 26. On the immanence of capitalism, its capacity to operate without extrinsic reference as a system which "contains its own good," and thus as a cult without limit, see Weber, *Benjamin's -abilities*, 255.

32. For a subtle account of Hieronimo offering "a new vision of subjectivity, authorized neither by birth nor by inherited content, but founded upon the very force of its discursive activities themselves," see James Siemon, "Sporting Kyd," *English Literary Renaissance* 24, no. 3 (Autumn 1994): 581. For Siemon, the fraught character of that literary emergence is related to Kyd's own attempts to accrue a noninstrumental form of discursive capital from the middling social position of the scrivener.

33. On that scene as representing the indigestibility of law, see Mazzio, *Inarticulate Renaissance*, 120. The contradictions of the spare blood script scene will flower in the scene of the ghost's appearance to Hamlet, a traumatic infraction that was also already known in advance—"O my prophetic soul."

34. "Drawing—the Single Trait: Toward a Politics of Singularity" in *Crediting God: Sovereignty and Religion in the Age of Global Capitalism*, ed. Miguel Vatter (New York: Fordham University Press, 2011), 23–35.

35. Francis Bacon, *The Major Works*, ed. Brian Vickers (Oxford: Oxford University Press, 2008), 347.

36. Lorna Hutson, *The Invention of Suspicion: Law and Mimesis in Shakespeare and Renaissance Drama* (Oxford: Oxford University Press, 2007), 3–30, 107–15, 234. Luke Wilson also argues for the intimate relation between contemporary developments in legal reasoning and the emergence of intention-driven drama. *Theaters of Intention: Drama and the Law in Early Modern England* (Stanford, CA: Stanford University Press, 2000), 25–67.

37. Hutson, *Invention of Suspicion*, 262.

38. Ibid., 278, 271–74.

39. Ibid., 115.

40. Ibid.

41. Ibid., 292.

42. On the relation between condign violence and reflexive thought, see Lezra, *Wild Materialism*, 171–72.

43. This is the right, belated, point to engage the debate over whether delay *is* a concern in the play. To the argument that it is an anachronistic preoccupation, one is tempted to point to something like the First Player's speech. But that misses the symptomatic force of the historical phenomenon Margareta De Grazia traces, the fact that the issue does not emerge as a significant concern until the nineteenth century and the era of characterological criticism. To argue from that, however, that the latter response is an imposition is to assume that historical proximity means critical accuracy; it would be as easy to argue that it's the delay in its reception that bears out the truth of delay's significance. The larger point concerns the question of evidentiary status. Delay's relation to speculative thought as such, and to the event as missed event, suggests that it is not so much a matter of empirical assertion—a listing of instances in the play—as of that which opens the possibility of speculative assertion and referential argument. It is, in that sense, a phenomenon borne out in its effects, including its delayed inscription within the historical debate. See De Grazia, *Hamlet Without Hamlet* (Cambridge: Cambridge University Press, 2007).

44. See Pye, *The Vanishing*, 106–7.

45. Mazzio, *Inarticulate Renaissance*, 133.

46. For Garrett Sullivan, Hieronimo's subjectivity is based on his withholdingness in the scene; "Tragic Subjectivities," 77.

47. Positions very roughly occupied by Francis Barker, *The Tremulous Private Body: Essays on Subjection* (London: Methuen, 1984); Catherine Belsey, *The Subject of Tragedy: Identity and Difference in Renaissance Drama* (London: Routledge, 1985); and Alan Sinfield, *Faultlines* (Oxford: Oxford University Press, 1992), as well as Maus, *Inwardness*, and Hutson, *The Invention of Suspicion*.

48. William Prynne, *Histrio-mastix, The Players Scourge* (London, 1633), fol. 556a. As Erne points out in *Beyond the Spanish Tragedy* (95), Prynne echoes Braithwaite's *English Gentlewoman*.

49. For a supple account of the phantasmatic character of suture—that which alone sustains a subject within a contingent social horizon—see Lezra, *Wild Materialism*, 122.

50. Maus, *Four Revenge Tragedies,* 348–49.

51. *Hamlet,* ed. G. R. Hibbard, *The Oxford Shakespeare* (Oxford: Oxford University Press, 1987), 2.2.441, 448, 459–73. Subsequent *Hamlet* references will be to this edition and cited in the text. The argument that follows concerning the scene expands and reorients analyses I have provided in other contexts.

52. Shakespearean distraction thus confirms and transvalues Augustine's view of life itself as a distraction or deviation in relation to divine ends. See *Confessions,* 9.29.

53. Paul de Man, "Autobiography as De-Facement," in *The Rhetoric of Romanticism* (New York: Columbia University Press, 1984), 74–81.

54. Jane Bellamy, *Translations of Power: Narcissism and the Unconscious in Epic History* (Ithaca, NY: Cornell University Press, 1992), 60–81. On Troy as *eremia,* see also, Adrian Poole, "Total Disaster: Euripides' *The Trojan Women,*" *Arion* 3, no. 3 (1976): 265. On the reiteration of the allusions to the cities in flames, see David Quint, *Epic and Empire* (Princeton, NJ: Princeton University Press, 1993), 65. On the specifically Renaissance dimension of *translatio,* as against Medieval metonymic and genealogical readings, and its bearing on historical self-consciousness, see Thomas M. Greene, *The Light in Troy: Imitation and Discovery in Renaissance Poetry* (New Haven, CT: Yale University Press, 1982), 87, and James Simpson, *Oxford English Literary History,* vol. 2, *1350–1547: Reform and Cultural Revolution* (Oxford: Oxford University Press, 2002), 68. On Shakespeare and the *translatio imperii,* see Heather James, *Shakespeare's Troy: Drama, Politics, and the Translation of Empire* (Cambridge: Cambridge University Press, 1997). Insofar as it locates politic foundations in relation to a negation prior to formal law, the scene bears on the distinction between "what's forbidden in the founding of the polis and what's unthinkable" provided by Joan Copjec, *Imagine There's No Woman: Ethics and Sublimation* (Cambridge, MA: MIT Press, 2002), 41. That law before law corresponds to Carl Schmitt's account of *nomos,* a primal, instituting cut or division prior to positive law Schmitt associates with the walls of the city. See Schmitt, *The Nomos of the Earth in the International Law of Jus Publicum Europaeum,* trans. G. L. Ulmen (New York: Telo Press, 2006), 78, and Sitze, introduction to Galli, *Political Spaces,* lxix–lxx.

55. *Dido Queene of Carthage* in *The Complete Works of Christopher Marlowe,* vol. 1, *Translations,* ed. Roma Gill (Oxford: Clarendon Press, 1998), 2.1.263–64, 255–58.

56. "stupet obtutuque haeret defixus in uno," Virgil, *Eclogues, Georgics, Aeneid Books 1–6,* ed. G. P. Goold, trans. H. Rushton Fairclough (Cambridge, MA: Harvard University Press, 1916), bk. 1, line 495.

57. "illi membra novus soluit formidine torpore," Virgil, *Aeneid Books 7–12, Appendix Vergiliana*, ed. G. P. Goold, trans. H. Rushton Fairclough (Cambridge, MA: Harvard University Press, 1918), bk. 12, line 867.

58. "extemplo Aeneas solvuntur frigore" (Virgil, *Aeneid*, bk. 1, line 92). David Quint in *Epic and Empire* (78–80) notes the reiterations in his analysis of the *Aeneid*'s own recursive, self-eroding logic.

59. Andrew Benjamin, "Spacing as the Shared: Heraclitus, Pindar, Agamben," in *Politics, Metaphysics, and Death: Essays on Giorgio Agamben's "Homo Sacer,"* ed. Andrew Norris (Durham, NC: Duke University Press, 2005), 150–54, and Carl Schmitt, *Nomos*, 67–79. As Hanna Arendt points out, *nomos* means wall as well as law. *The Human Condition* (Chicago: University of Chicago Press, 1958), 63–64.

60. As a judgment on the locus and possibility of judgment, the legislative act of *nomos* remains radically blind, necessarily beyond the field of determinable meanings and judgments it opens. (One can posit, and one can mean, but one cannot posit meaning, as de Man succinctly puts it.) As such, the political-interpretive force entailed in such a scene bears, not on the relativity of meanings, but on a more primordial, preanthropological positing bound up with "the ontology of names" (A. Benjamin, "Spacing as the Shared," 145), and particularly with the arbitrary materiality of the proper name. In that regard, the scene's status as primal scene, in the psychic as well as the political sense, may be evident less in its character as a drama of literary rivalry—a systematic, even if potentially illimitable, structure of negation and self-affirmation (Homer, Virgil/Marlowe, Shakespeare)—than in an at once more overt and far more opaque play of signifiers gravitating around the fragmentary site of political/subjective foundations: "neutral to his will"; "Ilium"; "gules"; "Pyrrhus": in all these signifiers one might hear "William," or "Gulielmus" as the birth certificate heraldically puts it. Political and aesthetic determinations reach a vanishing point in a form of senseless inscriptive phenomenalization prior to thought, and an occluded subject *morcele* in advance of ego.

61. On the relation between exemption and exemplification, see Giorgio Agamben, *Homo Sacer: Sovereign Power and Bare Life*, trans. Daniel Heller-Roazen (Stanford, CA: Stanford University Press, 1998), 21–22. On the state of exception positing sovereignty, see Bruno Gulli, "The Ontology and Politics of Exception" in *Giorgio Agamben: Sovereignty and Life*, ed. Matthew Calarco and Steven DeCaroli (Stanford, CA: Stanford University Press, 2007), 235. On the exception opening the possibility of the agency of the act, its "tak[ing] exception to me," see Derrida, *Politics of Friendship*, trans. George Collins (London: Verso,

2006), 68–69. On the decision's inextricability from the norm it would adjudicate, and sovereignty as a sub-set of its own divisive self-definition, see Lezra, *Wild Materialism* 22, 86–96. On such anteriority of the act in Machiavelli, see Miguel E. Vatter, *Between Form and Event: Machiavelli's Theory of Political Freedom* (Dordrecht, NL: Kluwer, 2000), 140.

62. On law's definitionally self-exceeding character, see Maurice Blanchot, *The Infinite Conversation*, trans. Susan Hanson (Minneapolis: University of Minnesota Press, 1992), 434, and Peter Fitzpatrick, "Bare Sovereignty," in *Politics, Metaphysics, and Death,* 62–65. On sovereignty as not external to *nomos*, but its actualization, see A. Benjamin, "Spacing as the Shared," 158.

63. Schmitt, *Hamlet or Hecuba*, 44. For analyses of such an account of aesthetics and history as nonmimetic intrusion in Schmitt, see Rust and Lupton, introduction to *Hamlet or Hecuba*; Lupton, "Invitation to a Totem Meal: Hans Kelsen, Carl Schmitt and Political Theology," in Paul Cefalu and Brian Reynolds, ed. *The Return of Theory in Early Modern Studies* (Houndsmills, Basingstone, Hampsire: Palgrave Macmillan, 2011), 133; Johannes Türk, "The Intrusion: Carl Schmitt's Non-Mimetic Logic of Art," *Telos* no. 142 (Spring 2008): 49–90; and Eric L. Santner, *The Royal Remains: The People's Two Bodies and the Endgames of Sovereignty* (Chicago: University of Chicago Press, 2011), 145–46.

64. On the decision and the caesura of time, see Derrida, *Adieu*, 116. On the polis not just as the city-state but as the site out of which historical time happens, see Heidegger, *Introduction to Metaphysics*, trans. Gregory Fried and Richard Polt (New Haven, CT: Yale University Press, 2000), 152, and Dennis J. Schmidt, *On Germans and Other Greeks: Tragedy and Ethical Life* (Bloomington: Indiana University Press, 2001), 248. On Shakespearean "untimeliness" and the limits of historicist history, see Jonathan Gil Harris, "Shakespeare After 5/11," in *Shakespeare after 9/11: How a Social Trauma Reshapes Interpretation, Shakespeare Yearbook*, vol. 20, ed. Douglas Brooks, Matthew Biberman, Julia Lupton (New York: Mellen, 2011), 153–59.

65. Pye, *The Vanishing*, 111–14, and Pye, "Senseless Illium," in *Shakespeare after 9/11*, 171–75.

66. Pye, *The Vanishing,* 116–17, and Pye, "Senseless Illium," 176–77.

67. Julia Lupton, *Thinking with Shakespeare: Essays on Politics and Life* (Chicago: University of Chicago Press, 2011), 89–91.

68. On the transition, see Carlo Galli, *Political Spaces*, 19–24. Galli articulates that historical moment in terms of the transition from Machiavelli to Hobbes and in a form pertinent to our account: "Machiavelli is incapable of 'construction' because he lacks not only the modern notion of the subject who is able to represent himself and his powers in

the State, but also, and more important, the logic and the regulating finality that sustain modern rationalism's entire political thought" (22). *Hamlet* articulates the (aesthetic) conditions for the possibility of that "regulating finality." On Hobbes's production of the rationalized space of the political as against prior theatrical conceptions of politics, see Paul A. Kottman, *A Politics of the Scene* (Stanford, CA: Stanford University Press, 2008), 54–77.

69. Nancy, *Creation of the World*, 6.

70. Schmitt, for one, focuses on the anxious regnal gap between Elizabeth and James in his analysis of the play.

71. Nancy, *Creation of the World*, 73.

4. "TO THROW OUT OUR EYES FOR BRAVE OTHELLO"

1. See Edward Pechter, *"Othello" and Interpretive Traditions* (Iowa City: University of Iowa Press, 1999), 71–72.

2. All Shakespeare references in this chapter are to *The Norton Shakespeare*, 2nd ed., ed. Stephen Greenblatt (New York: Norton, 2008).

3. E. A. J. Honigmann, *Othello, The Arden Shakespeare, Third Edition* (London: Thomas Learning, 2001), 291.

4. *A Midsummer Night's Dream*, 4.1.189.

5. On these claims in relation to Shakespearean drama, see Pye, *The Vanishing: Shakespeare, the Subject, and Early Modern Culture* (Durham, NC: Duke University Press, 2000), 86–104, 11–17. On the emerging concept of a subject drawing infinitude into itself, see Ernst Cassirer, *The Individual and the Cosmos in Renaissance Thought,* trans. Mario Domandi (New York: Barnes and Nobles, 1963), 189.

6. Julia Reinhard Lupton, *Citizen-Saints: Shakespeare and Political Theology* (Chicago: University of Chicago Press, 2005), 11 and passim. Lupton also addresses the relation between citizenship and judicial sacrifice (3, 117–18). On early modern citizenship and the claim to universality, see also Peter Fitzpatrick, *Modernism and the Grounds of Law* (Cambridge: Cambridge University Press, 2001).

7. For a fine account of the relation between substitutable office, military discipline, and erotic anxiety, see Julia Genster, "Lieutenancy, Standing In, and Othello," *ELH* 57 (1990): 785–809. See also, Michael Neill, who suggests the connection between displacement and the mercantilist themes in the play. "Changing Places in Othello," *Shakespeare Survey* 37 (1984): 118–21.

8. On the homoerotic and homosocial dimensions of the play, see Jonathan Dollimore, *Sexual Dissonance: Augustine to Wilde, Freud to*

Foucault (Oxford: Clarendon Press, 1991), 157–62; Robert Matz, "Slander, Renaissance Discourses of Sodomy, and Othello," *ELH* 66, no. 2 (1999): 261–76; and Ian Smith, "Barbarian Errors: Performing Race in Early Modern England," *Shakespeare Quarterly* 49, no. 2 (1998): 182–85.

9. On the play's punitive relation to its audience, see Michael Bristol, *Big-time Shakespeare* (London: Routledge, 1996), 200.

10. *The Comic Matrix of Shakespeare's Tragedies: Romeo and Juliet, Hamlet, Othello and King Lear* (Princeton, NJ: Princeton University Press, 1979).

11. Explicitly or implicitly, those readings of the play that focus on the objectifying gaze as the key to the question of race in the play, or more broadly on the tragic consequences of the demand for knowledge, operate within the terms of that aesthetic and speculative construction. On the play's scopic preoccupations, see Lynda Boose, " 'Let it be hid': Renaissance Pornography, Iago, and Audience Response," in *Autour d'Othello*, ed. Richard Marienstras and Dominique Guy-Blanquet (Paris: C.E.R.L.A., à L'Institute Charles V, 1987), 135–43, and Patricia Parker, "Othello and Hamlet: Spying, Discovery, Secret Faults" in *Shakespeare from the Margins: Language, Culture, Context* (Chicago: University of Chicago Press, 1996), 227–72. See also Arthur Little Jr., " 'An Essence that's not seen': The Primal Scene of Racism in Othello," *Shakespeare Quarterly* 44 (1993): 304–24, and Michael Neill, "Unproper Beds: Race, Adultery, and the Hideous in Othello," *Shakespeare Quarterly* 40, no. 4 (1989): 383–95. Both authors draw the connection between such scopophilic intensities and race consciousness in the play. On the tragic will to knowledge in the play, see Stanley Cavell, *The Claim of Reason: Wittgenstein, Skepticism, Morality, and Tragedy* (Oxford: Oxford University Press, 1979), 481–92.

12. See Parker, *Shakespeare from the Margins*, 244.

13. The reflexive conception of cannibalism, the idea that it is a matter not of eating others but of eating one's own, or rather that it abolishes the distinction between those categories of self and other, active and passive, recurs for Shakespeare in the "barbarous Scythian" "that makes his generation his messes" from *King Lear*, and in *Tempest*'s Caliban, the anagrammatic cannibal who amounts to the "thing of darkness" one must acknowledge as "one's own." Montaigne, too, famously reads the cannibal as a cultural reflex image: "Savor [my body parts] well," the victim proclaims, "you will find in them the taste of your own flesh." "On Cannibals," in *The Complete Essays of Montaigne*, trans. Donald Frame (Stanford, CA: Stanford University Press, 1948), 158. On the cannibal as a figure for the reverting force of the conqueror, see Roland Greene, *Unrequited Conquests: Love and Empire in the Colonial Americas* (Chicago: University of Chicago Press, 1999), 121.

14. Stephen Greenblatt, *Renaissance Self-Fashioning* (Chicago: University of Chicago Press, 1980), 238. Pechter also points out the recursive character of the speech: " 'Such was my process,' [Othello] says, referring at once to his experience and his relation of that experience, his life and his life story" (*"Othello" and Interpretive Traditions*, 41). Also see James L. Calderwood, who speaks of Othello as "a voice telling about himself telling about himself" ("Speech and Self in Othello," *Shakespeare Quarterly* 38 [1987]: 294).

15. Emily C. Bartels suggests that Brabantio's dream implies he was aware of what his invitations to Othello would encourage. "Making More of the Moor: Aaron, Othello, and the Renaissance Refashionings of Race," *Shakespeare Quarterly* 41 (1990): 450.

16. Parker, *Shakespeare from the Margins*, 48–52.

17. Jean Laplanche has argued in various contexts that the primal scene of psychoanalysis amounts to just such an occasion of indeterminately motivated seduction, a scene within which adult and child alike are enigmatically inscribed. See especially, Laplanche and Jean-Bertrand Pontalis, "Fantasy and the Origins of Sexuality" in *International Journal of Psychoanalysis* 49 (1968), and John Fletcher's introduction to Jean Laplanche, *Essays on Otherness* (London: Routledge, 1999).

18. Greenblatt in *Renaissance Self-Fashioning* (252) points out the way Lodovico's line emphasizes the textual character of Othello's life.

19. "Othello dies," Kenneth Gross observes, "folded into, strangely continuous with his story, even though it's a story that divides him against himself." "Slander and Skepticism in Othello," *ELH* 56, no. 4 (Winter 1989): 842. Ania Loomba argues that Othello's last speech graphically portrays him as a "near schizophrenic" subject split between "Christian and Infidel, the Venetian and the Turk, the keeper of the State and its opponent." *Gender, Race, Renaissance Drama* (Manchester: Manchester University Press, 1989), 48. I argue that such splitting inscribes Othello within a certain, dominant conception of the performative subject. On Othello's performativeness, see Greenblatt, *Renaissance Self-Fashioning*, 245; Karen Newman, " 'And wash the Ethiop white': Femininity and the Monstrous in *Othello*" in *Shakespeare Reproduced: The Text in History and Ideology*, ed. Jean Howard and Marion O'Connor (London: Methuen, 1987), 150; and Smith, "Barbarian Errors," 168–86. Peter Berek has a provocative account of the Jew, and especially the Marrano Jew, as the embodiment of cultural anxieties over performative identities; "The Jew as Renaissance Man," *Renaissance Quarterly* 51, no. 1 (1987): 293–303.

20. Timothy Murray offers a forceful account of the way the ordering narrative of the state functions to put right the scene of racial transgression represented at the close. *Like a Film: Ideological Fantasy on*

Screen, Camera, and Canvas (London: Routledge, 1993), 111. On Othello and the institution of the state, see Mitchell Greenberg, *Canonical States: Oedipus, Othering, and Seventeenth Century Drama* (Minneapolis: University of Minnesota Press, 1994), 30. Thomas Moisan argues that the intervention of the state at the close functions to domesticate the elements of the domestic narrative that resist traditional tragic closure. "Relating Things to the State: The 'State' and the Subject of Othello, in *"Othello": New Critical Essays*, ed. Philip C. Kolin (London: Routledge, 2002), 199.

21. On the curious intermixing of private and public spheres in the play, see Edward Snow, "Sexual Anxiety and the Male Order of Things in *Othello*," *English Literary Renaissance* 10, no. 3 (1980): 402n22. On the mutually constitutive opposition between the domestic sphere and the sphere of the state during the era, see Richard Helgerson, *Adulterous Alliances: Home, State, and History in Early Modern European Drama and Painting* (Chicago: University of Chicago Press, 2000).

22. Moisan, "Relating Things to the State": 195. On "interpellation," the constitutive "hailing" of the subject into a symbolic field, see Jacques Lacan, *Ecrits: A Selection*, trans. Alan Sheridan (New York: Norton, 1977), 29–42, and *The Seminar of Jacques Lacan: Book VII: The Ethics of Psychoanalysis, 1959–1960*, ed. J.-A. Miller, trans. Dennis Porter (New York: Norton, 1992), 43–138.

23. Geraldo U. de Sousa draws attention to this distinction between the domains of state archival history and non-European oral prehistory in the play. *Shakespeare's Cross-Cultural Encounters* (New York: St. Martin's Press, 1999), 118. Michel de Certeau explores the structuring, mutually determining opposition between orality and writing in the constitution of modern (ethnographic) historiography during the Renaissance in *The Writing of History*, trans. Tom Conley (New York: Columbia University Press, 1988), 209–43.

24. Citing Derrida's deconstructive account of the speech / writing opposition, Jonathan Goldberg articulates the problematic nature of developmental accounts of the cultural passage from orality to literacy at the advent of modernity. *Writing Matter: From the Hands of the English Renaissance* (Stanford, CA: Stanford University Press, 1990), 15–55.

25. On the dialectical relation between law and fiction in the early modern English context—the way in which "literary authority might invent itself *as such* by drafting off its juridical counterpart"—see Bradin Cormack, *A Power to Do Justice: Jurisdiction, English Literature, and the Rise of Common Law, 1509–1625* (Chicago: University of Chicago Press, 2007), 43. Constituted thus, the literary functions in continuity with rather than subversion of law (43). In Cormack's account, the jurisdictional

crises provoked by the ascendency of common law in the era prompts law to such newly prominent forms of definitional self-consciousness (33). Othello's reference to the "circumcised dog" is obviously pertinent to an account of symbolic inscription. The reference defines Othello, as Boose observes, in relation to an alien form of cultural marking, and Julia Reinhard Lupton brilliantly describes the double-edged character of that marker, an inscription whose self-negatingly suicidal force typologically fulfills the Moor's return to the Christian fold, even as it inevitably reinstates in the process the outward, Hebraic signature, thus locating Othello within a Judeo-Islamic covenant even while intimating the possibility of another, radical citizenship between distinct universals (*Citizen-Saints*, 118–23). I am arguing that the claims to universal subjecthood in Othello's reflexive self-negation are related to an aesthetic economy bound up with the categories of fiction and state and continuous with the play's own performative effects. The instability of that aesthetic formation, thus of its version of universalism, appears, I will argue, not as a thematic issue but as a radical shift in the problem of reference as such that appears with Shakespeare's middle and late drama.

26. Quentin Skinner, *The Foundations of Modern Political Thought*, vol. 1, *The Renaissance* (Cambridge, London, New York: Cambridge University Press, 1978). On the historical emergence of abstract law, and its structuring opposition to "what is most concrete," see Habermas, *Structural Transformation of the Public Sphere*, trans. Thomas Burger (Cambridge, MA: MIT Press, 1991), 54; Philip Corrigan and Derek Sayer, *The Great Arch: English State Formation as Cultural Revolution* (Oxford: Blackwell, 1985), 99–106; and Fitzpatrick, *Modernism and the Grounds of Law*, 132. On the phantasmatic nature of the modern state, see Jacqueline Rose, *States of Phantasy* (Oxford: Clarendon, 1996), 9, and Pye, *Vanishing*, 102–4.

27. On the emergence of the concept of the literary in early modern England, see Louis Montrose, "The Elizabethan Subject and the Spenserian Text," in *Literary Theory/Renaissance Texts*, ed. Patricia Parker and David Quint (Baltimore, MD: Johns Hopkins University Press, 1986), 303–40, and Robert Matz, *Defending Literature in Early Modern England: Renaissance Literary Theory in Social Context* (Cambridge: Cambridge University Press, 2000), 1–24.

28. Michael Neill in "Changing Places in Othello" (125) comments on the way hands become "an object of furious scrutiny" in the play.

29. John Kerrigan points out the slide of the voice from inside to outside. *On Shakespeare and Early Modern Literature: Essays* (Oxford: Oxford University Press, 2001), 11.

30. Harry Berger Jr., "Impertinent Trifling: Desdemona's Handkerchief," *Shakespeare Quarterly* 47, no. 3 (Autumn 1996): 235–50.

31. For the gesturing hand as a substitute for speech, see Helkiah Crooke, *Microcosmographia: A Description of the Body of Man* (London: Jaggard, 1615), 730.

32. Greenblatt suggests such a reading in *Renaissance Self-Fashioning*, 234.

33. My account of the problem of reference derives from the late work of Paul de Man. See especially, "Hypogram and Inscription," in *The Resistance to Theory* (Minnesota: University of Minnesota Press, 1986) and "Sign and Symbol in Hegel's Aesthetics," *Critical Inquiry* 8 (Summer 1982): 761–75. Jonathan Goldberg in *Writing Matter* (59–107) offers a far-reaching analysis of the ideology of "right writing" and the assertions of force, especially pedagogical force, around writing's impossible founding moment. For an evocative account of the unmoored quality of language in the play, see Kenneth Gross, *Shakespeare's Noise* (Chicago: University of Chicago Press, 2001), 120–21.

34. Gross in *Shakespeare's Noise* (118) points to Othello's hysterical and empty "posture of pointing" at the play's conclusion.

35. My account here of the relation between force and the radical uncertainties of reference is indebted to the work of Cynthia Chase. See especially, "The Witty Butcher's Wife: Freud, Lacan, and the Conversion of the Resistance to Theory," *Modern Language Notes* 102, no. 5 (December 1987): 1008–10. See also de Man's reading of deixis in Hegel in *The Resistance to Theory*, 42. Likening the gesture to Fortinbras's at the close of Hamlet, Timothy Murray also suggests the significance of Lodovico's indeterminately deictic "this"; he associates it with Jean Laplanche's "enigmatic signifier" and sees its obscurity of reference operating in the service of traumatizing visual censorship. *Drama Trauma: Specters of Race and Sexuality in Performance, Video, and Art* (New York and London: Routledge, 1997), 37. For an account of deixis as the nonsignifying limit of linguistic tropology, and thus in relation to the Lacanian "Thing," see Julia Reinhard Lupton and Kenneth Reinhard, *After Oedipus: Shakespeare in Psychoanalysis* (Ithaca, NY: Cornell University Press, 1993), 179–89.

36. On miscegenation as the play's "primal scene," see Little, "'An essence that's not seen,'" 319.

37. Snow, "Sexuality and the Male Order of Things," 385; Neill, "Unproper Beds," 395.

38. For an insightful account of the role of hands in the play as indexes of alienated agency especially in relation to the (premodern) conception of the political body and lineage, see Katherine Rowe, *Dead*

Hands: Fictions of Agency, Renaissance to Modern (Stanford, CA: Stanford University Press, 1999), 52–85. Rowe also comments on the play's tendency toward reflexive, self-referential punning around the figure of the hand (57–58; 62–63). James Kuzner reads the returned hand in relation to the failure of possibilities of intersubjective consent in the play. "*And here's they hand*": *Titus Andronicus* in a Time of Terror" in *Shakespeare After 9/11: How a Social Trauma Reshapes Interpretation*, ed. Brooks, Biber, and Lupton (Lewiston, NY: Mellen, 2011), 193–94.

39. For a crystallizing account of debates over the status of race during the era—whether it exists as color-consciousness at all or in an as yet unconsolidated form admixed with theological determinates—see Ania Loomba, *Shakespeare, Race, and Colonialism* (Oxford: Oxford University Press, 2002), 22–39, 91–111.

5. AESTHETICS AND ABSOLUTISM IN *THE WINTER'S TALE*

1. Jean Bodin, *The Six Bookes of a Commonweale*, ed. Douglas McRae (London, 1606; repr., Cambridge, MA: Harvard University Press, 1962), 159–62, 169–73.

2. See Carl Schmitt, *Political Theology: Four Chapters on the Concept of Sovereignty*, trans. George Schwab (Chicago: Chicago University Press, 1985), 48.

3. Ibid., 26, 63, 65.

4. Ibid., 34, 63–65. On Schmitt's association between the perceived abstraction of the liberal democratic political sphere and the autonomy of the aesthetic, see Victoria Kahn, "Hamlet or Hecuba: Carl Schmitt's Decision," *Representations* 83 (Summer, 2003): 73. On Schmitt's analysis as a commentary on the increased subjection of life to objectivized orders such as economy and bureaucratic politics, see Slavoj Žižek, "Carl Schmitt in the Age of Post-Politics," in *The Challenge of Carl Schmitt*, ed. Chantal Mouffe (London: Verso, 1999), 144.

5. See especially, Chantal Mouffe, *The Return of the Political* (London: Verso, 1993), 117–33.

6. Schmitt, *Political Theology*, 5.

7. On the self-dividing character of the sovereign decision, see Jacques Derrida, *The Politics of Friendship*, trans. George Collins (London: Verso, 2006), 68–69, and Jacques Lezra, *Wild Materialism: The Ethic of Terror and the Modern Republic* (New York: Fordham University Press, 2010), 68–69.

8. Paul Hirst, "Carl Schmitt's Decisionism," in *The Challenge of Carl Schmitt*, 11.

9. Schmitt, *Political Theology*, 2.

10. On the impasses of the political decision as a feature of the Reformation era particularly, see chapter 1.

11. Schmitt, *Political Theology*, 31–32.

12. On abdication as an expression of sovereign will, see Franco Moretti, "The Great Eclipse," in *Signs Taken for Wonders: Essays in the Sociology of Literary Forms*, trans. Susan Fischer, David Forgacs, and David Miller (London: Verso, 1988), 46.

13. On the *ex nihilo* character of Renaissance artistic production, see Julia Reinhard Lupton, *Afterlives of the Saints: Hagiography, Typology, and Renaissance Literature* (Stanford, CA: Stanford University Press, 1996), 67–69.

14. Michel Foucault, "Governmentality" in *The Foucault Effect*, ed. Graham Burchell, Colin Gorden, and Peter Miller (Chicago: University of Chicago Press, 1991), 95.

15. *The Winter's Tale*, ed. Stephen Orgel (Oxford: Oxford University Press, 1996), 1.2.178–80. Subsequent references to the play will be to this edition and cited in the text.

16. René Girard, *Violence and the Sacred,* trans. Patrick Gregory (Baltimore, MD: Johns Hopkins University Press, 1979), 143–68.

17. On the phrase, "standing in," as an allusion to Polixenes's standing in Leontes's place, see Howard Felperin, " 'Tongue-tied, Our Queen?': The Deconstruction of Presence in *The Winter's Tale*," in *Shakespeare: The Last Plays*, ed. Kiernan Ryan (London: Longman, 1999), 195.

18. On Shakespeare's Romances occupying the transition between medieval conceptions of liberties to an "emerging identity between subjectivity and citizenship," see Simon Palfrey, *Late Shakespeare: A New World of Words* (Oxford: Clarendon, 1997), 50. On the mixed character of absolutism, its articulation of feudal forms in relation to fundamentally bourgeois bureaucratic transformations, see Perry Anderson, *Lineages of the Absolutist State* (London: Verso, 1974). On the relation between surrogacy and structures of office, see Julia Genster, "Lieutenancy, Standing In, and Othello," *ELH* 57 (1990): 785–809. The triangulated structure of the initiating scene of desire in the play of course includes the possibilities of homoerotic affiliation: it's not a coincidence that all erupts for Leontes at the moment Polixines plans to depart. Still, to fix on homosexual identification as the scene's explanatory secret is to allay the greater threat of the radically open, dissolvative desire it represents. On the homosocial dimensions of the opening scenes, see Michael D. Bristol, "In Search of the Bear: Spatiotemporal Form and the Heterogeneity of Economies in *The Winter's Tale*," *Shakespeare Quarterly* 42, no. 2 (Summer 1991): 155.

19. I borrow this spatial conception of citizenship from Julia Lupton; see Lupton, *Citizen-Saints: Shakespeare and Political Theology* (Chicago: University of Chicago Press, 2005), 11 and passim.

20. On Leontes as embodying the new "self-centered, rationalist" subject of the bourgeois era—more a "man" than a king—see William Morse, "Metacriticism and Materiality: The Case of Shakespeare's *The Winter's Tale*," *ELH* 58, no. 2 (Summer 1991): 291, 289.

21. René Girard, *A Theater of Envy: William Shakespeare* (New York: Oxford University Press, 1991), 316–18. Stephen Orgel implies this aspect of jealousy in the play when he associates it with the "self-generating and autonomous nature of consciousness itself"; see Orgel, introduction to *The Winter's Tale* (Oxford: Oxford University Press, 1996), 19. Northrup Frye describes Leontes's jealousy as a "parody of creation out of nothing." *Fables of Identity: Studies in Poetic Mythology* (New York: Harcourt, 1963), 115.

22. Carol Thomas Neely notes the motif in the context of a reading of the play as a hard-won celebration of fertility and reproductive love. "*The Winter's Tale*: Women and Issue" in *Shakespeare: The Last Plays*, 169–71.

23. On Leontes's unconscious metatheatricalness, see David Young, *The Heart's Forest: A Study of Shakespeare's Pastoral Plays* (New Haven, CT: Yale University Press, 1972), 124.

24. Felperin in "'Tongue-tied, Our Queen?,'" (196–98) reads the passage as epitomizing the play's larger preoccupation with linguistic indeterminacy and the fall from interpretive innocence.

25. Understood as an infinitization of the social and symbolic order, the signifying transformation I am pointing to anticipates the process of political disincorporation that marks the advent of the modern state form. See Claude Lefort, "The Genesis of Ideology in Modern Societies," in *The Political Forms of Modern Society: Bureaucracy, Democracy, Totalitarianism*, ed. John Thompson (Cambridge, MA: MIT Press, 1986). That process amounts to the historical displacement of the sovereign exception by the (political) logic of the "universal exception," the logic according to which, in Jacques Derrida's gnomic formulation, "every other is every other": all are equivalent, even as, precisely because of the illimitability of the structure, each one is radically other—a cipher. *The Gift of Death*, trans. David Wills (Chicago: University of Chicago Press, 1996), 87.

26. On absolutism's preoccupation with purely formal unity—the state conceived as a system of ratios—see Bodin, *Six Bookes of a Commonweale*, 741–46, 786–94. On Bodin's emphasis on the state as "self-originating," and his "displacement of the center of theoretical consideration from the question of legitimacy to that of the life of the State and its sovereignty as a united body," see Michael Hardt and

Antonio Negri, *Empire* (Cambridge, MA: Harvard University Press, 2000), 98.

27. Ivan Nagel, *Autonomy and Mercy: Reflections on Mozart's Operas*, trans. Marion Faber and Ivan Nagel (Cambridge, MA: Harvard University Press, 1991), 54. See also, Perry Anderson, *Lineages of the Absolutist State* (London: Verso, 1974), 51.

28. On the Enlightenment era relation between autonomous authority and grace, see Nagel, *Autonomy and Mercy*, 52–57, 145–48, and Slavoj Žižek, *Tarrying with the Negative: Kant, Hegel, and the Critique of Ideology* (Durham, NC: Duke University Press, 1993), 169–74.

29. Read in this way, oracular law bears out Derrida's account of what Montaigne termed the "mystical foundation of authority." Rather than being external to it—a matter of its enforcement—force is intrinsic to law and its performative constitution. "The very emergence of justice and law, the founding and justifying moment that institutes law implies a performative force, which is always an interpretive force," a groundless "coup de force . . . that in itself is neither just nor unjust." "Force of Law: The 'Mystical Foundation of Authority,'" in *Deconstruction and the Possibility of Justice*, ed. Drucilla Cornell, Michael Rosenfield, and David Carlson (New York and London: Routledge, 1992), 13. On the convergence of law with its interpretation in the context of early modern legal centralization, see Bradin Cormack, *A Power to Do Justice: Jurisdiction, English Literature, and the Rise of Common Law, 1509–1625* (Chicago: University of Chicago Press, 2007), 43.

30. Derrida comments on the inevitable fragility of that opposition in "Force of Law," 38–40.

31. On the aesthetic as the privileged category of "reflexive self-designation," see Thierry de Duve, "Five Remarks on Aesthetic Judgment," in *Aesthetics and Sublimation*, ed. Joan Copjec, *Umbr(a)* 1 (1999): 70. On the romance genre and structures of return, see Constance Jordan, *Shakespeare's Monarchies: Ruler and Subject in the Romances*, (Ithaca, NY: Cornell University Press, 1997), 107, and Young, *Heart's Forest*, 138. On that genre's self-consciousness, see Simon Palfrey, *Late Shakespeare*, 40, and Young, *Heart's Forest*, 125–29. On the reflexive self-consciousness of the play, and the interpretive self-awareness it prompts, see Stephen Miko, *"Winter's Tale," Studies in English Literature* 29, no. 2 (Spring, 1989): 259–75.

32. Hardt and Negri point to the relation between absolutism and the newfound emphasis on the state's capacity "to construct its own origin and structure" (*Empire*, 98). On self-origination and the emerging conception of the autonomy of the political domain, see also Moretti, "Great Eclipse," 45, 47. My account of the play's articulation

of the state as aesthetic formation is not inconsistent with Stanley Cavell's observation that the play moves from incestuous, paternal bonds to a version of social contract; see Cavell, *Disowning Knowledge in Seven Plays of Shakespeare* (Cambridge: Cambridge University Press, 2003), 217.

33. Andrew Gurr sees the abruptness of the transition as a joke on Florio's literal-minded definition of tragic-comedy as "half a tragedy and half a comedy." "The Bear, the Statue, and Hysteria in *The Winter's Tale*," *Shakespeare Quarterly* 34, no. 4 (Winter 1988): 422. Shakespeare may also have in mind the opportune and oddly self-conscious conclusion of *Pandosto*, where the title character "fell in a melancholy fit and—to close up the comedy with a tragical strategem—he slew himself" (Orgel, *The Winter's Tale*, 274). On the self-conscious artifice of the tragic-comic hinge scene, see C. B. Hardman, "Theory, Form, and Meaning in Shakespeare's *The Winter's Tale*," *The Review of English Studies* 36, no. 142 (May 1985): 232–33.

34. A fact intimated by the Chorus's reference to the "growth . . . of that wide gap" rather than the growth of what occurred within that interval (4.1.6–7). On editors' bewilderment with the formulation, see Orgel's note on the line in *The Winter's Tale*, 159.

35. The relation between self-sufficiency and self-consumption may be implied by Autolycus's name—the wolf himself, but also the auto-wolf, a turn on Erasmus's *homo homini lupus*; "man is a wolf to man" (*Adages*, 1.1.69–70). On the character's self-createdness, see Palfrey, *Late Shakespeare*, 118.

36. On the class scope of the genre, see Simon Palfrey, *Late Shakespeare*, 36–39, and David Lee Miller, *Dreams of the Burning Child: Sacrificial Sons and the Father's Witness* (Ithaca, NY: Cornell University Press, 2003), 19.

37. On Autolycus's association with "unregulated exchange" and the "development of the placeless market, see, respectively, Miller, *Dreams of the Burning Child*, 127, and Michael D. Bristol, "In Search of the Bear," 163. On the prominence of the economic metaphor in the play, see Stanley Cavell, *Disowning Knowledge*, 200.

38. Roy Battenhouse, "Theme and Structure in *The Winter's Tale*," *Shakespeare Survey* 33 (1980): 138. Julia Lupton offers a particularly nuanced argument according to which "the statue scene . . . stages the visual conditions of Catholic image worship," but in an iconoclastically canceling form which nevertheless lets it retain "vestigial thaumaturg[ical]" force. *Afterlives of the Saints: Hagiography, Typology, and Renaissance Literature* (Stanford, CA: Stanford University Press, 1996), 216, 218.

39. Note Leonard Barkan's observation that both the oracle and the statue are "connected to resolutions in the affairs of men that seem beyond their individual actions." " 'Living Sculptures': Ovid, Michelangelo, and The Winter's Tale," *ELH* 48, no. 4 (Winter 981): 660.

40. Palfrey, *Late Shakespeare*, 111.

41. *Disowning Knowledge*, 194. All comes back to that ear in Palfrey's formulation: "The dancing saltiers, the miraculously metamorphosing 'statue' return to the queen's ear wherein the tale was first whispered" (*Late Shakespeare*, 111).

42. Such an emphasis on the consumptive violence of the play's aesthetic self-reflection should be contrasted with John J. Joughin's subtle argument for the play's offering the prospect of an Adornian "affinity through distance" and an aesthetic truth "truer than truth only cognition." "Shakespeare, Modernity and the Aesthetic: Art, Truth and Judgment in *The Winter's Tale*" in *Shakespeare and Modernity: Early Modern to Millennium*, ed. Hugh Grady (London: Routledge, 2000), 82. It is, I have argued, precisely where the aesthetic would pass beyond cognition toward it's own autogenetic grounds that its irresolvable relation to force becomes most outright.

43. Kahn in "Hamlet or Hecuba" (70) similarly argues, against Schmitt, that in Hobbes artifice functions as the grounds of the sovereign decision, the basis of his *auctoritas*.

44. With that, the entire sustaining conception of sovereignty as a law capable of suspending itself dissolves. For the structure, see Slavoj Žižek, *Tarrying with the Negative*, 192.

45. On the homogenization of social space and the positivization of law as defining features of totalitarian political structures, see Claude Lefort, *The Political Forms of Modern Society*, 286–87, 299–301.

6. THE BEATING MIND: *THE TEMPEST* IN HISTORY

1. Carl Schmitt, *The Nomos of the Earth in the International Law of the Jus Publicum Europaeum*, trans. G. L. Ulmen (New York: Telos Press, 2003), 145.

2. Shakespeare, *The Tempest*, ed. Stephen Orgel (Oxford: Clarendon Press, 1987), 1.2.397–99. Future references to the play will be to this edition and cited parenthetically.

3. Pascal, *Pensées*, in *Oeuvre completes*, L'Intégrale (Paris: Éditions du Seuil, 1963) 5:294. See also Schmitt, *Nomos*, 95. On *ius gentium* as a "law of division," see Annabel S. Brett, *Changes of State: Nature and the Limits*

of the City in Early Modern Natural Law (Princeton, NJ: Princeton University Press, 2011), 197.

4. Jeffrey Knapp, *An Empire Nowhere: England, America, and Literature from* Utopia *to* The Tempest (Berkeley: University of California Press, 1992), 220–42.

5. Francisco Suárez, *De legibus ac Deo legislatore*, ed. L. Pereña, 6 vols. (Madrid: CSIC 1971–1981), lib. 3, cap. 33, n. 12. Cited in Brett, *Changes of State*, 177.

6. A negotiability Annabel Brett's fine-grained project traces. See Brett, *Changes of State*, passim.

7. Schmitt, *Nomos*, 101–7.

8. Francisco de Vitoria, *Political Writings*, ed. Anthony Pagden and Jeremy Lawrance (Cambridge: Cambridge University Press, 1991), 274, 263, 265.

9. Schmitt, *Nomos*, 148.

10. On the connection between absolutist sovereignty and the historically novel question of the individual, see Roberto Esposito, *Bios: Biopolitics and Philosophy*, trans. Timothy Campbell (Minneapolis: University of Minnesota Press, 2008), 60–61.

11. For the modern, "subtractive" version of liberty—liberty purely as the absence of impediment—see Esposito, *Bios*, 60–73.

12. On imperial responsibility as responsibility for rather than to, see Peter Patrick, *Modernism and the Grounds of Law* (Cambridge: Cambridge University Press, 2001), 181.

13. Brett, "The Development of the Idea of Citizen's Rights" in *States and Citizens*, ed. Quentin Skinner and Bo Strath (Cambridge: Cambridge University Press, 2003), 98, 110.

14. On the mixture of compression and pleonastic iteration in the play, see Russ McDonald, "Reading *The Tempest,*" in *Critical Essays on Shakespeare's "The Tempest,"* ed. Virginia Vaughan and Alden Vaughan (London: Twayne, 1998), 218–19. For a beautiful account of the lability of character and language in the play and its social implications, see Simon Palfrey, *Late Shakespeare: A New World of Words* (Oxford: Oxford University Press, 1997), 25–27, 144, 230.

15. Palfrey, *Late Shakespeare*, 26.

16. Shakespeare, *King Lear* (conflated text), *The Norton Shakespeare*, 2nd ed., ed. Stephen Greenblatt (New York: Norton, 2008), 2.4.54–55.

17. On imprinting as cultural, pedagogical and sexual reproduction in the play, see Jonathan Goldberg, *Tempest in the Caribbean* (Minneapolis: University of Minnesota Press, 2004), 124–28. Joan Pong Linton emphasizes the mimetological contradictions internal to the play's gendered forms of cultural imprinting. *The Romance of the New World:*

Gender and the Literary Formations of English Colonialism (Cambridge: Cambridge University Press, 1998), 155–170.

18. Orgel, *Introduction*, 50. Jeffrey Knapp considers distraction in the play more broadly as both the impediment and the vehicle for the cultivation of a colonialism based on "temperate homebodiedness" (*Empire Nowhere*, 220–42).

19. Ernst Kantorowicz, *The King's Two Bodies: A Study in Medieval Political Theology* (Princeton, NJ: Princeton University Press, 1997), 159, and Claude Lefort, *The Political Forms of Modern Society: Bureaucracy, Democracy, Totalitarianism*, trans. David Thompson (Cambridge, MA: MIT Press), 306.

20. Ethel Person, ed., *On Freud's "A Child is Being Beaten,"* (New Haven, CT: Yale University Press, 1997). For the classic analysis of the intransitivity of the scene, see Jean Laplanche, *Life and Death in Psychoanalysis*, trans. Jeffrey Mehlman (Baltimore, MD: Johns Hopkins University Press, 1976).

21. Jacques Lacan, *The Four Fundamental Concepts of Psychoanalysis*, ed. J.-A. Miller, trans. Alan Sheridan (New York: Norton, 1981), 76.

22. For a Cavellian account of the scene as a reflection of Prospero's avoidance of mutuality, see Sarah Beckwith, *Shakespeare and the Grammar of Forgiveness* (Ithaca, NY: Cornell University Press, 2011), 168–70.

23. The structural relation between reflexive reason and revenge is apparent in the passage from Montaigne whose phrases echo through Prospero's articulation of forgiveness. Montaigne speaks of the distinction between goodness and the higher order of virtue: "He that through a natural facility and genuine mildness should neglect to condemn injuries received, should no doubt perform a rare action and worthy commendation; but he who being stung to the quick with any wrong or offence received, should arm himself with reason against this furiously blind desire of revenge, and in the end after a great conflict yield himself master over it, should doubtless do much more." *The Essayes of Michael Lord of Montaigne*, trans. John Florio, ed. Henry Morley (London: Routledge, 1893), 211. The difference involves more than the intensity of the affront; it's a distinction between goodness as natural inclination and a virtue founded on the capacity to reflexively recognize one's blind, reiterative inclination. On the relation between the passage and *The Tempest*, see Paul Yachnin, "Eating Montaigne," in *Reading Renaissance Ethics*, ed. Marshall Grossman (London: Routledge, 2007), 169–70, and Eleanor Prosser, "Shakespeare, Montaigne, and the 'Rarer Action,'" *Shakespeare Studies* 1 (1965): 261–64.

24. On the relation between cannibalism and humanism's "threatened ideal of incorporative reading"—a matter of European readers'

relations to "their own kind"—see Yachnin, 164. On the reflexivity of the European preoccupation with the cannibal in general, see Roland Greene, *Unrequited Conquests: Love and Empire in the Colonial Americas* (Chicago: University of Chicago Press, 1999), 121, and the account of *Othello* in chapter 4 above.

25. Giorgio Agamben, *Homo Sacer: Sovereign Power and Bare Life*, trans. Daniel Heller-Roazen (Stanford, CA: Stanford University Press, 1998), 38.

26. On bare life as "the first and immediate referent" of the sovereign ban, see ibid., 29, 107. More broadly, Caliban reformulates the question of sovereignty, focusing it not on what lies beyond the structure of the sovereign ban—Agamben's antinomian preoccupation—but on whether the movement of the ban does or does not belong to the sovereign. The continuation of Caliban's ditty—"'Ban, 'Ban, Ca-caliban / Has a new master—get a new man"—seems to offer the promise of an entire minia-ture political genealogy from the originative self-banning ban to mastery to the getting of a man indistinguishable from that new subjection. But the question is precisely the genealogical one, how one passes from the reiterative, backward and forward, doing and undoing of the first line— the figuration in small of all those dispersive voices that may or may not have inhabited the island before the magician's arrival—and the conver-sion of that movement into a developmental form. The political aesthetic instance, and the instance of sovereignty, is the force that manages that conversion. Insofar as such force amounts to an ambiguously reiterative banning of banning, it will always be an uncertain gesture, a force that calls for no end of force. My account here contrasts with Julia Lupton's suggestive Agambenian analysis of Caliban as protosymbolic creaturely ground. *Citizen-Saints: Shakespeare and Political Theology* (Chicago: University of Chicago Press, 2005), 161–80.

27. "A true repertory of the wreck and redemption of Sir Thomas Gates" cited in Orgel, *The Tempest*, appendix B, 209, 211.

28. Walter Benjamin, "Theses on the Philosophy of History," in *Illuminations*, ed. Hannah Arendt (New York: Schocken, 1969), 253–64.

7. HOBBES AND THE HYDROPHOBES: THE FATE OF THE AESTHETIC IN THE TIME OF THE STATE

1. On Hobbes's "neutralized space" as constituted against a prior conception of space as animated by the political—the shift from the Machiavellian city to the Hobbesian state—see Carlo Galli, *Political Spaces and Global War*, ed. Adam Sitze, trans. Elisabeth Fay (Minneapo-lis: University of Minnesota Press, 2010), 27–28.

2. Thomas Hobbes, *Leviathan*, ed. Edwin Curley (Indianapolis, IN: Hackett, 1994), 3. Subsequent references will be to this edition and cited in the text.

3. Victoria Kahn, *Wayward Contracts: The Crisis of Political Obligation in England, 1640–1674* (Princeton, NJ: Princeton University Press, 2004), 1–12. Among other things, Kahn's analysis implicitly answers the claim that Hobbes's reference to "art" is historically limited to techne— craft or making—as yet unaffiliated with more ambitious creative stakes; the point is evident enough in the link he draws from the outset between art and divine *fiat*.

4. Simon Palfrey, *Late Shakespeare: A New World of Words* (Oxford: Oxford University Press, 1997), 158.

5. Kahn, *Wayward Contracts*, 134–51.

6. On the absence in Hobbes of a stabilizing intellectual faculty "independent of the . . . sociopolitical processes that move [it]," see Gordon Hull, *Hobbes and the Making of Modern Political Thought* (London: Continuum, 2009), 87.

7. On the at once immanent and transcendent character of the modern "machine" of governance, see Giorgio Agamben, *The Kingdom and the Glory: For a Theological Genealogy of Economy and Government*, trans. Lorenzo Chiesa (Stanford, CA: Stanford University Press, 2011), 230. What I am describing as Hobbes's instrumentalist and contractualist conception of the social and linguistic domains is of a piece with the signifying logic implied by eighteenth century neoclassical discourse more broadly, where the affirmation of the contingent, antiessentialist character of language is able to underwrite a consensualist understanding of truth claims insofar as such contingency operates within the stabilizing horizon of a probabilistic and economistic notion of meaning. On the relation between the contingency of language and social assent during the era, see Richard W. F. Kroll, *The Material Word: Literate Culture in the Restoration and Early Eighteenth Century* (Baltimore, MD: Johns Hopkins University Press, 1991), esp. 13–27.

8. On the abstraction of war as a foundational procedure in Hobbes, see Michel Foucault, *Society Must Be Defended: Lectures at the Collège de France, 1975–76* (New York: Picador, 2003), 92. See also Friedrich Balke, " 'The War Has Not Ended': Thomas Hobbes, Carl Schmitt, and the Paradoxes of Countersovereignty," in *Crediting God: Sovereignty and Religion in the Age of Global Capitalism,* ed. Miguel Vatter (New York: Fordham University Press, 2011), 185–87. On the modern constitution of Europe as an internal space incorporating the division that will become the seed of its own destruction, see Sitze, introduction to Galli, *Political Spaces*, lvi–lvii.

9. Kahn, *Wayward Contracts*, 135–37.

10. *De Cive: The English Version*, ed. Howard Warrender (Oxford: Oxford University Press, 1983), 67.

11. On Hobbes's thoroughgoing nominalism, see Hull, *Hobbes and the Making of Modern Political Thought*, 70–86.

12. On the fear of death as a fiction, see Kahn, *Wayward Contracts*, 153–54.

13. On Hobbes's contractual emphasis in this context, see Annabel S. Brett, *Changes of State: Nature and the Limits of the City in Early Modern Natural Law* (Princeton, NJ: Princeton University Press, 2011), 164–67.

14. See Hull, *Hobbes and the Making of Modern Political Thought*, 89–90, and Carl Schmitt, *The Leviathan in the State Theory of Thomas Hobbes: Meaning and Failure of a Political Symbol*, trans. George Schwab and Erna Hilfstein (Chicago: University of Chicago Press, 2008), 73. On the sovereign as the point of indistinction between nature and civil law, see Giorgio Agamben, *Homo Sacer: Sovereign Power and Bare Life*, trans. Daniel Heller-Roazen (Stanford, CA: Stanford University Press, 1998), 79, and Miguel Vatter, "Strauss and Schmitt as Readers of Hobbes and Spinoza: On the Relation between Political Theology and Liberalism," *CR: The New Centennial Review* 4, no. 3 (Winter 2004): 171.

15. See Hull, *Hobbes and the Making of Modern Political Thought*, 86, 102–3. On "nature" as a condition of "semiotic meltdown," see ibid., 105.

16. On the asociality of the modern "democracy of individuals," see Galli, *Political Spaces*, 46. On the aporetic relation between law and modern autonomy, see Samuel Weber, "Drawing on the Single Trait: Toward a Politics of Singularity," in *Crediting God*, 230.

17. On Locke's essentialism, Annabel S. Brett, "the Development of the Idea of Citizen's Rights," in *States and Citizens*, ed. Quentin Skinner and Bo Strath (Cambridge: Cambridge University Press, 2003), 110.

18. Roberto Esposito, *Bios: Biopolitics and Philosophy* (Minneapolis: University of Minnesota Press, 2008), 57.

19. Ibid., 58.

20. Ibid., 58, 59.

21. Ibid., 59.

22. Ibid., 30.

23. Ibid., 166.

24. Ibid., 46.

25. Ibid., 46, 63, 171.

26. What Derrida refers to as the "heteronomical and dissymmetrical warp of a law of originary sociality" which is "perhaps the very

essence of law." *The Politics of Friendship*, trans. George Collins (London: Verso, 1997), 231.

27. Jacques Derrida, *Rogues: Two Essays on Reason*, trans. Pascale-Anne Brault and Michael Naas (Stanford, CA: Stanford University Press, 2005), 109. On law's exorbitance in relation to itself, the fact that there is no "simple outside to law as the very condition of law," see Patrick Fitzpatrick, "Bare Sovereignty," in *Politics, Metaphysics, and Death: Essays on Giorgio Agamben's Homo Sacer,* ed. Andrew Norris (Durham, NC: Duke University Press, 2005), 62.

28. On the permeability of the art/nature distinction in the early modern era, see Hull, *Hobbes and the Making*, 28–30, and Horst Bredekamp, *The Lure of Antiquity and the Cult of the Machine: The Kunstkammer and the Evolution of Nature, Art and Technology* (Princeton, NJ: Markus Wiener, 1995).

29. The reflexive turn to the reader's own interpretive act, and the conception of that act in comparative terms—a matter of considering one's judgment in relation to other readers—is a feature of neoclassical discursive paradigms generally. See Kroll, *Material Word*, 53–54.

30. Kahn, *Wayward Contracts*, 150–51.

31. The account of the image I pursue in the following paragraphs modifies and recontextualizes my earlier analysis: see Pye, *The Regal Phantasm: Shakespeare and the Politics of Spectacle* (London: Routledge, 1990), 73–76.

32. *The Bible: Authorized King James Version,* ed. Robert Carroll and Stephen Prickett (Oxford: Oxford Unviersity Press, 2008).

33. Thus the proliferative and punitive character of the Leviathan in Schmitt's account: "Whoever utilizes such images, easily glides into the role of the magician who summons forces that cannot be matched by his arm, his eye, or any other measure of his human ability. He runs the risk that instead of encountering an ally he will meet a heartless demon who will deliver him into the hands of his enemies" (*The Leviathan in the State Theory*, 82). For Schmitt the self-betraying demon is, of course, the anti-Semitism that torques his reading of Hobbes's image from beginning to end. On the "anamorphic consolidation of the sovereign" in the frontispiece image, see Horst Bredekamp, "Thomas Hobbes's Visual Strategies," in *The Cambridge Companion to Hobbes's Leviathan*, ed. Patricia Springborg (Cambridge: Cambridge University Press, 2007), 43–44. On the self-referential performativeness of Hobbes theory of sovereignty, see Matthias Bohlender, *Die Rhetorik des Politischen. Zur Kritik der Politischen Theorie* (Berlin: Oldenbourg Akademieverlag, 1995), 160–62, and Björn Quiring, *Shakespeare's Curse: The Aporias of Ritual Exclusion in Early Modern Royal Drama* (London: Routledge, 2014), 67–68.

34. That one does not contract *with* the leviathan is explicit enough: "Canst thou draw out leviathan with a hook? or his tongue with a cord which thou lettest down? . . . Will he make a covenant with thee?" (*Job* 41:1–4).

35. "There will be no extrapolitical archaic ghosts left to tag along" in Hobbes's new political universe, Hull argues in *Hobbes and the Making of Modern Political Thought*, 121. None but one: the sovereign.

36. As opposed to the porous, dispersed aesthetic space opened in late Shakespeare, what emerges with the neutral, economic space of the state is the sovereign specifically as an included/excluded other, something like a specifiable political unconscious. The founder of political thought as systematic certainty is also the thinker who articulates a politics of primary process. "Mental discourse," the "train of thoughts," is of two sorts, Hobbes claims, the first systematic and causal, the second, "unguided, without design," where "thoughts are said to wander, and seem impertinent to one another, as in a dream." And yet, even in this "wild ranging of the mind, a man may oft-times perceive the way of it, and the dependence of one thought upon another. For in a discourse of our present civil war, what could seem more impertinent than to ask (as one did) what was the value of a Roman penny? Yet the coherence to me was manifest enough. For the thought of the war introduced the thought of the delivering up the king to his enemies; the thought of that brought in the thought of delivering up of Christ; and that again the thought of the 30 pence which was the price of that treason; and thence easily followed that malicious question; and all this in a moment of time, for thought is quick" (12).

A lot to read in a Roman penny, even if we imagine that coin represents the image of the ruler. But forced reading is precisely to the point, insofar as the unconscious amounts to the expulsive conjuring through which the betrayer betrays himself. Including Hobbes. We can hear in the account of those who self-annulingly "deliver up" their king at least the structural equivalent of that "lay[ing] down" of "a man's right" through which he becomes free to "enjoy his own original right," that is, the sacrifice that founds the Hobbesian social contract (81). That association with the foundations of contract and exchange suggests the deeper meaning of the relation between sacrifice and coinage, the sovereign as what one gives up in exchange, but also as what one gives up to establish exchange and thus to give the king his incomparable worth.

37. Paul Kottman, *A Politics of the Scene* (Stanford, CA: Stanford University Press, 2008), 82–83.

38. On the sovereign as a height or depth beyond any comparable or measurable height and depth, see Jean-Luc Nancy, *The Creation of the*

World, or Globalization, trans. François Raffoul and David Pettigrew (Albany: SUNY Press, 2007), 104.

39. Hobbes, *De Cive*, 125.

40. Quentin Skinner describes the metaphor in these terms. See *Hobbes and Republican Liberty* (Cambridge: Cambridge University Press, 2008), 111–12.

41. On metaphors leading to "contention and sedition," see *Leviathan*, 26.

42. On sovereignty's character as definitionally internal and external to itself, see Jacques Lezra, *Wild Materialism: The Ethic of Terror and the Modern Republic* (New York: Fordham University Press, 2010), 86.

43. On *nomos* as primordial, destabilizing "cut," see Sitze, introduction to Galli, *Political Spaces*, lxxiii. The violence of that division—again, what forcibly "establishes" a relation to nonrelation—can be felt in the atavism of Schmitt's sacramental fantasy of history's "cutting up" and "eating" of the Leviathan (*The Leviathan in the State Theory of Thomas Hobbes*, 74). On the sacrificial force that precedes and conditions the possibility of "any 'free' intentional acts, including the act of entry into contract," see Lezra, *Wild Materialism*, 168.

44. Schmitt, *Leviathan in the State Theory*, 79–80. Carlo Galli reads Schmitt's *nomos* as the realization of this aquatic irony in relation to the maritime underpinnings of the European state—that "potent element that is neither statual nor even statualizable." "Hamlet or Hecuba," in *Political Theology and Early Modernity*, ed. Graham Hammill and Julia Lupton (Chicago: University of Chicago Press, 2012), 67.

45. *The Tempest*, ed. Stephen Orgel (Oxford: Clarendon Press, 1987). References to the play will be to this edition and cited in the text.

46. On the dangerous loss of distinction between source and response in the political theological context—God's glory as the celebration of his glory—see Agamben, *Kingdom and Glory*, 221.

47. With Hobbes, Agamben claims, "the absolute capacity of the subjects' bodies to be killed forms the new political body of the West" (*Homo Sacer*, 125).

48. Like money, the state "has a life of its own"; see David Runciman, "The Concept of the State: The Sovereignty of a Fiction," in *States and Citizens*, 35.

49. Kroll describes the formation of probabilistic norms in the era specifically as against the "numinous and so elusive authority of 'mere voice'" (*Material Word*, 50–51). On the splitting off of conscience from the sphere of politics in Hobbes, see Reinhart Koselleck, *Critique and Crisis: Enlightenment and the Pathogenesis of Modern Society* (Cambridge, MA: MIT Press, 1988), 36, and Schmitt, *Leviathan in the State Theory*, 73.

On the paradoxical exacerbation of conscience—the way in which asymmetrical indebtedness as a purely structural consequence of sociality becomes internalized as inexplicable and intractable guilt—see Samuel Weber, *Benjamin's -abilities* (Cambridge, MA: Harvard University Press, 2008), 260–61.

Bibliography

Adams, Barry. "The Audiences of *The Spanish Tragedy*." *JEGP* 68 (1969): 221–36.

Adorno, Theodor W. *Aesthetic Theory*. Edited and translated by Robert Hullot-Kentor. Minneapolis: University of Minnesota, 1997.

Agamben, Giorgio. *Homo Sacer: Sovereign Power and Bare Life*. Translated by Daniel Heller-Roazen. Stanford, CA: Stanford University Press, 1998.

———. *The Kingdom and the Glory: For a Theological Genealogy of Economy and Government*. Edited by Lorenzo Chiesa and Matteo Mandarini. Stanford, CA: Stanford University Press, 2011.

———. *The Man Without Content*. Translated by Georgia Albert. Stanford, CA: Stanford University Press, 1999.

Alberti, Leon Battista. *On Painting*. Translated by John R. Spencer. New Haven: Yale University Press, 1966.

Althusser, Louis. *Machiavelli and Us*. Translated by Gregory Elliott. London: Verso, 1999.

Anderson, Perry. *Lineages of the Absolute State*. London: Verso, 1974.

Arasse, Daniel. "Annonciation/ énonciation." *VS, Quaderni di studi semiotici* 37 (January–April 1984): 3–17.

———. *Leonardo da Vinci: the Rhythm of the World*. Translated by Rosetta Translations. New York: Konecy and Konecky, 1998.

Arendt, Hannah. *The Human Condition*. Chicago: University of Chicago Press, 1958.

Bacon, Francis. *The Major Works*. Edited by Brian Vickers. Oxford: Oxford University Press, 2008.

Balke, Friedrich. "'The War Has Not Ended': Thomas Hobbes, Carl Schmitt, and the Paradoxes of Countersovereignty." In *Crediting God: Sovereignty and Religion in the Age of Global Capitalism,* edited by Miguel Vatter, 179–89. New York: Fordham University Press, 2011.

Barkan, Leonard. "'Living Sculptures': Ovid, Michelangelo, and The Winter's Tale." *ELH* 48, no. 4 (Winter 1981): 639–67.

———. *Transuming Passion: Ganymede and the Erotics of Humanism.* Stanford, CA: Stanford University Press, 1991.

———. *Unearthing the Past: Archaeology and Aesthetics in the Making of Renaissance Culture.* New Haven, CT: Yale University Press, 1999.

Barker, Francis. *The Tremulous Private Body: Essays on Subjection.* London: Methuen, 1984.

Bartels, Emily C. "Making More of the Moor: Aaron, Othello, and the Renaissance Refashionings of Race." *Shakespeare Quarterly* 41 (1990): 433–54.

Barzman, Karen-edis. *The Florentine Academy and the Early Modern State: The Discipline of* Disegno. Cambridge: Cambridge University Press, 2000.

Battenhouse, Roy. "Theme and Structure in *The Winter's Tale.*" *Shakespeare Survey* 33 (1980): 123–38.

Baxandall, Michael. *Painting and Experience in Fifteenth-Century Italy.* Oxford: Oxford University Press, 1988.

Beckwith, Sarah. *Shakespeare and the Grammar of Forgiveness.* Ithaca, NY: Cornell University Press, 2011.

Bell, Robert H. *Shakespeare's Great Stage of Fools.* New York: Palgrave Macmillan, 2011.

Bellamy, Jane. *Translations of Power: Narcissism and the Unconscious in Epic History.* Ithaca, NY: Cornell University Press, 1992.

Belsey, Catherine. *The Subject of Tragedy: Identity and Difference in Renaissance Drama.* London: Methuen, 1985.

Belting, Hans. *Likeness and Presence: A History of the Image before the Era of Art.* Translated by Edmund Jephcott. Chicago: University of Chicago Press, 1994.

Benjamin, Andrew. "Spacing as the Shared: Heraclitus, Pindar, Agamben." In *Politics, Metaphysics, and Death: Essays on Giorgio Agamben's "Homo Sacer,"* edited by Andrew Norris, 145–72. Durham, NC: Duke University Press, 2005.

Benjamin, Walter. *Origin of the German Tragic Drama.* Translated by John Osborne. London: Verso, 1998.

———. "Theses on the Philosophy of History." In *Illuminations*, edited by Hannah Arendt. New York: Schocken, 1969.

———. "The Work of Art in the Age of Mechanical Reproduction." In *Illuminations: Essays and Reflections*, edited by Hannah Arendt, 217–52. New York: Schocken, 1969.

Berek, Peter. "The Jew as Renaissance Man." *Renaissance Quarterly* 51, no. 1 (1987): 128–62.

Berger, Harry Jr. "Impertinent Trifling: Desdemona's Handkerchief." *Shakespeare Quarterly* 47, no. 3 (Autumn 1996): 235–50.

———. "Second World Prosthetics: Supplying Deficiencies of Nature in Renaissance Italy." In *Early Modern Visual Culture*, edited by Peter Erickson and Clark Hulse. Philadelphia: University of Pennsylvania Press, 2000.

Bernstein, J. M. *The Fate of Art: Aesthetic Alienation from Kant to Derrida and Adorno*. University Park, PA: Penn State Press, 1992.

Blanchot, Maurice. *The Infinite Conversation*. Translated by Susan Hanson. Minneapolis: University of Minnesota Press, 1992.

Blunt, Anthony. *Artistic Theory in Italy, 1450–1600*. Oxford: Oxford University Press, 1963.

Bodin, Jean. *The Six Bookes of a Commonweale*. Edited by Douglas McRae. London, 1606. Reprint, Cambridge, MA: Harvard University Press, 1962.

Bohlender, Matthias. *Die Rhetorik des Politischen. Zur Kritik der Politischen Theorie*. Berlin: Oldenbourg Akademieverlag, 1995.

Boose, Lynda. " 'Let it be hid': Renaissance Pornography, Iago, and Audience Response." In *Autour d'Othello*, edited by Richard Marienstras and Dominique Guy-Blanquet, 135–43. Paris: C.E.R.L.A., à L'Institute Charles V, 1987.

Bredekamp, Horst. *The Lure of Antiquity and the Cult of the Machine: The Kunstkammer and the Evolution of Nature, Art and Technology*. Princeton, NJ: Markus Wiener, 1995.

———. "Thomas Hobbes's Visual Strategies." In *The Cambridge Companion to Hobbes's Leviathan*, edited by Patricia Springborg, 29–60. Cambridge: Cambridge University Press, 2007.

Brett, Annabel S. *Changes of State: Nature and the Limits of the City in Early Modern Natural Law*. Princeton, NJ: Princeton University Press, 2011.

———. "The Development of the Idea of Citizen's Rights." In *States and Citizens*, edited by Quentin Skinner and Bo Strath, 97–114. Cambridge: Cambridge University Press, 2003.

Bristol, Michael. *Big-time Shakespeare*. London: Routledge, 1996.

———. "In Search of the Bear: Spatiotemporal Form and the Heterogeneity of Economies in *The Winter's Tale*." *Shakespeare Quarterly* 42, no. 2 (Summer 1991): 145–67.

Bruster, Douglas. *Shakespeare and the Question of Culture: Early Modern Literature and the Cultural Turn*. Houndsmills, UK: Palgrave, 2003.

Burt, Richard. *Licensed by Authority: Ben Jonson and the Discourses of Censorship*. Ithaca, NY: Cornell University Press, 1993.

Calderwood, James L. "Speech and Self in Othello." *Shakespeare Quarterly* 38 (1987): 293–303.

Cambell, Stephen J. "Vasari's Renaissance and Its Renaissance Alternatives." In *Renaissance Theory*, edited by James Elkins and Robert Williams. New York: Routledge, 2008.

Cassirer, Ernst. *The Individual and the Cosmos in Renaissance Philosophy.* London: Dover, 2011.

Cavell, Stanley. *The Claim of Reason: Wittgenstein, Skepticism, Morality, and Tragedy.* Oxford: Oxford University Press, 1979.

———. *Disowning Knowledge in Seven Plays of Shakespeare.* Cambridge: Cambridge University Press, 2003.

Chase, Cynthia. "The Witty Butcher's Wife: Freud, Lacan, and the Conversion of the Resistance to Theory." *Modern Language Notes* 102, no. 5 (December 1987): 989–1013.

Chittolini, Giorgio. "The 'Private,' the 'Public,' the State." In *The Origins of the Modern State in Italy 1300–1600*, edited by Julius Kirchner, 34–61. Chicago: University of Chicago Press, 1995.

Cohen, Walter. *Drama of a Nation.* Ithaca, NY: Cornell University Press, 1985.

Collins, Bradley. *Leonardo, Psychoanalysis, and Art History.* Chicago: Northwestern University Press, 1997.

Copjec, Joan. *Imagine There's No Woman: Ethics and Sublimation.* Cambridge, MA: MIT Press, 2002.

Cormack, Bradin. *A Power to Do Justice: Jurisdiction, English Literature, and the Rise of Common Law, 1509–1625.* Chicago: University of Chicago Press, 2007.

Corrigan, Philip, and Derek Sayer. *The Great Arch: English State Formation as Cultural Revolution.* Oxford: Blackwell, 1985.

Crooke, Helkiah. *Microcosmographia: A Description of the Body of Man.* London: Jaggard, 1615.

Crum, Roger J., and John Paoletti. Introduction to *Renaissance Florence: A Social History,* edited by Roger J. Crum and John Paoletti, 1–16. Cambridge: Cambridge University Press, 2006.

Crum, Roger J., and David Wilkins. "In the Defense of Florentine Republicanism: Saint Anne and Florentine Art, 1343–1575." In *Interpreting Cultural Symbols: St. Anne in Late Medieval Society,* edited by Kathleen Ashley and Pamela Sheingorn, 131–68. Athens: University of Georgia Press, 1990.

Damisch, Hubert. *The Origin of Perspective.* Translated by John Goodman. Cambridge, MA: MIT Press, 1994.

Da Vinci, Leonardo. *The Literary Works of Leonardo da Vinci.* Edited by Carlo Pedretti. 2 vols. Berkeley: University of California Press, 1977.

————. *The Notebooks of Leonardo da Vinci.* Translated by E. Mac-Curdy. 2 vols. London: Reprint Society, 1954.

Dawson, Anthony, and Paul Yachnin. *The Culture of Playgoing in Shakespeare's England: A Collaborative Debate.* Cambridge: Cambridge University Press, 2001.

de Certeau, Michel. *The Writing of History.* Translated by Tom Conley. New York: Columbia University Press, 1988.

De Grazia, Margareta. *Hamlet Without Hamlet.* Cambridge: Cambridge University Press, 2007.

de Man, Paul. *Aesthetic Ideology.* Edited by Andrzej Warminski. Minneapolis: University of Minnesota Press, 1996.

————. "Autobiography as De-Facement." In *The Rhetoric of Romanticism*, 67–82. New York: Columbia University Press, 1984.

————. "Hypogram and Inscription." In *The Resistance to Theory*, 27–53. Minneapolis: University of Minnesota Press, 1986.

de Sousa, Geraldo U. *Shakespeare's Cross-Cultural Encounters.* New York: St. Martin's Press, 1999.

De Vitoria, Francisco. *Political Writings.* Edited by Anthony Pagden and Jeremy Lawrance. Cambridge: Cambridge University Press, 1991.

Derrida, Jacques. *Adieu to Emmanuel Levinas.* Translated by Pascale-Anne Brault and Michael Naas. Stanford, CA: Stanford University Press, 1999.

————. *The Beast and the Sovereign.* Vol. 1. Translated by Geoffrey Bennington. Chicago: University of Chicago Press, 2009.

————. "Force of Law: The 'Mystical Foundation of Authority.'" In *Deconstruction and the Possibility of Justice*, edited by Drucilla Cornell, Michael Rosenfield, and David Carlson, 3–67. New York and London: Routledge, 1992.

————. *The Gift of Death.* Translated by David Wills. Chicago: University of Chicago Press, 1996.

————. *The Politics of Friendship.* Translated by George Collins. London: Verso, 2006.

————. *Rogues: Two Essays on Reason.* Translated by Pascale-Anne Brault and Michael Naas. Stanford, CA: Stanford University Press, 2005.

————. *Specters of Marx: The State of the Debt, the Work of Mourning, and the New International.* Translated by Peggy Kamuf. New York and London: Routledge, 1994.

————. *The Truth in Painting.* Translated by Geoffrey Bennington and Ian McLeod. Chicago: University of Chicago Press, 1987.

————. "What is Relevant Translation?" Translated by Lawrence Venuti. *Critical Inquiry* 27, no. 2 (Winter 2001): 174–200.

Didi-Huberman, Georges. *Confronting Images: Questioning the End of a Certain History of Art.* Translated by John Goodman. University Park, PA: Penn State Press, 2009.

Dollimore, Jonathan. *Sexual Dissonance: Augustine to Wilde, Freud to Foucault.* Oxford: Clarendon Press, 1991.

Dovev, Lea. "The Musical Hand in Leonardo da Vinci's Anatomical Drawings." *Reinsprung 11: Zeitschrift für Bildkritik* (2012): 20–33.

Duve, Thierry de. "Five Remarks on Aesthetic Judgment." In *Aesthetics and Sublimation,* edited by Joan Copjec, *Umbr(a)* 1 (1999): 13–34.

Eagleton, Terry. *The Ideology of the Aesthetic.* Oxford: Wiley-Blackwell, 1991.

Erne, Lukas. *Beyond the Spanish Tragedy: A Study of the Works of Thomas Kyd.* Manchester, UK: Manchester University Press, 2001.

Esposito, Roberto. *Bios: Biopolitics and Philosophy.* Translated by Timothy Campbell. Minneapolis: University of Minnesota Press, 2008.

Evans, Malcolm. *Signifying Nothing: Truth's True Contents in Shakespeare's Text.* Athens: University of Georgia Press, 1986.

Farago, Claire. "Aesthetics before Art: Leonardo through the Looking Glass." In *Compelling Visuality: The Work of Art In and Out of History,* edited by Claire Farago and Robert Zwijnenberg, 45–92. Minneapolis: University of Minnesota Press, 2003.

———. "The Concept of the Renaissance Today: What is at Stake." In *Renaissance Theory,* edited by James Elkins and Robert Williams, 69–94. New York: Routledge, 2008.

Felperin, Howard. "'Tongue-tied, Our Queen?': The Deconstruction of Presence in *The Winter's Tale.*" In *Shakespeare: The Last Plays,* edited by Kiernan Ryan, 187–205. London: Longman, 1999.

Fitzpatrick, Peter. "Bare Sovereignty." In *Politics, Metaphysics, and Death: Essays on Giorgio Agamben's Homo Sacer,* edited by Andrew Norris, 43–74. Durham, NC: Duke University Press, 2005.

———. *Modernism and the Grounds of Law.* Cambridge: Cambridge University Press, 2001.

Foucault, Michel. "Governmentality." In *The Foucault Effect,* edited by Graham Burchell, Colin Gorden, and Peter Miller, 87–104. Chicago: University of Chicago Press, 1991.

———. *Society Must be Defended: Lectures at the Collège de France, 1975–76.* Translated by David Macey. New York: Picador, 2003.

Freud, Sigmund. *Leonardo da Vinci: A Study in Psychosexuality.* Translated by A. A. Brill. New York: Moffat, 1947.

———. *On Freud's "A Child is Being Beaten."* Edited by Ethel Person. New Haven, CT: Yale University Press, 1997.

Frienkel, Lisa. *Reading Shakespeare's Will: The Theology of Figure from Augustine to the Sonnets.* New York: Columbia University Press, 2002.

Frye, Northrup. *Fables of Identity: Studies in Poetic Mythology.* New York: Harcourt, 1963.

Galli, Carlo. *Political Spaces and Global War.* Edited by Adam Sitze and translated by Elizabeth Fay. Minneapolis: University of Minnesota Press, 2010.

Genster, Julia. "Lieutenancy, Standing In, and Othello." *ELH* 57 (1990): 785–809.

Girard, René. *A Theater of Envy: William Shakespeare.* New York: Oxford University Press, 1991.

———. *Violence and the Sacred.* Translated by Patrick Gregory. Baltimore, MD: Johns Hopkins University Press, 1977.

Goldberg, Jonathan. *Tempest in the Caribbean.* Minneapolis: University of Minnesota Press, 2004.

———. *Writing Matter: From the Hands of the English Renaissance.* Stanford, CA: Stanford University Press, 1990.

Grady, Hugh. *Shakespeare and Impure Aesthetics.* Cambridge: Cambridge University Press, 2009.

Green, André. *Révélations de l'inachèvement: A propos du cartoon de Londres de Léonard de Vinci.* Paris: Flammarion, 1992.

Greenberg, Mitchell. *Canonical States: Oedipus, Othering, and Seventeenth Century Drama.* Minneapolis: University of Minnesota Press, 1994.

Greenblatt, Stephen. "Psychoanalysis and Renaissance Culture." In *Literary Theory/Renaissance Texts,* edited by Patricia Parker and David Quint. Baltimore, MD, and London: Johns Hopkins University Press, 1986.

———. *Renaissance Self-Fashioning.* Chicago: University of Chicago Press, 1980.

———. *Shakespearean Negotiations: The Circulation of Social Energy in Renaissance England.* Berkeley: University of California Press, 1988.

Greene, Roland. *Unrequited Conquests: Love and Empire in the Colonial Americas.* Chicago: University of Chicago Press, 1999.

Greene, Thomas M. *The Light in Troy: Imitation and Discovery in Renaissance Poetry.* New Haven, CT: Yale University Press, 1982.

Gross, Kenneth. *Shakespeare's Noise.* Chicago: University of Chicago Press, 2001.

———. "Slander and Skepticism in Othello." *ELH* 56, no. 4 (Winter 1989): 819–52.

Gulli, Bruno. "The Ontology and Politics of Exception." In *Giorgio Agamben: Sovereignty and Life,* edited by Matthew Calcarco and Steven DeCaroli, 219–42. Stanford, CA: Stanford University Press, 2007.

Gurr, Andrew. "The Bear, the Statue, and Hysteria in *The Winter's Tale.*" *Shakespeare Quarterly* 34, no. 4 (Winter 1988): 420–25.

Habermas, Jürgen. *The Philosophical Discourse of Modernity.* Translated by Fredrick Lawrence. Cambridge, MA: MIT Press, 1987.

———. *Structural Transformation of the Public Sphere.* Translated by Thomas Burger. Cambridge, MA: MIT Press, 1991.

Halpern, Richard. "Marlowe's Theater of Night: *Doctor Faustus* and Capital." *ELH* 71, no. 8 (Summer 2004): 455–95.

Hammill, Graham. *The Mosaic Constitution: Political Theology and Imagination from Marlowe to Milton.* Chicago: University of Chicago Press, 2012.

———. *Sexuality and Form: Caravaggio, Marlowe, and Bacon.* Chicago: University of Chicago Press, 2002.

Hammill, Graham, and Julia Lupton. Introduction to *Political Theology and Early Modernity,* edited by Graham Hammill and Julia Lupton, 1–22. Chicago: University of Chicago Press, 2012.

Hardman, C. B. "Theory, Form, and Meaning in Shakespeare's *The Winter's Tale.*" *The Review of English Studies* 36, no. 142 (May 1985): 228–35.

Hardt, Michael, and Antonio Negri. *Empire.* Cambridge, MA: Harvard University Press, 2000.

Harris, Jonathan Gil. "Shakespeare After 5/11." In *Shakespeare after 9/11: How a Social Trauma Reshapes Interpretation, Shakespeare Yearbook* 20, edited by Douglas Brooks, Matthew Biberman, and Julia Lupton, 153–59. New York: Mellen, 2011.

———. *Untimely Matter in the Time of Shakespeare.* Philadelphia: University of Pennsylvania Press, 2009.

Hauser, Arnold. *The Social History of Art.* Vol. 2, *Renaissance, Mannerism, Baroque.* London: Routledge, 1999.

Haverkamp, Anselm. *Shakespearean Genealogies of Power.* London: Routledge, 2011.

Hawkes, David. *Faustus Myth: Religion and the Rise of Representation.* Gordansville, VA: Palgrave, 2007.

Heidegger, Martin. *Introduction to Metaphysics.* Translated by Gregory Fried and Richard Polt. New Haven, CT: Yale University Press, 2000.

———. "The Origin of the Work of Art." In *Poetry, Language, Thought,* translated by Albert Hofstadter, 15–86. London: Harper and Row, 1977.

Helgerson, Richard. *Adulterous Alliances: Home, State, and History in Early Modern European Drama and Painting.* Chicago: University of Chicago Press, 2003.

Hirst, Paul. "Carl Schmitt's Decisionism." In *The Challenge of Carl Schmitt*, edited by Chantal Mouffe, 7–17. London: Verso, 1999.

Hobbes, Thomas. *De Cive: The English Version*. Edited by Howard Warrender. Oxford: Oxford University Press, 1983.

———. *Leviathan*. Edited by Edwin Curley. Indianapolis: Hackett, 1994.

Holly, Michael Ann. "Mourning and Method." In *Compelling Visuality: The Work of Art In and Out of History*, edited by Claire Farago and Robert Zwijnenberg, 60–69. Minneapolis: University of Minnesota Press, 2003.

Hull, Gordon. *Hobbes and the Making of Modern Political Thought*. London: Continuum, 2009.

Hulse, Clark. *The Rule of Art: Literature and Painting in the Renaissance*. Chicago: Chicago University Press, 1990.

———. "Tudor Aesthetics." In *The Cambridge Companion to English Literature, 1500–1600*, edited by Arthur F. Kinney, 29–63. Cambridge: Cambridge University Press, 2000.

Hutson, Lorna. *The Invention of Suspicion: Law and Mimesis in Shakespeare and Renaissance Drama*. Oxford: Oxford University Press, 2007.

James, Heather. *Shakespeare's Troy: Drama, Politics, and the Translation of Empire*. Cambridge: Cambridge University Press, 1997.

Jordan, Constance. *Shakespeare's Monarchies: Ruler and Subject in the Romances*. Ithaca, NY: Cornell University Press, 1997.

Joughin, John J. "Shakespeare, Modernity and the Aesthetic: Art, Truth and Judgment in *The Winter's Tale*." In *Shakespeare and Modernity: Early Modern to Millennium*, edited by Hugh Grady, 61–84. London: Routledge, 2000.

Kahn, Victoria. "Hamlet or Hecuba: Carl Schmitt's Decision." *Representations* 83 (Summer 2003): 67n96.

———. *Machiavellian Rhetoric*. Princeton, NJ: Princeton University Press, 1994.

———. "Political Theology and Liberal Culture: Strauss, Schmitt, Spinoza, and Arendt." In *Political Theology and Early Modernity*, edited by Graham Hammill and Julia Lupton, 23–47. Chicago: University of Chicago Press, 2012.

———. *Wayward Contracts: The Crisis of Political Obligation in England, 1640–1674*. Princeton, NJ: Princeton University Press, 2004.

Kantorowicz, Ernst. *The King's Two Bodies: A Study in Medieval Political Theology*. Princeton, NJ: Princeton University Press, 1997.

Kemp, Anthony. *The Estrangement of the Past: A Study in the Origins of Modern Historical Consciousness*. Oxford: Oxford University Press, 1990.

Kemp, Martin. "From 'Mimesis' to 'Fantasia': The Quattrocento Vocabulary of Creation, Inspiration, and Genius in the Visual Arts." *Viator: Medieval and Renaissance Studies* 8 (1977): 347–91.

———. *Leonardo da Vinci: The Marvelous Works of Nature and Man.* Cambridge, MA: Harvard University Press, 1981.

Keenan, Thomas. *Fables of Responsibility: Aberrations and Predicaments in Ethics and Politics.* Stanford, CA: Stanford University Press, 1997.

Kerrigan, John. *On Shakespeare and Early Modern Literature: Essays.* Oxford: Oxford University Press, 2001.

———. *Revenge Tragedy: Aeschylus to Armageddon.* New York: Oxford University Press, 1998.

Knapp, Jeffrey. *An Empire Nowhere: England, America, and Literature from Utopia to The Tempest.* Berkeley: University of California Press, 1992.

Koerner, Joseph Leo. *The Moment of Self-Portraiture in German Renaissance Art.* Chicago: University of Chicago Press, 1993.

———. *The Reformation of the Image.* Chicago: University of Chicago Press, 2004.

Kofman, Sarah. *The Childhood of Art: An Interpretation of Freud's Aesthetic.* Translated by Winifred Woodhull. New York: Columbia University Press, 1988.

Kosselleck, Reinhart. *Critique and Crisis: Enlightenment and the Pathogenesis of Modern Society.* Cambridge, MA: MIT Press, 1988.

Kottman, Paul A. *A Politics of the Scene.* Stanford, CA: Stanford University Press, 2007.

Kroll, Richard W. F. *The Material Word: Literate Culture in the Restoration and Early Eighteenth Century.* Baltimore, MD: Johns Hopkins University Press, 1991.

Kuzner, James. *"And here's thy hand": Titus Andronicus* in a Time of Terror." In *Shakespeare After 9/11: How a Social Trauma Reshapes Interpretation*, edited by Brooks, Biber and Lupton, 191–201. Lewiston, NY: Mellen, 2011.

Kyd, Thomas. *The Spanish Tragedy.* In *Four Revenge Tragedies*, edited by Katherine Eisaman Maus. Oxford: Oxford University Press, 1995.

Lacan, Jacques. *Ecrits: A Selection.* Translated by Alan Sheridan. New York: Norton, 1977.

———. *The Four Fundamental Concepts of Psychoanalysis.* Edited by J.-A. Miller. Translated by Alan Sheridan. New York: Norton, 1981.

———. *The Seminar of Jacques Lacan.* Book 7, *The Ethics of Psychoanalysis 1959–1960.* Translated by Dennis Porter. New York: Norton, 1992.

Laclau, Ernesto. *Emancipations.* London: Verso, 2007.

Ladner, Gerhart B. *Ad Imaginem Dei: The Image of Man in Medieval Art.* Latrobe, PA: Archabbey Press, 1965.

Laplanche, Jean. *Essays on Otherness*. Edited by John Fletcher. London: Routledge, 1999.

———. *Life and Death in Psychoanalysis*. Translated by Jeffrey Mehlman. Baltimore, MD: Johns Hopkins University Press, 1976.

Laplanche, Jean, and Jean-Bertrand Pontalis. "Fantasy and the Origins of Sexuality." *International Journal of Psychoanalysis* 49 (1968): 1–18.

Latini, Brunetto. *La rettorica*. Edited by Francesco Maggini. Florence: Le Monnier, 1968.

Lefort, Claude. "The Death of Immortality?" In *Democracy and Political Theory*, translated by David Macey, 256–82. Minneapolis: University of Minnesota Press, 1988.

———. *Machiavelli in the Making*. Translated by Michael Smith. Evanston, IL: Northwestern University Press, 2012.

———. "The Permanence of the Theological-Political." In *Democracy and Political Theory*, translated by David Macey, 213–55. Minneapolis: University of Minnesota Press, 1988.

———. *The Political Forms of Modern Society: Bureaucracy, Democracy, Totalitarianism*. Translated by David Thompson. Cambridge, MA: MIT Press, 1986.

Lezra, Jacques. "The Instance of the Sovereign: The Primal Scenes of Political Theology." In *Political Theology and Early Modernity*, edited by Graham Hammill and Julia Lupton, 183–211. Chicago: University of Chicago Press, 2012.

———. *Wild Materialism: The Ethic of Terror and the Modern Republic*. New York: Fordham University Press, 2010.

Linton, Joan Pong. *The Romance of the New World: Gender and the Literary Formations of English Colonialism*. Cambridge: Cambridge University Press, 1998.

Little, Arthur Jr. "'An Essence that's not seen': The Primal Scene of Racism in Othello." *Shakespeare Quarterly* 44 (1993): 304–24.

Loomba, Ania. *Gender, Race, Renaissance Drama*. Manchester: Manchester University Press, 1989.

———. *Shakespeare, Race, and Colonialism*. Oxford: Oxford University Press, 2002.

Lupton, Julia Reinhard. *Afterlives of the Saints: Hagiography, Typology, and Renaissance Literature*. Stanford, CA: Stanford University Press, 1996.

———. *Citizen-Saints: Shakespeare and Political Theology*. Chicago: University of Chicago Press, 2005.

———. "Invitation to a Totem Meal: Hans Kelsen, Carl Schmitt, and Political Theology." In *The Return of Theory in Early Modern Studies*, edited by Paul Cefalu and Bryan Reynolds, 121–42. Houndsmills, UK: Palgrave, 2011.

―――. *Thinking with Shakespeare: Essays on Politics and Life.* Chicago: University of Chicago Press, 2011.

Lupton, Julia Reinhard, and Kenneth Reinhard. *After Oedipus: Shakespeare in Psychoanalysis.* Ithaca, NY: Cornell University Press, 1993.

Marani, Pietro. *Leonardo da Vinci: The Complete Paintings.* New York: Abrams, 2000.

Marin, Louis. *On Representation.* Translated by Catherine Porter. Stanford, CA: Stanford University Press, 2001.

Marlowe, Christopher. *Dido Queene of Carthage.* In *The Complete Works of Christopher Marlowe.* Vol. 1, *Translations*, edited by Roma Gill. Oxford: Clarendon Press, 1998.

―――. *The Tragical History of Doctor Faustus A-Text.* In *Doctor Faustus and Other Plays*, edited by David Bevington and Eric Rasmussen. Oxford: Oxford University Press, 1995.

Matz, Robert. *Defending Literature in Early Modern England.* Cambridge: Cambridge University Press, 2000.

―――. "Slander, Renaissance Discourses of Sodomy, and *Othello.*" *ELH* 66, no. 2 (1999): 261–76.

Maus, Katharine Eisaman. *Inwardness and Theater in the English Renaissance.* Chicago: University of Chicago Press, 1995.

Mazzacane, Aldo. "Law and Jurists in the Formation of the Modern State in Italy." In *The Origins of the State in Italy 1300–1600*, edited by Julius Kirshner, 62–73. Chicago: University of Chicago Press, 1995.

Mazzio, Carla. *The Inarticulate Renaissance: Language Trouble in an Age of Eloquence.* Philadelphia: University of Pennsylvania Press, 2009.

McDonald, Russ. "Reading *The Tempest.*" In *Critical Essays on Shakespeare's "The Tempest,"* edited by Virginia Vaughan and Alden Vaughan, 15–28. London: Twayne, 1998.

McKeon, Michael. "The Origins of Aesthetic Value." *Telos* 57 (September 1983): 63–82.

―――. *The Origins of the English Novel, 1600–1740.* Baltimore, MD: Johns Hopkins University Press, 2002.

―――. "Politics of Discourses and the Rise of the Aesthetic in Seventeenth Century England." In *Politics of Discourse: The Literature and History of Seventeenth Century England*, edited by Kevin Sharpe and Steven Zwicker, 35–51. Berkeley: University of California Press, 1987.

McMillin, Scott. "The Figure of Silence in *The Spanish Tragedy.*" *ELH* 39, no. 1 (1972): 27–48.

Miko, Stephen. "*Winter's Tale.*" *Studies in English Literature* 29, no. 2 (Spring 1989): 259–75.

Miller, David Lee. *Dreams of the Burning Child: Sacrificial Sons and the Father's Witness.* Ithaca, NY: Cornell University Press, 2003.

Milner, Stephen J. "The Florentine *Piazza Della Signoria* as Practical Place." In *Renaissance Florence: A Social History* edited by Roger J. Crum and John Paoletti, 83–103. Cambridge: Cambridge University Press, 2006.

Moisan, Thomas. "Relating Things to the State: The 'State' and the Subject of *Othello*." In *"Othello": New Critical Essays*, edited by Philip C. Kolin, 189–202. London: Routledge, 2002.

Montaigne, Michel de. *The Complete Essays of Montaigne.* Translated by Donald Frame. Stanford, CA: Stanford University Press, 1948.

———. *The Essayes of Michael Lord of Montaigne.* Translated by John Florio. Edited by Henry Morley. London: Routledge, 1893.

Montrose, Louis. "The Elizabethan Subject and the Spenserian Text." In *Literary Theory/Renaissance Texts*, edited by Patricia Parker and David Quint, 303–40. Baltimore, MD: Johns Hopkins University Press, 1986.

———. "The Poetics and Politics of Culture." In *The New Historicism*, edited by H. Aram Veeser, 15–36. New York: Routledge, 1989.

Moretti, Franco. *Signs Taken for Wonders.* London: Verso, 1988.

Morse, William. "Metacriticism and Materiality: The Case of Shakespeare's *The Winter's Tale*." *ELH* 58, no. 2 (Summer 1991): 283–304.

Mouffe, Chantal. *The Return of the Political.* London: Verso, 1993.

Murray, Timothy. *Drama Trauma: Specters of Race and Sexuality in Performance, Video, and Art.* New York: Routledge, 1997.

———. *Like a Film: Ideological Fantasy on Screen, Camera, and Canvas.* London: Routledge, 1993.

Nagel, Alexander. "Leonardo and Sfumato." *Res: Anthropology and Aesthetics* 24 (Autumn 1993): 7–20.

Nagel, Alexander, and Christopher S. Wood. *Anachronic Renaissance.* New York: Zone Books, 2010.

Nagel, Ivan. *Autonomy and Mercy: Reflections on Mozart's Operas.* Translated by Marion Faber and Ivan Nagel. Cambridge, MA: Harvard University Press, 1991.

Nancy, Jean-Luc. *The Creation of the World, or Globalization.* Translated by François Raffoul and David Pettigrew. Albany: SUNY Press, 2007.

———. *The Ground of the Image.* New York: Fordham University Press, 2005.

Neely, Carol Thomas. "*The Winter's Tale*: Women and Issue." In *Shakespeare: The Last Plays*, edited by Kiernan Ryan, 169–86. London: Longman, 1999.

Negri, Antonio. *Insurgencies: Constituent Power and the Modern State.* Translated by Maurizia Boscagli. Minneapolis: University of Minnesota Press, 2009.

Neill, Michael. "Changing Places in Othello." *Shakespeare Survey* 37 (1984): 115–31.

———. "English Revenge Tragedy." In *A Companion to Tragedy*, edited by Rebecca Bushnell. Oxford: Blackwell, 2005.

———. "Unproper Beds: Race, Adultery, and the Hideous in Othello." *Shakespeare Quarterly* 40, no. 4 (1989): 383–412.

Newman, Karen. "'And wash the Ethiop white': Femininity and the Monstrous in *Othello*." In *Shakespeare Reproduced: The Text in History and Ideology*, edited by Jean Howard and Marion O'Connor, 143–62. London: Methuen, 1987.

Novellara, Pietro da. *Leonardo dopo Milano: La Madonna dei fusi*. Edited by A. Vezossi. Florence, 1982.

Oort, Richard Van. "Shakespeare and the Idea of the Modern." *New Literary History* 37, no. 2 (Spring 2006): 319–39.

Orgel, Stephen. Introduction to *The Winter's Tale* by William Shakespeare. Oxford: Oxford University Press, 1996.

Pagden, Sylvia Ferino. "From Cult Images to the Cult of Images: the Case of Raphael's Altarpieces." In *The Altarpiece in the Renaissance*, edited by Peter Humphrey and Martin Kemp, 165–89. Cambridge: Cambridge University Press, 1991.

Paleotti, Gabriele. *Discorso intorno alle imagini sacre e profane*. In *Trattati d'arte del cinquecento*. Edited by P. Barocchi. Bari: G. Laterza, 1960.

Palfrey, Simon. *Late Shakespeare: A New World of Words*. Oxford: Clarendon, 1997.

Panofsky, Erwin. *Perspective as Symbolic Form*. Translated by Christopher Wood. New York: Zone Books, 1996.

Parker, John. *The Aesthetics of Antichrist: From Christian Drama to Christopher Marlowe*. Ithaca, NY: Cornell University Press, 2007.

Parker, Patricia. *Shakespeare from the Margins: Language, Culture, Context*. Chicago: University of Chicago Press, 1996.

Pascal, Blaise. *Pensées*. In *Oeuvre completes*. L'Intégrale. Paris: Éditions du Seuil, 1963.

Pechter, Edward. *"Othello" and Interpretive Traditions*. Iowa City: University of Iowa Press, 1999.

Pedretti, Carlo. "The Angel in the Flesh." *Achademia Leonardi Vinci: Journal of Leonardo Studies* 4 (1991): 34–51.

Pocock, J. G. A. *The Machiavellian Moment: Florentine Political Thought and the Atlantic Republican Tradition*. Princeton, NJ: Princeton University Press, 2003.

Poole, Adrian. "Total Disaster: Euripides' *The Trojan Women*." *Arion* 3, no. 3 (1976): 257–87.

Procaccini, Alfonso. "Alberti and the 'Framing' of Perspective." *The Journal of Aesthetics and Art Criticism* 40, no. 1 (Autumn 1981): 29–39.

Prosser, Eleanor. "Shakespeare, Montaigne, and the 'Rarer Action.'" *Shakespeare Studies* 1 (1965): 261–64.

Prynne, William. *Histrio-mastix, The Players Scourge.* London, 1633.

Pye, Christopher. *The Regal Phantasm: Shakespeare and the Politics of Spectacle.* London: Routledge, 1990.

———. "Senseless Illium." In *Shakespeare after 9/11: How a Social Trauma Reshapes Interpretation, Shakespeare Yearbook* 20, edited by Douglas Brooks, Matthew Biberman, and Julia Lupton, 171–81. New York: Mellen, 2011.

———. *The Vanishing: Shakespeare, the Subject, and Early Modern Culture.* Durham, NC: Duke University Press, 2000.

Quint, David. *Epic and Empire.* Princeton, NJ: Princeton University Press, 1993.

Quiring, Björn. *Shakespeare's Curse: The Aporias of Ritual Exclusion in Early Modern Royal Drama.* London: Routledge, 2014.

Rancière, Jacques. *The Emancipated Spectator.* Translated by Gregory Elliott. London: Verso, 2011.

———. *The Politics of Aesthetics: The Distribution of the Sensible.* Translated by Gabriel Rockhill. New York: Continuum, 2004.

Redfield, Marc. "Derrida, Europe, Today." In *Late Derrida*, edited by Ian Balfour. *South Atlantic Quarterly* 106, no. 2 (Spring 2007): 373–92.

———. *The Politics of Aesthetics: Nationalism, Gender, Romanticism.* Stanford, CA: Stanford University Press, 2003.

The Revenger's Tragedy. In *Four Revenge Tragedies*, edited by Katherine Eisaman Maus, 93–174. Oxford: Oxford University Press, 1995.

Ripa, Cesare. *Iconologia; overo descrittione di diverse imagini cavate dall'antichita, e di propria inventione.* Edited by E. Mandowsky. Rome: 1603. Reprint, Hildesheim: 1970.

Rose, Jacqueline. *States of Phantasy.* Oxford: Clarendon, 1996.

Rossi, Paolo. *Philosophy, Technology, and the Arts in the Early Modern Era.* Translated by Salvator Attanasio. New York: Harper and Row, 1970.

Rowe, Katherine. *Dead Hands: Fictions of Agency, Renaissance to Modern.* Stanford, CA: Stanford University Press, 1999.

Runciman, David. "The Concept of the State: The Sovereignty of a Fiction." In *States and Citizens,* edited by Quentin Skinner and Bo Strath, 28–38. Cambridge: Cambridge University Press, 2003.

Rust, Jennifer, and Julia Lupton. Introduction to *Hamlet or Hecuba: The Intrusion of the Time into the Play* by Carl Schmitt. Translated by David Pan and Jennifer Rust. New York: Telos Press, 2009.

Santner, Eric L. *The Royal Remains: The People's Two Bodies and the Endgames of Sovereignty.* Chicago: University of Chicago Press, 2011.

Schiera, Piero. "Legitimacy, Discipline, and Institutions: Three Necessary Conditions for the Birth of the Modern State." In *The Origins of the Modern State in Italy 1300–1600*, edited by Julius Kirshner, 11–33. Chicago: University of Chicago Press, 1995.

Schmitt, Carl. *The Concept of the Political: Expanded Edition.* Translated by George Schwab. Chicago: University of Chicago Press, 2007.

———. *Hamlet or Hecuba: The Intrusion of the Time into the Play.* Translated by David Pan and Jennifer Rust. New York: Telos Press, 2009.

———. *The Leviathan in the State Theory of Thomas Hobbes: Meaning and Failure of a Political Symbol.* Translated by George Schwab and Erna Hilfstein. Chicago: University of Chicago Press, 2008.

———. *The Nomos of the Earth in the International Law of Jus Publicum Europaeum.* Translated by G. L. Ulmen. New York: Telos Press, 2006.

———. *Political Theology: Four Chapters on the Concept of Sovereignty.* Translated by George Schwab. Chicago: University of Chicago Press, 2006.

Schmidt, Dennis J. *On Germans and Other Greeks: Tragedy and Ethical Life.* Bloomington: Indiana University Press, 2001.

Semenza, Gregory M. Colón. "*The Spanish Tragedy* and Metatheatre." In *The Cambridge Companion to English Renaissance Tragedy*, edited by Emma Smith and Garrett A. Sullivan. Cambridge: Cambridge University Press, 2010.

Shakespeare, William. *As You Like It.* In *The Norton Shakespeare*, edited by Greenblatt, Cohen, Howard, and Maus. 2nd ed. New York: Norton, 2008.

———. *Hamlet.* Edited by G. R. Hibbard. *The Oxford Shakespeare.* Oxford: Oxford University Press, 1987.

———. *King Lear.* In *The Norton Shakespeare*, edited by Greenblatt, Cohen, Howard, and Maus. 2nd ed. New York: Norton, 2008.

———. *Othello.* In *The Norton Shakespeare*, edited by Greenblatt, Cohen, Howard, and Maus. 2nd ed. New York: Norton, 2008.

———. *The Tempest.* Edited by Stephen Orgel. Oxford: Clarendon Press, 1987.

———. *The Winter's Tale.* Edited by Stephen Orgel. Oxford: Oxford University Press, 1996.

Shearman, John. *Only Connect: Art and the Spectator in the Italian Renaissance.* Princeton, NJ: Princeton University Press, 1992.

Sidney, Philip. *Sidney's "The Defence of Poesy" and Selected Renaissance Literary Criticism.* Edited by Gavin Alexander. London: Penguin, 2004.

Siemon, James. "Sporting Kyd." *English Literary Renaissance* 24, no. 3 (Autumn, 1994): 553–82.

Simpson, James. *Oxford English Literary History*. Vol. 2, *1350–1547: Reform and Cultural Revolution*. Oxford: Oxford University Press, 2002.

Sinfield, Alan. *Faultlines*. Oxford: Oxford University Press, 1992.

Sitze, Adam. "Editor's Introduction." In Carlo Galli, *Political Spaces and Global War*, edited by Sitze and translated by Elizabeth Fay, xi–xxxv. Minneapolis: University of Minnesota Press, 2010.

Skinner, Quentin. *The Foundations of Modern Political Thought*. Vol. 1, *The Renaissance*. Cambridge: Cambridge University Press, 1978.

———. *Hobbes and Republican Liberty*. Cambridge: Cambridge University Press, 2008.

Smith, Ian. "Barbarian Errors: Performing Race in Early Modern England." *Shakespeare Quarterly* 49, no. 2 (1998): 168–86.

Snow, Edward. "Sexual Anxiety and the Male Order of Things in *Othello*." *English Literary Renaissance* 10, no. 3 (1980): 384–412.

Snyder, Susan. *The Comic Matrix of Shakespeare's Tragedies: Romeo and Juliet, Hamlet, Othello and King Lear*. Princeton, NJ: Princeton University Press, 1979.

Soussloff, Catherine. *The Absolute Artist: The Historiography of a Concept*. Minneapolis: University of Minnesota Press, 1997.

Steinberg, Leo. *Leonardo's Incessant Last Supper*. New York: Zone Books, 2001.

Suárez, Francisco. *De legibus ac Deo legislatore*. Edited by L. Pereña. 6 vols., Madrid: CSIC, 1971–81.

Sullivan, Garrett A. Jr. "Tragic Subjectivities." In *The Cambridge Companion to English Renaissance Tragedy*, edited by Emma Smith and Garrett A. Sullivan Jr., 73–85. Cambridge: Cambridge University Press, 2012.

Summers, David. *The Judgment of Sense: Renaissance Naturalism and the Rise of Aesthetics*. Cambridge: Cambridge University Press, 1987.

Thurschwell, Adam. "Cutting the Branches for Akiba: Agamben's Critique of Derrida." In *Politics, Metaphysics, and Death: Essays on Giorgio Agamben's Homo Sacer*, edited by Andrew Norris, 173–97. Durham, NC: Duke University Press, 2005.

Trachtenberg, Marvin. *Dominion of the Eye: Urbanism, Art, and Power in Early Modern Florence*. Cambridge: Cambridge University Press, 1997.

Trexler, Richard. *Public Life in Renaissance Florence*. Ithaca, NY: Cornell University Press, 1980.

Trilling, James. "The Image Not Made by Hands and the Byzantine Way of Seeing." In *The Holy Face and the Paradox of Representation*, edited by Herbert Kessler and Gerhard Wolf, 109–27. Rome: Nuova Alfa, 1998.

Türk, Johannes. "The Intrusion: Carl Schmitt's Non-Mimetic Logic of Art," *Telos*, no. 142 (Spring 2008): 73–89.

Vasari, Giorgio. *The Lives of the Artists*. Translated by Julia Conaway Bondanella and Peter Bondanella. Oxford: Oxford University Press, 1991.

———. *Vite de' più eccellenti pittori, scultore e architetti*. Milan: Società Tipografica de Classic Italiani, 1809.

Vatter, Miguel E. *Between Form and Event: Machiavelli's Theory of Political Freedom*. Dordrecht, NL: Kluwer, 2000.

———. "Strauss and Schmitt as Readers of Hobbes and Spinoza: On the Relation between Political Theology and Liberalism." *CR: The New Centennial Review* 4, no. 3 (Winter 2004): 161–214.

Veeser, H. Aram. Introduction to *The New Historicism*. Edited by H. Aram Veeser. New York: Routledge, 1989.

Virgil. *Eclogues, Georgics, Aeneid Books 1–6*. Edited by G. P. Goold. Translated by H. Rushton Fairclough. Cambridge, MA: Harvard University Press, 1916.

Virgil. *Aeneid Books 7–12, Appendix Vergiliana*. Edited by G. P. Goold. Translated by H. Rushton Fairclough. Cambridge, MA: Harvard University Press, 1918.

Warminski, Andrzej. "Introduction: Allegories of Reference." In Paul de Man, *Aesthetic Ideology*, edited by Warminski, 1–33. Minneapolis: University of Minnesota Press, 1996.

Weber, Samuel. *Benjamin's -abilities*. Cambridge, MA: Harvard University Press, 2008.

———. "Drawing—the Single Trait: Toward a Politics of Singularity." In *Crediting God: Sovereignty and Religion in the Age of Global Capitalism*, edited by Miguel Vatter, 221–52. New York: Fordham University Press, 2011.

Williams, Robert. *Art Theory: An Historical Introduction*. Oxford: Blackwell, 2004.

———. *Art, Theory, and Culture in Sixteenth Century Italy: From Techne to Metatechne*. Cambridge: Cambridge University Press, 2011.

———. "Italian Renaissance Art and the Systematicity of Representation." *Rinascimento* 43 (2004): 309–31.

Wilson, Luke. *Theaters of Intention: Drama and the Law in Early Modern England*. Stanford, CA: Stanford University Press, 2000.

Wilson, Richard. *Shakespeare in French Theory: The King of Shadows*. London: Routledge, 2007.

Woodridge, Linda. *English Revenge Drama: Money, Resistance, Equality.* Cambridge: Cambridge University Press, 2010.

Yachnin, Paul. "Eating Montaigne." In *Reading Renaissance Ethics*, edited by Marshall Grossman, 157–82. London: Routledge, 2007.

Young, David. *The Heart's Forest: A Study of Shakespeare's Pastoral Plays.* New Haven, CT: Yale University Press, 1972.

Žižek, Slavoj. "Carl Schmitt in the Age of Post-Politics." In *The Challenge of Carl Schmitt*, edited by Chantal Mouffe, 18–37. London: Verso, 1999.

———. "Neighbors and Other Monsters." In *The Neighbor: Three Inquiries in Political Theology* by Kenneth Reinhard, Eric Santner, and Slavoj Žižek. Chicago: University of Chicago Press, 2006.

———. *Tarrying with the Negative: Kant, Hegel, and the Critique of Ideology.* Durham, NC: Duke University Press, 1993.

Zorach, Rebecca. Introduction to *Renaissance Theory*. Edited by James Elkins and Robert Williams. New York: Routledge, 2008.

———. *The Passionate Triangle.* Chicago: University of Chicago Press, 2011.

Zwijnenberg, Robert. *The Writings and Drawings of Leonardo da Vinci: Order and Chaos in Early Modern Thought.* Translated by Caroline van Eck. Cambridge: Cambridge University Press, 1999.

Index